Old Age and Urban Poverty in the Developing World

The Shanty Towns of Buenos Aires

Peter Lloyd-Sherlock
Lecturer in Public Health
London School of Hygiene and Tropical Medicine
University of London

First published in Great Britain 1997 by
MACMILLAN PRESS LTD
Houndmills, Basingstoke, Hampshire RG21 6XS and London
Companies and representatives throughout the world

A catalogue record for this book is available from the British Library.

ISBN 0–333–68286–6

First published in the United States of America 1997 by
ST. MARTIN'S PRESS, INC.,
Scholarly and Reference Division,
175 Fifth Avenue, New York, N.Y. 10010

ISBN 0–312–17502–7

Library of Congress Cataloging-in-Publication Data
Lloyd-Sherlock, Peter.
Old age and urban poverty in the developing world : the shanty towns of Buenos Aires / Peter Lloyd-Sherlock.
p. cm.
Includes bibliographical references and index.
ISBN 0–312–17502–7 (cloth)
1. Aged—Argentina—Buenos Aires. 2. Poor—Argentina—Buenos Aires. 3. Poor aged—Argentina—Buenos Aires. 4. Poor—Housing–Argentina—Buenos Aires. I. Title.
HQ1064.A7L56 1997
305.26'0982'11—dc21 97–7122
CIP

This book is printed on paper suitable for recycling and made from fully managed and sustained forest sources.

10 9 8 7 6 5 4 3 2 1
06 05 04 03 02 01 00 99 98 97

Printed in Great Britain by
The Ipswich Book Company Ltd
Ipswich, Suffolk

OLD AGE AND URBAN POVERTY IN THE DEVELOPING WORLD

Also by Peter Lloyd-Sherlock

OLD AGE AND SOCIAL POLICY: Global Comparisons
(*editor with P. Johnson*)

Contents

List of Maps, Tables and Figures

MAPS

TABLES

FIGURES

Acknowledgements

A large number of people made important contributions to this book. Dr Colin Lewis of the London School of Economics supervised the PhD thesis on which large parts of the book were based. He remained essential to the project throughout its development, providing excellent guidance and constant encouragement. I would also like to thank the administrative staff of the Department of Economic History at the London School of Economics, as well as Bernardo Duggan and Anne Arthur. I would also like to thank Dr Paul Johnson and Dr Walter Little, the external examiners of the original thesis, for their support and feedback.

In Argentina, Silvia Simone and Nelida Redondo of CEPEV gave invaluable advice and key initial contacts in Villa Jardín and Villa Zavaleta. I am also very grateful to Laura Golbert, Rubén Lo Vuolo and other researchers at CIEPP for their kind support. I would also like to thank the residents of Villa Jardín, Villa Azul and Villa Zavaleta for their hospitality, understanding and co-operation.

Finally, I would like to thank the following organisations for their financial support: the Suntory Toyota International Centre for Economics and Related Disciplines, the Economic and Social Research Council, the University of London, the Carnegie Trust for the Universities of Scotland and the Leverhulme Trust. I am especially grateful to my parents who provided financial assistance on a rather more ad hoc basis.

List of Acronyms

ANSES	*Administración Nacional de Seguridad Social* (National Social Security Administration)
BNSE	*Bono Nacional Solidario de Emergencia* (National Emergency Food Voucher)
CELADE	*Centro Latinoamericano de Demografía* (Latin American Centre for Demography)
CEPAL	*Comisión Económica para América Latina* (Economic Commission for Latin America)
CEPEV	*Centro de Promoción y Estudios de la Vejez* (Centre for the Promotion and Study of the Elderly)
CMV	*Comisión Municipal de la Vivienda* (Municipal Housing Commission)
CNV	*Comisión Nacional de la Vivienda* (National Housing Commission)
CVL	*Centro 'La Virgen de Luján'* – Villa Zavaleta
CUNP	*Centro Urbana Nuevo Parroquia* (New Parish Urban Centre)
DMTA	*Dirección Municipal de la Tercera Edad* (Municipal Directorate for the Elderly)
DNA	*Dirección Nacional de la Ancianidad* (National Directorate for the Elderly)
ECLA(C)	Economic Commission for Latin America and the Caribbean
FEP	*Fundación Eva Perón* (Eva Perón Foundation)
FOC	*Fundación de Organización Comunitaria* (Foundation for Community Organisation)
GADIS	*Grupo de Análisis y Desarrollo Institucional y Social* (Institutional and Social Development Analysis Group)
GBA	Greater Buenos Aires
GDP	gross domestic product
GNP	gross national product
HAI	Help Age International
IAF	Inter-American Foundation
ILO	International Labour Office
IMF	International Monetary Fund
INDEC	*Instituto Nacional de Estadística y Censos* (National Statistics and Census Institute)

INSSJP	*Instituto Nacional de Servicios Sociales para Jubilados y Pensionados* (National Institute of Social Services for Pensioners)
MAEC	*Ministerio de Asuntos Exteriores y Culto* (Ministry of Foreign Affairs and Religion)
MCBA	*Municipalidad de la Ciudad de Buenos Aires* (Municipality of the Federal Capital)
MHSA	Ministry of Health and Social Action
NCV	*New Comisión Vecinal* – Villa Zavaleta
NGO	non-governmental organisation
NHT	*núcleo de habitación transitorio* (temporary housing camp)
ODA	Overseas Development Administration
OECD	Organisation for Economic Cooperation and Development
PAIS	*Programa Alimentario Integral Solidario* (Provincial Food Programme)
PAMBA	*Programa de Alimentación de la Municipalidad de la Ciudad de Buenos Aires* (Federal Capital Municipal Food Programme)
PAMI	*Programa de Asistencia Médica Integral* (Integral Medical Assistance Programme)
PAN	*Programa de Alimentación Nacional* (National Food Programme)
PBA	Province of Buenos Aires
STE	*Secretaría de la Tercera Edad* (Secretariat for the Elderly)
UIS	urban informal sector
UN	United Nations
UNICEF	United Nations Children's Fund

Glossary

aguinaldo	Annual bonus
Centro de Jubilados	PAMI pensioners' day centre
changas	Odd jobs
jubilación	Insurance pension
jubilado/a	Holder of insurance pension
Junta Vecinal	Neighbourhood association
libreta	Informal credit system
pensionado/a	Holder of assistance pension
Proceso	Military governments of 1976 to 1982
trámites	Paperwork
villa	Shanty town
villero/a	Shanty town resident

1 Ageing and Economic Welfare in the Developing World

INTRODUCTION

Across the developing world two tendencies are becoming increasingly marked. The first is the recognition that states are unable or unwilling to provide for the income needs of all groups who are outside the workforce, be they children, the unemployed, the disabled or the elderly. It is important, then, to assess the degree to which states currently provide for the income needs of these groups and the alternative sources of economic support available to them. This provides an empirical basis for current debates about the role of the public sector in welfare provision.

Secondly, many countries in the developing world are now facing a rapid acceleration in demographic ageing or will do so in the near future. As yet, this has generated insufficient interest, either from academics or policy-makers. Increases in the number and proportion of elderly may further reduce the capacity of states to support their non-economically active populations. Argentina is one of the few developing economies which have already undergone rapid demographic ageing and therefore it is instructive to see how the state and other actors have been able to meet this challenge.

This chapter begins with a brief analysis of demographic ageing patterns in the developing world, which allows the Argentine experience to be put into a broader context. It goes on to look at debates about the role of the state in meeting elderly welfare and to examine the actual experiences of different parts of the developing world. This considers both the operation of formal social security systems and other elements of elderly economic welfare, such as continued employment and family support. It shows that the majority of existing research has been more concerned with the nature of welfare institutions themselves than with the actual economic difficulties facing elderly populations. As such, the book advocates a more inclusive approach towards welfare studies, which should focus on the economic condition of specific groups and examine how different institutions and strategies at both the macro- and micro-levels combine to form patterns of resource opportunities and constraints.

DEMOGRAPHIC AGEING IN THE DEVELOPING WORLD

Over the past decade, increasing attention has been paid to the 'problem' of demographic ageing in the developed world.[1] Numerous studies have predicted that increases in the absolute and relative number of elderly in rich countries will have major consequences for their economies, social structures and political systems (OECD, 1988; Johnson and Falkingham, 1992). Most observe that greater provision will have to be made for healthcare and retirement benefits. In addition, providing informal care for the elderly will be a new challenge for households, which are already confronting profound social change. There is also much concern about the rising burden of economic dependency, as increasing numbers of retired elderly rely upon a diminishing active workforce. Possibilities to defer retirement have to be balanced against the risk of reducing employment opportunities for younger age groups. As yet, many of these questions have been unresolved and it is widely recognised that there is an urgent need for additional empirical research.

What about developing regions? Here, it would seem that the priority has largely remained controlling overall rates of population increase and easing the plight of the swollen younger cohorts. This is partly understandable, given the substantial increases in total population which are still projected to occur in many of these countries. The low priority afforded issues of population ageing and elderly welfare in developing countries was clearly apparent in the agenda of the 1994 Cairo International Conference on Population and Development. Participants agreed to 15 key principles for future population policy, none of which made even indirect mention of the aged.[2] Issues related to ageing were only briefly referred to in a separate sub-section hidden in the main body of the principal conference report.

This lack of interest certainly does not mean that future trends in demographic ageing in developing countries can be ignored. As shown in Table 1.2 it is projected that by 2025 almost one in eight people in developing regions will be aged 60 or more. The economic and social challenges posed by this ageing process will be complex and efforts must be taken to plan for these as far in advance as possible.

Tables 1.1 and 1.2 show that the process of demographic ageing (defined as an increase in the proportion of population falling within older age cohorts) in the developing world has so far been less pronounced than in developed regions and that it will continue to lag behind through to 2025. This is because most developing countries only began to experience the first stage of demographic transition (declining mortality) relatively recently and few have yet achieved the final stage (low, stable fertility). The relationships between demographic transition and population ageing are illustrated in

Figure 1.1. Arrival at stage three of demographic transition is particularly significant, since it has been well demonstrated that reduced fertility usually makes the most contribution to population ageing (Albert and Cattell, 1994: 37–46). This occurs because when the number of children being born in younger cohorts falls, the relative weight of the aged population increases. Conversely, the decline in crude death rates associated with the first stage of demographic transition is generally associated with reductions in infant mortality rather than increased longevity. As such, this tends to reduce the overall proportion of aged (although the absolute number will probably rise). Significant reductions in adult mortality are usually registered closer to the second phase of transition, thus compounding the effect of fertility decline.[3] Population ageing will go on for a time after birth rates have stabilised, until fertility levels are equal for all age cohorts: this explains the continued ageing experienced by many countries in the developed world.

Table 1.1: Estimated percentage of total population aged 60 and over by major world region, 1950–90

	1950	1955	1960	1965	1970	1975	1980	1985	1990
World	11.4	11.9	12.5	13.4	14.2	15.3	15.1	16.0	17.1
LDRs	6.3	6.2	6.1	6.0	6.0	6.1	6.3	6.6	6.9
Africa	5.1	4.9	4.8	4.9	5.0	4.9	4.9	4.9	4.8
Asia	6.7	6.6	6.5	6.4	6.4	6.5	6.8	7.2	7.7
L.Am.	5.6	5.7	5.9	6.0	6.1	6.3	6.5	6.8	7.2

Source: United Nations, 1993.

Table 1.2: Medium-variant projections for percentage of total population aged 60 and over by major world region, 1995–2025

	1995	2000	2005	2010	2015	2020	2025
DRs	17.6	18.5	18.8	19.9	21.3	23.0	24.5
LDRs	7.3	7.6	8.0	8.5	9.6	10.7	12.1
Africa	4.8	4.9	4.9	5.0	5.3	5.7	6.2
Asia	8.3	8.7	9.2	10.0	11.3	12.6	14.2
L.Am.	7.6	8.0	8.6	9.4	10.6	12.0	13.7

Source: United Nations, 1993.

There is still some disagreement whether all developing countries must inevitably experience the process of demographic transition as illustrated in Figure 1.1. Several studies have noted that whilst mortality declines were abrupt, reductions in fertility have been slower than was the case in the

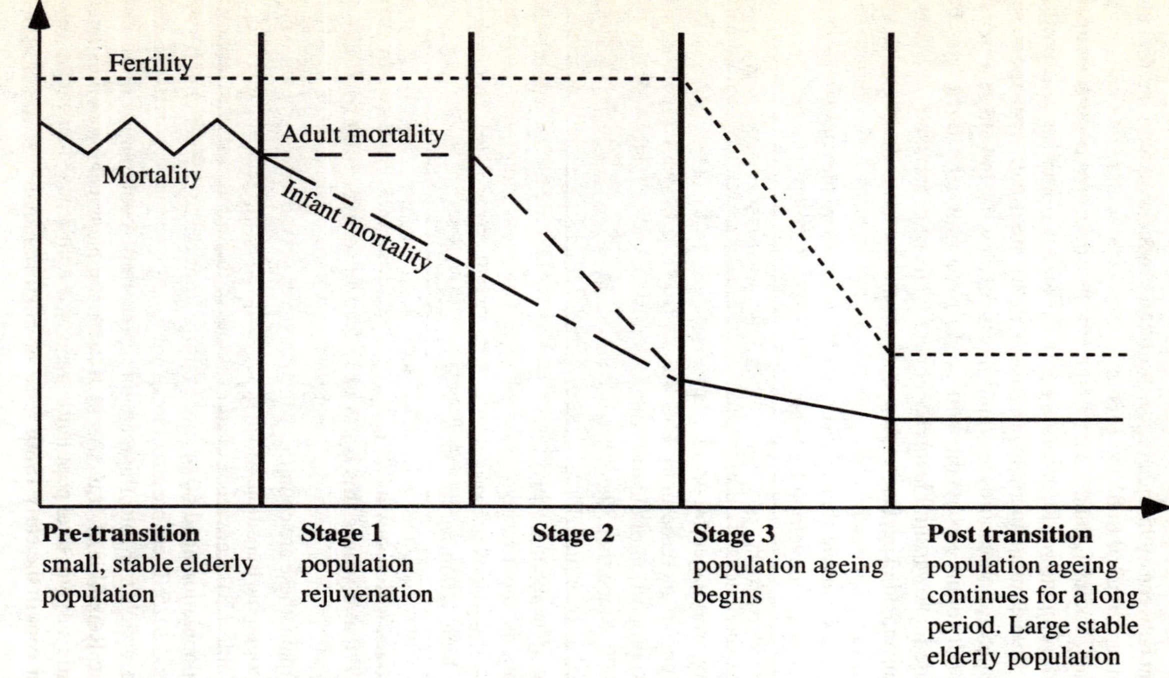

Figure 1.1 Demographic transition and population ageing

developed world. Nevertheless, there is increasing evidence, particularly in Asia and Latin America that the third stage of transition is starting to take effect. As a result, the pace of demographic ageing in the developing world as a whole is projected to accelerate sharply over the next three decades. Table 1.2 shows that the proportion aged 60 or over is set to rise from 7.3 to 12.1 per cent between 1995 and 2025. In absolute terms, the increase appears more dramatic: from 330 to 855 million.

In fact, Tables 1.1 and 1.2 understate the true impact of population ageing in the developing world, since they define the elderly in purely chronological terms. Studies of ageing in the developed world have questioned the validity of simple age thresholds in capturing the biological, social and cultural complexity of the process. In many developing countries a strong case could be made for lowering this threshold to perhaps 50 or 55 years, in line with their lower life expectancies and more premature lifecycle stages. A more sophisticated approach would, however, hinder international comparisons. Also, it is probable that by 2025 the divergence in chronological ageing between many developing countries and their developed counterparts will have been reduced.

The experiences of different developing regions are quite varied. In Africa the proportion aged 60 or over has been static and will not begin to show any signs of increase until well into the next century. Asia contains the highest proportion of elderly, although this declined slightly between 1950 and 1970. Since then, there has been a steady recovery, which is projected to speed up over time. Finally, Latin America has seen gradually accelerating demographic ageing, which shows no signs of abating by 2025. Whilst generalisations about large regions provide a useful starting point, it is more meaningful to look at the experiences of individual countries. These may be divided into a number of categories.

Countries which saw a fall in the proportion of elderly between 1950 and 1990 and where this is not projected to recover fully by 2025

In the main, these are countries which have not yet moved into the third phase of demographic transition. Much of sub-Saharan Africa falls into this category (see Table 1.3). Kenya is a clear example of this trend, with the proportion of its population aged 60 or more falling from 6.3 to 3.9 per cent between 1990 and 2025. There are also a small number of countries beyond sub-Saharan Africa which fall into this category. The most populous of these is the Islamic Republic of Iran. As in Kenya, the principal cause has been a dramatic surge in total population growth, which reached an annual rate of 4.4 per cent in the early 1980s.[4]

For countries such as Kenya and Iran, the falling proportion of elderly does not preclude substantial absolute increases in numbers. Between 1990 and 2025 their populations aged 60 and over are projected to rise from 1 064 000 to 3 077 000 (Kenya) and 3 322 000 to 8 511 000 (Iran). From an optimistic perspective, it may be hoped that lower dependency ratios will reduce the economic challenges posed by the absolute increase of elderly. More pessimistically, it may be wondered how productive employment opportunities and general economic growth will be able to keep pace with the overall rate of population change.

Table 1.3: Population aged 60 and over in Chad, Iran and Kenya, 1950–2025

	1950 %	1990 %	2025* %	1950 (1000)	1990 (1000)	2025* (1000)
Chad	6.8	5.8	6.2	181	321	796
Iran	8.3	5.6	6.8	1 396	3 322	8 511
Kenya	6.3	4.5	5.5	397	1 064	3 077

*Medium-variant projection
Source: United Nations, 1993, 1994.

Countries where the proportion of elderly fell or remained static up to 1990, but where large increases are projected to occur

This category includes countries from all the developing regions (see Table 1.4). The clearest example of this tendency is Pakistan, where the sharp fall in the proportion of elderly up to 1990 is matched by an equally impressive increase over the next 30 years. In Nigeria and South Africa the changes are not so pronounced, whereas in Mexico, the Philippines and Indonesia the projected increases are far in excess of the pre-1990 declines.

Again, the principal explanation for these trends is the timing of the demographic transition, which began its first stage between 1950 and 1990 and is projected to enter the third stage before 2025. For example, in Pakistan between 1950 and 1990 the mortality rate fell from 28.5 to 12.2 per 1000, whereas fertility scarcely shifted. Conversely, between 1990 and 2025 it is projected that the total fertility rate will fall from 6.75 to only 2.68. In absolute terms, the increase in elderly in these countries will be startling. Table 1.4 shows that the population aged 60 and over is set to roughly quadruple between 1990 and 2025. Clearly, these are countries which need to make urgent provision for their future elderly.

Table 1.4: Population aged 60 and over in Pakistan, Nigeria, South Africa, Mexico, the Philippines and Indonesia, 1950–2025

	1950 %	1990 %	2025* %	1950 (1000)	1990 (1000)	2025* (1000)
Pakistan	8.2	4.6	8.0	3 248	5 675	22 215
Nigeria	4.0	4.1	5.5	1 308	4 237	14 327
S. Africa	6.0	6.0	10.2	814	2 427	7 233
Mexico	6.6	5.6	12.7	1 872	4 918	18 189
Philippines	5.5	4.9	10.9	1 158	3 102	11 498
Indonesia	6.2	6.3	13.6	4 954	7 057	35 022

*Medium-variant projection
Source: United Nations, 1993, 1994.

Countries which have been experiencing demographic ageing since 1950

This category includes China and India, the most populous countries in the world. By 2025 China alone will contain more over-60-year-olds than the whole of Europe, and India will not be far behind. In these cases, the final phase of demographic transition had got underway well before 1990. For example, fertility rates in India fell from 5.97 in 1950 to 4.20 in 1990, whilst China's draconian family planning policies have caused an even sharper fall: 5.99 to 2.38 between 1950/55 and 1985/90.[5] In both cases this has led to a sharp surge in the rate of population ageing.

Table 1.5: Population aged 60 and over in Argentina, Brazil, China, India and Thailand, 1950–2025

	1950 %	1990 %	2025* %	1950 (1000)	1990 (1000)	2025* (1000)
Argentina	7.0	13.1	15.8	1 208	4 206	7 806
Brazil	4.2	7.1	15.4	2 259	10 677	36 026
China	7.5	8.8	18.8	41 072	99 522	274 077
India	5.6	7.1	12.7	20 098	58 296	173 120
Thailand	4.8	6.3	16.8	954	3 719	12 010

*Medium-variant projection
Source: United Nations, 1993, 1994.

In this category ageing population structures may have already led to a number of problems, such as the need to develop effective welfare structures and modify labour markets. As can be seen in Table 1.5, Argentina has one of the highest concentrations of elderly in the developing world.[6] Consequently, its experiences in the early 1990s may prefigure future developments elsewhere. It is, then, an ideal location for a case-study.

It is important to draw attention to a number of other issues related to population ageing. The first of these concerns relationships between ageing and gender. In the developed world a disproportionate share of the elderly are women (Table 1.6). The reasons for this differential are complex, partly reflecting higher male mortality due to violence in early adult life and due to disease in later adult life. In developing regions this relationship is much less apparent. Table 1.6 shows that in 1990 the ratio of men to women in the total population aged 60 or more was 0.93. The experiences of individual countries vary widely, however. As can be seen, in India in 1990 there were more elderly men than women, whereas in Brazil the reverse was true. It is unclear why the experiences of developing countries should differ so sharply from those of the rest of the world and between themselves. One possible explanation is that women suffer greater socio-economic disadvantage relative to men in some poorer countries.[7] Nevertheless, in almost all developing countries it can be seen that the proportion of women is usually higher in the very old age groups. Also, it is projected that there will be a slight rise in the proportion of elderly who are female by 2025. The consequences of these gender imbalances are complex and must be considered when developing policy. Unfortunately, very little research has been carried out in this area to date.

Table 1.6: Gender ratios among the elderly in the developed and developing world*

	1990		2025	
	60+	70+	60+	70+
Developed regions	0.67	0.56	0.78	0.68
Developing regions	0.93	0.85	0.90	0.84
India	1.06	0.99	0.93	0.86
Brazil	0.89	0.84	0.93	0.72

*Ratio of men to women.
Source: calculated from Bulatao et al, 1990.

Special care must be taken when using demographic data aggregated at the level of individual countries, since these may mask important disparities between different regions. The development process can lead to heightened geographical socio-economic variations within the same country. On the one hand, richer areas may enjoy higher life expectancy and lower fertility, leading to disproportionate numbers of aged. This has certainly been the case in Buenos Aires, as is demonstrated in Chapter 2. On the other hand, the selective out-migration of younger age groups may create the same effect in poor rural districts. For example, in the poor Brazilian state of Paraíba 7.7 per cent of the population was aged 60 or more in 1980, compared to a national figure of 6.1 per cent.[8] Clearly the relative importance of these counter-acting processes may have very significant implications for the economic welfare of the elderly in developing countries.

Finally, it is important to examine relationships between population ageing and socio-economic class. It is vital that we are able to predict whether the elderly populations of developing countries will include substantial numbers of poorer and more vulnerable socio-economic groups or whether population ageing is and will largely remain a phenomenon of more privileged groups. The overall incidence of old age and poverty depends on two separate processes. The first of these is whether the poor are more or less likely to reach old age than is society as a whole. Whilst it is highly desirable that population ageing should not exclude the poor, it is also the case that this scenario would entail a far greater challenge in areas such as welfare provision. Secondly, the extent of old age and poverty reflects the possibility that people may fall into poverty as a result of becoming elderly. Unfortunately, data combining population ageing and socio-economic indicators are unavailable for most developing countries. A limited amount of information about Argentina is provided in Chapter 2.

SOCIAL SECURITY AND PENSION FUNDS IN DEVELOPING COUNTRIES

Whilst it would be misleading to claim that measures to provide for the economic needs of groups such as the elderly were not a matter of debate until recently, there would appear to have existed a general welfarist consensus among international agencies, academics and most governments regarding the role of the state. More recently, however, traditional views about this role have been challenged by the emergent neo-liberal orthodoxy. On the surface, the principal reason for the breakdown of the welfarist consensus has been the mounting 'crisis' (perceived or otherwise) of public sector social security programmes in both developed and developing regions. It is, however, difficult to separate these new welfare debates from general ideological trends regarding the role of the state. Indeed, it is questionable whether they are primarily concerned with the economic welfare of the elderly or are essentially an extension of ideological dogma into a new battle ground.

The traditional welfarist approach is typified by work of the International Labour Office (ILO), which argues that the economic needs of the elderly should be met primarily through social security programmes. These are defined as:

> the protection which society provides for its members, through a series of public measures, against the economic and social distress that otherwise would be caused by the stoppage or substantial reduction of earnings resulting from [various contingencies including] invalidity, old age and death. (ILO 1984:3)

This definition suggests that social security is essentially a public sector mechanism. It identifies objectives rather than techniques. Recognising this, the ILO puts forward various approaches for achieving these goals, the principal ones being social insurance and social assistance.

Social insurance.[9] This is financed by contributions from workers, employers and the state. It is a legal obligation and a legal entitlement. Most social insurance programmes follow one of two models. The standard approach is to guarantee affiliates a fixed benefit value, irrespective of the time they have been actively contributing, so long as they meet the fund's basic eligibility requirements. Provident funds operate along different lines, providing affiliates the capitalised value of their contributions, often in a lump sum form, when they withdraw from the scheme. In this case, the value of benefits for those who enter the scheme late (perhaps because they move from informal to formal employment) or those who leave early (perhaps through injury or premature death) the value of the lump sum will be less.

Social assistance. This is financed by the state alone and is (in theory) generally available, though often means-tested. Usually, the aim is to bring income up to a community-determined minimum.

Other elements of social security. These include a large range of services, the most important of which are related to healthcare. Since this book is primarily concerned with the *economic* welfare of the elderly, forms of social security which perform other functions are not specifically examined here.

The acceleration in demographic ageing in developed and developing regions has both increased the need for and placed a particularly heavy financial strain on social welfare programmes. In response, policy-makers have begun to look for new models of welfare provision. The most favoured alternative has been put forward by neo-liberal economists and institutions such as the World Bank and International Monetary Fund (IMF). This approach is based on the premise that the public sector is intrinsically less efficient than the free market in allocating resources and therefore state participation in all areas of the economy should be kept to a minimum. This includes the field of welfare, where provision should be limited to those in extreme need, leaving the rest to the 'trickle-down' of wealth resulting from economic growth. The neo-liberal approach also emphasises direct intervention by the private and voluntary sectors in the provision of welfare (World Bank, 1991:65–9). Since the early 1990s, neo-liberals have paid particular attention to welfare programmes for the elderly, arguing that the public sector is simply incapable of dealing with the population ageing 'crisis' which is about to occur. In recent publications, the World Bank has put forward new models for social insurance management based on what is known as the 'three pillar approach'. This seeks to substantially increase the role of private firms and to reduce the participation of the state to providing a minimum safety net (World Bank, 1994:12–48). Similarly, neo-liberals have stressed the need to replace existing social assistance programmes with more rigorously targeted emergency relief programmes for those in extreme poverty (Graham, 1994:1–20).

In developing countries, the concept of social security is rarely as clear-cut as the above definitions and debates suggest. Tremendous diversity can be found both in the form and the scale of their welfare programmes. Tables 1.7, 1.8 and 1.9 show the level of development of formal social security schemes in selected developing countries. These have been grouped into three loose categories: countries with relatively little formal provision, those with moderate levels and those with (by developing world standards) comprehensive social security programmes. These categories are highly arbitrary and contain a large amount of internal variation. Nevertheless, they provide a useful starting point for analysis.

Table 1.7: Selected developing countries with little formal social security

		% labour force covered	Pensioners as % of over 60s	Pension spend as % of GDP
Chad	1989	1.1	na	0.0
Côte D'Ivoire	1989	9.3	5.7	na
El Salvador	1989	12.4	4.3	0.4
Ghana	1989	13.2	na	na
India	1990	10.5	na	0.6
Pakistan	1989	3.8	na	0.6

Source: World Bank, 1994:356–60.

Table 1.8: Selected developing countries with moderate levels of formal social security

		% labour force covered	Pensioners as % of over 60s	Pension spend as % of GDP
China	1989	23.7	22.5	2.6
Colombia	1989	24.5	10.0	0.8
Morocco	1989	17.4	20.0	1.2
Peru	1992	25.7	17.6	0.7
Philippines	1990	19.1	7.0	0.6

Source: World Bank, 1994:356–60.

Table 1.9: Selected developing countries with relatively comprehensive levels of formal social security

		% labour force covered	Pensioners as % of over 60s	Pension spend as % of GDP
Argentina	1989	53.2	72.4	4.6
Brazil	1989	50.3	47.1	2.9
Chile	1992	62.2	na	5.7
Egypt	1989	62.2	na	3.0
Malaysia	1991	44.6	na	1.6

Source: World Bank, 1994:356–60.

It is possible to make a number of regional generalisations about the degree of formal social security provision in developing countries. Almost all sub-Saharan African countries fall into the first category, whereas the majority of Latin American countries fall into the category of relatively comprehensive provision. For Asia, the pattern is much more varied, with several countries falling into each of the groupings. These geographical trends partly result from the common historical experiences, colonial roots and institutional traditions of different regions. To some extent they also reflect the varying levels of general socio-economic development which have been achieved. As such, it is possible to examine the development of social security within a regional framework. The following section gives a brief summary of existing arrangements in sub-Saharan Africa and Asia. It then provides a more detailed analysis of Latin American experiences, which provide a general context for the later chapters on Argentina.

Before looking at these individual regions, a number of additional observations can be made about the data presented in Tables 1.7, 1.8 and 1.9. It would appear that there are often discrepancies between the proportion of labour force covered, the proportion of over-60-year-olds with pensions and the overall cost of social security. In part, these reflect the amount of time that schemes have been operating in different countries. When programmes are first established, or when coverage is extended to large new sections of the population, it is to be expected that only a small proportion of affiliates will be old enough to retire. As a result, the ratio of pensioners to elderly is lower than the ratio of affiliates to the total workforce and overall expenditure on benefits is low. This can clearly be seen in the case of the Philippines where national social insurance was only extended to the bulk of the population in the early 1970s. Over time, it is to be expected that an equilibrium between the proportion of affiliates and pensioners will be reached. If this is accompanied by population ageing and a decline in affiliation (perhaps due to a contraction in formal employment), it is possible that the proportion of pensioners will be higher than affiliation rates. This is clearly the case in Argentina, where overall expenditure is consequently higher. In this respect, the Argentine scenario may foreshadow that of several other developing countries.

Social security in Asia

Formal social security arrangements are particularly diverse in this region, reflecting the sharp differences in prosperity, development ideology, history and institutional traditions found between different Asian countries.[10] On the one hand, several countries have taken a markedly minimalist approach. For example, Pakistan only set up a national social insurance scheme in 1976, whilst Thailand did not do so until 1991. On the other hand, several Asian countries have a long history of social security. National social insurance was first established in India in 1948, with the help of experts from the ILO. By 1965 the programme provided for over two million affiliates, growing to six million in 1989 (Midgely, 1984:120; Government of India, 1990:130). This programme was complemented by the creation of a provident fund in 1952. The provident scheme provides a more limited range of benefits but had been able to include over 14 million workers by 1989.[11] In China a national insurance programme was first established in 1951 and, after considerable disruption during the Cultural Revolution of 1966 to 1976, the system had expanded to embrace 95 per cent of urban workers by 1993 (Fennel and Zhu, 1996:80–104). Even in these two cases, however, formal social security provision has remained extremely limited in rural districts. This, in part, reflects the view that other arrangements are more feasible in the countryside. For example, rural old age relief in China is usually delegated to local village enterprises. However, the bias towards cities also reflects the lack of economic and political power enjoyed by rural workers relative to their urban counterparts. The extension of social security programmes in these countries, as in much of the developing world, has been a highly politicised process, in which genuine welfare issues are all too frequently subsumed by political negotiation. Urban workers are relatively well educated, organised and informed and therefore are more likely to benefit from this process.

A number of Asian countries, most notably Singapore and Malaysia, have developed national provident funds, which have been praised for their contributions to both elderly welfare and economic development. The Malaysian provident fund was set up in 1951, principally in order to provide lump sum retirement benefits, and by 1980 contained 3.7 million affiliates (69 per cent of the economically active population). To date, the scheme has not been extended to agricultural workers. Nevertheless, it is claimed that the fund is popular and provides a reasonable measure of income security for those living in urban areas (Midgely, 1984:144–6). Singapore's central provident fund was catering for almost 80 per cent of the workforce in 1984, by which time it had accumulated assets worth more than half the country's annual GDP. These have been used to promote both welfare and development. As well as providing monthly retirement pensions, the scheme has been a source of subsidised housing credits. Since the late 1960s, the central provident fund has accounted for around 15 per cent of gross national savings and, as such, has been a key element in the country's successful growth strategy (Huff, 1994:334–6). In addition to the provident fund the Singaporian government has set up an assistance programme, which provides the elderly means-tested benefits worth half the minimum insurance pension.

In several respects, the Malaysian and Singaporian funds do not conform with either the traditional welfarist approach to social insurance nor the model advocated by neo-liberals. Both schemes are administered by central government and were established primarily as forced saving schemes. Their success in developing fully capitalised, financially buoyant pension programmes which would appear to follow technocratic prescriptions rather more than political machinations, challenges the generalisations made about the public sector by organisations such as the World Bank. It also begs the question whether these programmes could be emulated elsewhere. Provident funds which appear to be organised along similar lines have been set up in a range of Asian and African countries, particularly former British colonies, yet, as will be seen, these have been on a far smaller scale and, more often than not, have generated financial deficits. In Latin America by contrast, the concept of government-managed provident funds is virtually unheard of.

Social security in sub-Saharan Africa

In this region social welfare provision for all groups is poorly developed. Few sub-Saharan African countries possessed social insurance or assistance schemes for their native populations before the end of the Second World War. A limited number of pension programmes existed for European expatriates working in the public sector and fiscal inducements were sometimes made for companies to develop their own in-house pension programmes. Since the late 1940s, more efforts have been made to establish occupation-specific schemes, although these have mainly been restricted to privileged groups of white collar urban workers. Overall, the proportion of elderly benefiting from social insurance and provident funds has grown as schemes have matured, although it still only accounts for a small minority of the total.

This limited development of pension programmes reflected a scarcity of financial resources and the low priority usually afforded to welfare programmes. The extension of contributory insurance has also been obstructed by the prevalence of informal employment both in the rural and urban sectors. Given the low proportion of population which is elderly (currently around 5 per cent are aged 60 or more), it is not surprising that those welfare schemes which do exist are more inclined to target other groups. The tendency is particularly apparent in Francophone Africa, which has emulated the traditional emphasis given to child benefit programmes found in France and Belgium (Midgely, 1984:121). In Côte d'Ivoire, for example, only 29 per cent of social security expenditure in 1986 went to old age, invalidity and survivors' benefits, whilst in Chad the figure was as low as 4.5 per cent (ILO, 1990:32–41).

In much of the region, particularly in the former British colonies, the preferred form of provision for old age has been through provident funds. These have, however, been far less effective than in countries such as Singapore or Malaysia and have been criticised for providing very low returns on investment and suffering from widespread corruption. In addition, the development of provident funds in the region has been obstructed by the weakness of local capital markets.

The cases of Zambia and Ghana are fairly typical of the region. In the former, social insurance programmes are limited to providing protection against work injuries, whilst the coverage of its provident fund has been restricted to less than 14 per cent of the workforce. Although the Zambian government also developed a programme of social assistance specifically targeting the elderly, the scale of this initiative was insignificant.[12] In recognition of the failings of the provident fund, a major reform was enacted in 1993, signalling a shift towards a more comprehensive social insurance system (International

Social Security Association, 1992:26–7). Ghana's national provident fund grew rapidly (from 335 000 to 1 500 000 affiliates between 1965 and the late 1980s), although this still excluded around 86 per cent of the workforce. Moreover, the scheme was highly skewed towards urban areas. A survey in 1971 found that only 7 out of 180 retired people living in rural districts received any benefit (Araba Apt and Grieco, 1994:113–14; Araba Apt, 1996:65). Even for the fortunate minority, retirement pensions were usually insufficient to meet basic subsistence requirements.

As such, it can be concluded that the general impact of these welfare initiatives on the economic well-being of the elderly in countries such as Ghana and Zambia has been minimal. It is to be expected, therefore, that the great majority of elderly in sub-Saharan Africa mainly depend upon other forms of income, such as family support and continued employment. These are examined later in the chapter.

Social security in Latin America

There are a number reasons for focusing on the experiences of this particular region. It is clear that Latin America has, perhaps more than any other developing region, a common set of distinctive institutional traditions and structures. Consequently, the formal welfare systems of Argentina, Brazil and Mexico have much more in common with each other than they do with most countries in Africa or Asia. This is reflected both in the scale of provision and in the form it has taken. During the early and middle decades of the twentieth century, the traditional welfarist public sector approach to social security was more in evidence in Latin America than in any other part of the developing world. By the end of this period social security programmes in the largest Latin American countries included the majority of their workforces, both urban and rural (Table 1.10). Since then, there has been a pronounced shift towards a more neo-liberal welfare ideology, which has seen the implementation of sweeping social security reforms in much of the region, including Argentina. This change has occurred in response to the particularly severe problems facing welfare systems and the public sector as a whole in the region. It also mirrors a more general ideological lunge from state-led development to radical free-market liberalism. This has been most apparent in Chile, whose social security system was largely privatised in 1980. The Chilean experience has been fêted as highly successful and is now considered a model for much of the region and beyond.

Given the scale of social security programmes and the intensity of recent reforms, it is not surprising that these issues have attracted considerable academic attention. Indeed, the volume of publications concerned with social security in Latin America far outweighs those devoted to the rest of the developing world put together. Nevertheless, this research has overlooked a number of issues which are highly relevant to the economic welfare of the elderly.

Table 1.10: Economically active population covered by social insurance in selected Latin American countries, 1960–85

	1960	1970	1980	1985
Argentina	55.2	68.0	69.1	79.1
Brazil	23.1	27.0	87.0	na
Chile	70.8	75.6	61.2	79.2
Colombia	8.0	22.2	28.1	30.2
Mexico	15.6	28.1	42.0	40.2

Source: Mesa-Lago, 1991a.

The perceived 'crisis' of social security programmes in Latin America can be divided into three overlapping issues, relating to their administration, finances and welfare impact.

Administrative problems

Most accounts of the historical evolution of social security systems in Latin America trace the upgrading of isolated charitable initiatives and occupational pension schemes into large-scale publicly administered programmes, embracing, in many cases, the majority of the population. The timing of this process varied by country, but occurred approximately from the end of the nineteenth century to the 1970s. Numerous explanations have been put forward to explain this development. Considerable attention has been paid to political factors, such as the actions of autonomous pressure groups or policies of co-optation.[13] Revisionist accounts have laid more emphasis on the economic significance of social insurance as a means of generating forced savings (Araujo Oliveira and Fleury Teixeira, 1986; Lewis, 1993). Studies of social assistance refer to a gradual change in attitudes towards poverty and public responsibility, although they also stress the importance of political factors (Tenti, 1989).

The politicised origins of Latin American social insurance are reflected in the structures of the welfare organisations and the various services they provide. Whilst the administration of social security in developed countries is typically performed by single, centralised units, Latin American systems have been shown to be highly stratified and fragmented.[14] They often incorporate national and local agencies as well as bodies responsible for particular occupational groups or contingencies. These problems have been exacerbated by the tendency of Latin American governments to treat social security agencies as sources of privileged public sector employment, used to reward political loyalties.

The disorganised administration of social insurance has created various problems. First, programmes are shown to have been inefficient: the share of budgets allocated to management has been significantly higher than in other regions (Mesa-Lago, 1991b:201–3). Secondly, it is inegalitarian, enabling the survival of privileged funds for powerful interest groups (Dieguez and Petrecolla, 1977). Thirdly, it is blamed for high levels of evasion, both by employers and workers, thus reducing the revenue and coverage afforded by insurance programmes. Administrative stratification also fosters corruption, which undermines the credibility of the system and discourages participation.[15] Another potentially significant consequence of organisational fragmentation is the creation of obstacles and delays for pursuing benefit claims. Existing studies make scant reference to this problem, reflecting, in large part, problems of quantification at the macro-level.

Neo-liberals put forward strong arguments that pension fund administration can be improved through increased private sector participation and the elimination of monopolies. In the case of Chile there is evidence that the 1980 reform led to major improvements in efficiency (Baeza and Simonetti, 1986; Castañeda, 1992). However, some studies note that when marketing and publicity expenditure is taken into account the overall cost of the new system may be as much as 40 per cent higher than the old public one (Arellano, 1985). Moreover, the experiences of countries such as Malaysia and Singapore indicate that a public sector monopoly does not in itself inevitably lead to financial inefficiency. Indeed, even World Bank economists have admitted that:

> All pension systems require good government...A country that is deemed unable to run well a funded or unfunded public pension system...would most likely be unable to regulate and supervise a private pension system.[16]

This does not auger well for the newly privatised pension systems in countries such as Peru, Colombia and Argentina.

Throughout Latin America, social assistance programmes have been developed on a much smaller scale than insurance programmes. Accounts of assistance schemes often draw attention to the high levels of wastage caused by inefficient implementation, clientelism and corruption.[17] There is also much debate about their success in targeting those individuals in greatest need. Nevertheless, neo-liberals have argued that carefully structured and clearly targeted assistance programmes may be able to avoid the institutional problems characteristic of the region's mass social insurance funds. Again, they draw attention to the successful targeting of assistance in Chile during the 1970s and 1980s (Castañeda, 1992).

Financial problems

Considerable attention has been paid to the ways in which Latin American social insurance is financed. This draws attention to the huge amounts of funds involved and mounting financial deficits.[18] The administrative problems outlined above have been compounded by a number of other effects. These include a general failure to project the long-term financial requirements of pension schemes. This was understandable at the beginning of the century when the economic and demographic data needed for such forecasts were often absent. However, as this data became more available there have been few attempts to achieve long-run equilibrium. In the absence of effective taxation systems, social insurance contributions became a major source of public revenue in some countries. In others the problem was not so much state borrowing as its failure to meet its own contribution obligations. Whichever occurred, the direct result was public indebtedness and the depletion of the financial resources of social insurance programmes. As initial surpluses based on high ratios of workers to beneficiaries began to dry up, many programmes were forced to switch from fully-funded financing (which finances benefits from the interest accrued by contributions) to a pay-as-you-go system (which employs annual fund income to cover expenditure). Resistance to higher levies from both labour and employers meant that the main cost was usually borne by the pensioners themselves, with benefits sharply devalued by inflation.

Neo-liberals point out that transferring management to the private sector reduces the risk of government pilfering and political interference with financial decision-making. There is some truth in this, although it is disingenuous to make generalisations about the financial prowess of the private sector. In Brazil, for example, both private and state-run pension funds have been found to be corrupt and inefficient and by 1995 both had accumulated large actuarial deficits (Matijasic, 1993). Also, the removal of contributing affiliates to the private sector increases the immediate financial difficulties of pre-existing public funds, since they are left with no source of income other than direct government transfers to cover the cost of those already retired. This is reflected in continued high levels of expenditure on social security in Chile (Table 1.9).

Welfare impact

The general welfare impact of social security should take into account the proportion of the population included, the contingencies provided for and the value of benefits. Table 1.10 provides a positive picture, indicating that, by the 1980s, social insurance schemes included a substantial part of the economically active populations of the larger Latin American economies. These data should be treated with considerable caution, however. A general, undiscriminating use of top-line official data may mask the true impact of these programmes. Several studies have shown that the figures presented in Table 1.10 may often be misleading and underestimate true levels of evasion.[19] It should also be stressed that the most widely cited figures are based on *affiliation* to insurance programmes, not the receipt of benefits. Insufficient contributions, bureaucratic obstacles and delays could mean that the two do not automatically coincide. Studies of the Chilean system reveal that the proportion of the workforce covered has in fact fallen significantly since the privatisation.[20] This reflects the preference of private insurers to concentrate their efforts on attracting affiliates with high and reliable income streams.

Existing research on social insurance in the region makes occasional references to groups which are not included, stressing variations in affiliation between different occupation groups. This pattern reflects two sets of effects. The first is the politicised, ad hoc extension of systems in which more powerful interest groups such as the military, organised urban labour and the civil service were able to command coverage superior to that of weaker groups, such as rural labour and the self-employed.[21] This has led to a degree of urban bias in formal social security provision, although high overall coverage means that this bias is usually less obvious than in other developing regions. Secondly, there are various 'economic' effects, such as the difficulty of monitoring evasion in small-scale, informal production units and the inability or unwillingness of the poorest sectors of the population to make regular contributions (Mesa-Lago, 1983; Tokman, 1991). Consequently, the rise in poverty and expansion of the informal sector in recent decades have been identified as formidable obstacles to the diffusion of social insurance.

Whilst existing studies have gone into some detail in explaining the effects of poverty and informality on social insurance, there are a number of weaknesses in their interpretations. These result from a general tendency to consider such relationships from a large-scale institutional perspective rather than the users' viewpoint. The first is an unresolved debate within writing on the informal sector about the extent to which informality is a safety net for inadequate welfare or is a means of avoiding payment of social security and tax levies: in other words, whether it is *driven by* inadequate protection or *driven from* inappropriate measures.[22] Other issues include the effects of education, access to information and bureaucratic obstacles to affiliation. This is particularly significant for self-employed workers, on whom falls the full burden of responsibility for handling paperwork and dealing with government agencies. These issues can only be examined effectively through micro-level studies.

Latin American social security programmes generally provide a narrower range of benefits than those in developing countries. For example, few provide effective unemployment benefits. However, those contingencies of greatest significance to the elderly (old age, widowhood and invalidity) are included in every country. As a result, old age pensions account for the great majority of expenditure in the region. Usually eligibility criteria are based on a minimum period of contributions and a minimum retirement age. These compare favourably with systems in developed countries. It should not be assumed, however, that eligibility for benefits automatically determines access to them. This relationship must be tested, again through the use of micro-level surveys.

The financial difficulties facing social security programmes in recent years have often led to sharp falls in benefit values. Benefits values may also vary widely between different occupational groups in an individual country. No research has specifically studied changes of benefit values over time and their capacity to meet the basic needs of their recipients. It is possible that the welfare gains from the expansion of nominal coverage in some Latin American countries have been more than off-set by falls in the real values of pensions.

Another gap in existing research is a tendency to ignore initiatives which are not implemented at the national level. Several Latin American countries have complex geographical hierarchies of social insurance which include provincial and municipal funds. In countries such as Argentina, Brazil and Chile, there has been a shift towards the decentralisation of assistance schemes. It is argued that this process can improve access to and the targeting of benefits and assistance. Again, the verification of this claim requires analysis from a grassroots perspective and should be placed in the broader context of social policy reform.

Thus, despite the large amount of material which has been published, there are a number of significant gaps in existing studies of formal social security in Latin America. These often result from a preoccupation with the institutions themselves rather than their impact on individuals and households. They also reflect a failure to integrate analyses of social insurance with other social policies and factors which may influence the economic livelihood of target populations. By focusing an enquiry on particular groups as opposed to a particular organisation, it is possible to examine these issues and to assess the consequences of large-scale institutional failures at the grassroots level.

OTHER ASPECTS OF ELDERLY ECONOMIC WELFARE

One weakness of both the welfarist and the neo-liberal approaches to elderly economic welfare is that they assume that this issue can be largely reduced to the provision of social security and old age pensions (be they managed privately or by the state). This ignores the simple fact that across the developing world a large proportion of elderly do not presently receive such support and it is highly unlikely that they will do so in the foreseeable future. It also presupposes that those elderly who receive pensions have no other source of income and that this benefit is for their sole consumption and does not comprise just part of the often complex income maintenance strategies of households. It is, then, vital to develop studies of these relationships at the micro-level. Such a focus may provide insights into the interface between public policy and the dynamics of micro-economic behaviour.

During the past twenty years increasing priority has been given to this sort of micro-level research in developing regions.[23] Studies have examined a range of issues, such as the role of women, kinship networks, employment strategies and nutrition. However, very few of these make specific or even passing reference to the welfare of the elderly. This reflects the fact that rapid demographic ageing is yet to occur in most of the developing world. In Latin America, the few existing studies of the elderly pay very little attention to economic issues, but stress psychological, sociological and medical aspects of ageing.[24] The financial welfare of the elderly is presumed to be governed almost entirely by social security policy.[25]

One central concern of sociological research is the extent to which economic relationships between the elderly and other household members may been affected by recent socio-economic change. The 'golden age' argument posits that the elderly enjoyed considerable power and prestige in less modern societies. However, historical and anthropological research across the world has found as many examples which support this view as contradict it (Tout, 1989:10–11; Kertzer and Laslett, 1995). In many cases, the concept of a protracted old age simply does not exist for pre-modern societies: people continue to work so long as they are physically able to and this is quickly followed by their death. This process does not necessarily preclude the veneration of the elderly, especially if those few who do not die quickly were more high-ranking members of society in the first place (Silverman and Maxwell, 1982:46-69; Minois, 1987; Keith et al, 1994).

Regardless of what may have happened in times past, there is general agreement that the rapid modernisation of recent decades has had an unfavourable effect on the social relations of the elderly. This occurs for a range of reasons. First, the increased access to education and the technological sophistication of labour processes renders the skills of the elderly obsolete. At the same time, the separation of workplace from home, associated with urbanisation and industrialisation, increases the social isolation of the aged. Finally, it is argued that increased longevity and the expansion of elderly population cohorts intensifies competition for resources between them and other age groups (Cowgill, 1974:123–46). For developed countries, these negative social effects of modernisation have nevertheless been accompanied by a general improvement in the economic welfare of the majority of elderly, thanks to the upgrading of social security.

To date, the vast majority of empirical research into these issues has been carried out in the developed world. There is, however, a broad consensus that the experiences of developing countries are not dissimilar as regards the social position of the aged. For example, as long ago as the early 1960s one anthropological study of rural Mexico observed:

> It appears to be the consensus that less and less respect for old people is being shown...there are more sources of conflict between the older and younger generations because of recent social and economic changes.
> (Lewis, 1963:411–12)

As the shift towards nuclear family structures, along with urbanisation and increased geographical mobility have occurred particularly abruptly in many developing countries, it is to be expected that the social relations of the elderly will be adversely affected. At the same time, the absence of formal social security in many such countries will have meant that these social trends have been paralleled by (and may also have contributed towards) growing economic hardship for the elderly. Thus, whereas the social problems of the elderly in developed countries may have been compensated for by economic factors, both effects are more likely to be negative in the developing world.

Even so, the social and economic impact of modernisation should not be considered a foregone conclusion. Very little substantial research has been undertaken to verify these claims, the notable exception being Nana Araba Apt's study of ageing in Ghana. This largely supports the view that modernisation is detrimental to the social and economic status of the elderly.[26] Nevertheless, it is conceivable that in some cases poor elderly in rural areas may benefit financially from remittance payments sent by children who have migrated away.[27] Likewise, one survey in São Paulo, Brazil found that elderly who were living alone were just as likely to receive economic and other forms of support from their children (Ramos, 1992).

Since the 1960s notable advances have been made in micro-economic theory relating to the family in developed regions. These have paid particular attention to fertility and marriage patterns as well as economic relations between parents and children. References to the elderly are largely restricted to explanations for the increased number living alone in countries such as the USA. These posit that since most elderly receive social security benefits, they no longer require family support and so are free to live alone. At the same time, they argue that the pace of economic and technological modernisation means that the elderly have fewer relevant skills to offer younger family members. The first of these explanations is in line with the neo-liberal view that universal public pension programmes undermine 'informal' systems of support for the elderly (World Bank, 1994:67). This is a key issue for developing regions where 'informal' support is particularly prominent, but little has been done to test the relationship in this specific context. Moreover, an important weakness in current micro-economic theory is the failure to recognise that, in cases where more women take on salaried employment, the role of the elderly as 'investors in household capital' (rearing children and other domestic duties) could in fact be increased, making them a more integral part of the family. To date, most research in this area has mainly examined the negative impact of reduced female time available for domestic care of the aged.

The main focus of micro-economic research in developing countries has centred upon the old age security motive for having children (Liebenstein,1957; Lindert, 1983; Setapa, 1993). There is considerable controversy concerning the extent to which individuals in developing countries decide to raise large numbers of children in order to increase their own welfare when they become elderly. In many respects, this unresolved debate has been more strongly concerned with lowering fertility and population growth rates than with the impact of demographic ageing. As fertility levels are now falling in most developing countries, it would be constructive for micro-economists to shift their attention to those issues being studied in the developed world.

The failure of micro-economists, both in developed and developing regions, to carry out more considered studies of the aged reflects a more general tendency to assume that elderly individuals are simply the passive recipients of economic support, be it from social security systems or family members. This view is dangerously simplistic. In developed countries small but significant sectors of the elderly population may continue to make income transfers to their children and grandchildren. Also, the elderly are more likely to be home-owners and to have accumulated savings (Johnson and Falkingham, 1992:59–71). In some developing countries regular pensions payments, no matter how ungenerous they may seem, may provide an important guaranteed source of monthly income in households where younger members are forced to rely upon the vagaries of informal employment. In these cases some form of intergenerational contract may exist, through which the elderly obtain care from family members in exchange for the transfer of resources, including inheritance rights.

Another weakness of micro-economic theory is that it assumes the elderly no longer work. Whilst this assumption may be reasonably valid in many developed countries, it clearly does not hold for poorer parts of the world. Table 1.11 shows that in developing regions 44.8 per cent of 60- to 64-year-olds and 27.9 per cent of those aged 65 or more were defined as economically active in 1990. The lowest rates of recorded activity were in Latin America, reflecting the greater presence of social security programmes in this region.

In fact, these ILO figures probably underestimate the true extent of elderly employment. Given the low qualitative and quantitative coverage of formal pension schemes in developing countries, it is only to be expected that many elderly will seek additional forms of income. The limited research conducted in these countries suggests that the aged are more likely to be involved in informal, part-time employment of a nature which is often under-reported in official surveys.[28] It is important to assess whether this tendency reflects a genuine preference to work on a casual basis or is due to the exclusion of the elderly from more formalised employment opportunities. Definitions of unemployment and underemployment for the elderly are often less clear-cut than for other age groups.[29] Activity rates for the elderly may be artificially lowered by assuming that all those elderly who no longer work have chosen to retire and are not seeking fresh employment.

Table 1.11: Rates of economic activity[30] by age group in selected developing countries and regions, 1950–2025

	1950		1990		2025	
Age	60–64	65+	60–64	65+	60–64	65+
Developed Regions	52.6	28.1	32.6	8.3	31.1	5.4
Developing Regions	57.5	39.8	44.8	27.9	33.8	13.5
Africa	65.1	50.4	56.1	36.6	43.4	21.5
Asia	57.2	38.0	44.9	24.0	33.2	13.1
Latin America	50.2	38.6	38.4	18.9	31.7	9.0

Source: ILO, 1986b.

Elderly employment rates can influence the group's economic welfare in two ways. First, in the most direct sense, they comprise an additional source of income for elderly workers. Secondly, elderly employment affects the overall level of economic dependency. This may influence levels of development and productivity and, as such, the economic welfare of society as a whole.

Table 1.12: Proportion of population in dependent age groups for developed and developing regions, 1950–2025 (%)

		1950	1990*	2025*
Developed Regions				
	Total	54.8	50.4	57.5
	0–14	43.0	32.3	28.7
	65+	11.8	18.1	28.8
Developing Regions				
	Total	71.5	66.7	52.2
	0–14	65.0	59.3	39.9
	65+	6.6	7.4	12.2
Africa				
	Total	84.3	92.5	67.4
	0–14	78.5	86.7	60.7
	65+	5.8	5.9	6.7
Asia				
	Total	68.7	61.0	48.5
	0–14	61.8	52.9	34.3
	65+	6.8	8.0	14.3
Latin America				
	Total	78.2	72.7	49.3
	0–14	72.0	64.9	35.6
	65+	6.2	7.8	13.8

*Projected
Source: United Nations, 1993.

Whilst rates of elderly economic activity are higher in developing regions than in developed ones, they are declining sharply. Table 1.11 shows that by 2025 rates will have reached the same level as those attained by developed regions in 1990. This reflects the expansion of welfare systems and, as such, should be interpreted as a welcome effect. Nevertheless, declining elderly employment will reinforce the impact of population ageing on crude economic dependency rates (the proportion of the population which is inactive versus the rest). As such it might be expected that dependency rates will increase significantly for developing countries over the next few decades. To some extent, however, the impact of ageing will be off-set by a range of other effects. Table 1.12 gives dependency ratios as calculated simply according to chronological age and shows that the reduction in the proportion of population aged 14 or under is far more significant than the rise in the elderly. Hence there will be an overall decline in the relative size of the population in 'dependent' age groups for all developing regions between 1990 and 2025.

Table 1.13 provides a more sophisticated measure, taking into account the rates of economic activity for different age groups. This also reveals that overall levels of participation in the salaried labour force are in fact set to rise slightly in most of the developing world. The increase mainly reflects a projected decline in the proportion of adolescents (aged 11 to 20), whose continued education reduces economic activity.

Table 1.13: Economic activity rate of population aged 10 or over for developed and developing regions, 1950–2025 (%)

	1950	1990*	2025
Developed Regions	46.5	48.4	45.6
Developing Regions	47.7	43.6	44.3
Africa	44.2	37.6	40.2
Asia	49.5	47.0	46.6
Latin America	35.2	35.1	39.5

*Projected
Source: World Bank, 1994:356–60.

In the light of these figures, it might be argued that the economic challenges posed by population ageing in developing regions have been exaggerated and that the 'burden' of swollen elderly cohorts in 2025 would appear insubstantial in comparison with the costs of providing for the under-working-age populations of the 1990s. To some extent this is true. It should, however, be stressed that the particular needs of the elderly, both in pure economic terms as well as regards healthcare and other issues are very different to those of young children and thus require specific policy initiatives. Also, it is questionable whether many of the poorer developing countries will be able to effectively absorb large cohorts of younger adults into their workforces. This may well cause further increases in unemployment and under-employment, which will intensify intergenerational resource conflict and damage the economic welfare of all groups, elderly included.

The projected rise in participation will occur in spite of a a slight decline in recognised female economic activity, from 30.8 to 29.6 per cent between 1990 and 2025 (ILO 1986b:21). The only exception is Latin America, where rates of elderly activity are already low and where female participation will experience a moderate increase. Although the continued low level of incorporation of women into the salaried labour force may shore up their traditional role as carers for the elderly, it may also weaken the economic capacity of families to provide for their most vulnerable members.[31]

The economic welfare of the elderly, particularly those in poverty, may also be influenced by institutions operating at the level of the community. A number of studies have stressed the significant potential advantages that can be offered by well-organised local initiatives.[32] These can perform a range of functions, including the provision of informal credit, risk pooling, direct assistance, the channelling of resources from other actors (such as government programmes), the promotion of self-help strategies and generally raising awareness of elderly concerns at the community level. They may also serve to reduce the social isolation and prestige loss of the elderly associated with modernisation. As such, community-level initiatives may help bridge the gap between household-level survival strategies and macro-level public policy. Several studies have identified the key role played by traditional informal mutual aid societies in parts of sub-Saharan Africa (Araba Apt and Grieco, 1994:114; World Bank, 1994:52–4). Research in Latin America has observed the flourishing of informal grassroots organisations in the region since the 1970s (Assies, Burgwal and Salman, 1990). Since the 1960s, non-governmental organisations (NGOs) have become increasingly prominent in developing regions and have taken a major role in promoting grassroots and community-level initiatives. Existing studies of NGOs and the programmes they develop generally place more emphasis on the evolution and nature of the organisations themselves than their concrete impact on target groups. This is partly because such schemes often provide indirect forms of assistance which are not easily quantifiable. Very little research considers the importance of community initiatives for the elderly. This is surprising, given the prominent role played by the aged in new social movements in countries such as Argentina.[33]

The economic welfare of the elderly in developing countries is a complex issue, which deserves much greater scrutiny than it has attracted to date. Existing research has been over-compartmentalised, both geographically and thematically. There remains a major gulf between, on one hand, the research of macro-economists and political scientists into pensions and social security and, on the other, that of micro-economists, sociologists and anthropologists into other aspects of elderly economic welfare. Studies need to take into account relationships between the elderly, their households and families, as well as the numerous sources of income other than pensions which may be available to them. It is also important to consider patterns of consumption and expenditure among the elderly, in which healthcare is often prominent. A comprehensive analysis of these issues must combine analyses of large-scale institutions and micro-level relations, as well as relevant influences at intervening levels, such as community initiatives.

INSTITUTION VERSUS PROBLEM-SPECIFIC APPROACHES TO WELFARE

As has been shown, most of the literature dealing with the economic welfare of groups such as the elderly is primarily interested in the institutions created to this end rather than their actual impact on the daily lives of these groups. Thus, micro-level studies focus on the form and dynamics of households, whilst analyses of social security systems emphasise their structure and organisational efficiency. These issues are important enough to justify the academic attention which has been devoted to them. However, the institutional focus has led to a number of gaps in research. Little has been done to assess relationships *between* the various forms of institutions and strategies or the ways in which they combine to form patterns of resource opportunities and constraints for particular groups. This can only be done by complementing an institutional approach with a group and problem-specific one.

This book focuses on a specific contingency (the maintenance of income when elderly) for a narrowly defined group (shanty town residents in Greater Buenos Aires). These parameters were selected for a number of reasons. The elderly already account for a large share of social expenditure in many developing countries. With the acceleration of demographic ageing over the next decades, this will pose even greater challenges. As has been seen, formal social security programmes in developing countries usually favour urban areas. In this respect, it might be concluded that elderly survival strategies in rural areas are of particular interest. It should, however, be borne in mind that by the early twenty-first century the great majority of people in developing countries will be living in cities. Thus, although the economic problems of elderly living in rural areas are a matter of considerable concern, this book takes an urban focus. Greater Buenos Aires was selected since it already contains far higher proportions of elderly than most other large Latin American and Third World cities. In addition, Argentina has a long-established social security system which has suffered from problems characteristic of the region. To narrow the focus of enquiry still further it was elected to restrict the investigation to those elderly in a condition of poverty, since it is likely that this group suffers most hardship from any shortcomings in social policy. Thus, much of this book deals specifically with the cases of a number of shanty towns. This narrow definition of target group is coupled with a strictly economic focus. As such, the book is only concerned with the *economic* welfare of the elderly, excluding, so far as is possible, healthcare and other issues from its enquiry.

This book maps out the full range of income maintenance institutions and strategies potentially available to elderly shanty town residents, noting areas of complementarity, overlap and conflict between them. In this way it is able to integrate both micro- and macro-scale perspectives of the same phenomenon. The case-studies also clarify the relationship between state and non-state action in the realm of welfare. At the same time, a number of more specific questions are posed. These include the effect of gender and past employment on elderly income maintenance, gaps between potential and actual access to institutional support and the economic impact of local organisations.

A central contention of this book is that the economic welfare of the elderly in any developing country cannot be properly understood without reference to the recent economic and social changes and the particular institutional traditions of the country in question. Chapter 2 provides this background context for Argentina, explaining the timing of demographic ageing and drawing attention to the dramatic shift in the country's economic fortunes during the lifetimes of its elderly population. The subsequent chapters form a progression from macro- to micro-level perspectives. They begin with an analysis of elderly economic welfare in Argentina and Greater Buenos Aires as a whole, go on to examine the cases of particular poor urban neighbourhoods and finally consider individual experiences. This hierarchical structure enables an accumulation of information, so that the later chapters are presented in the light of findings of the earlier ones. Thus, although Chapter 5 is primarily concerned with the experiences of individuals, its findings are only meaningful when placed in national, regional and local contexts.

The principal objective of this book is to provide insights into and a policy framework for what will become a major new issue for developing regions in the near future. It is vital that we develop a more sophisticated and comprehensive understanding of the economic welfare of the elderly in these regions. This should not entail unproven generalisations nor should it involve transferring models and assumptions from Europe and North America. Whilst demographic ageing is in itself a desirable process, it must not be considered a costless one. If the material needs of the elderly are not provided for effectively, ageing may simply constitute an extension of privation and misery rather than an enrichment of lifetime opportunities.

2 Ageing and Poverty in Argentina

INTRODUCTION: THE BOOM AND BUST OF ARGENTINE DEVELOPMENT

Argentina's elderly of the 1990s had been born into one of the most prosperous countries in the world, a country which had enjoyed half a century of rapid and sustained economic growth and whose future prospects looked bright. The tremendous fertility of the Pampas region had been the base for the export of farm produce to Britain and other European countries. By the interwar years, living conditions in Argentina were much closer to those in countries such as Australia and Canada than they were to the rest of Latin America. Buenos Aires was a thriving, international metropolis, the largest city on the Atlantic coast of the Americas after New York. The Argentina of the 1930s and 1940s had a large middle class, universal education and a rapidly expanding welfare system.

By the 1990s, the country's fortunes had shifted dramatically. For the 50 years preceding 1930 the gross domestic product (GDP) grew at an average annual rate of around 5 per cent a year (Diaz Alejandro 1970:3). Over the following 60 years, annual growth averaged only around 2 per cent and the 1980s saw GDP fall by more than 1 per cent a year.[1] Decades of economic underperformance had reduced Argentina to the status of 'just another middle income developing country'. Per capita wealth was by now close to or even below that of several other Latin American countries. Poverty and inequality had risen markedly and in Buenos Aires the grandiose architecture of the *belle époque* now stood side by side with slums and shanty towns.

Not surprisingly, Argentina's disastrous economic decline has been the subject of intense academic debate and conflicting interpretations. Since these are not a central concern of this book, this chapter will simply provide a general overview of social and economic change since the 1930s. This focuses on the shifting economic and social opportunities open to those population cohorts born in the interwar period. Later chapters will examine how such changes may have influenced these cohorts' economic welfare upon reaching old age.

This chapter begins by examining patterns of population ageing in Argentina. It shows that the high proportion of elderly was, in large part, a consequence of the long economic 'boom' period. The chapter then goes on to look at changes since the 1930s, paying particular attention to patterns of employment opportunities, wages, poverty and general living conditions.

POPULATION AGEING IN ARGENTINA

Figure 2.1 shows that gradual demographic ageing began to occur in Argentina after the First World War, that it accelerated during the 1950s and slowed down again by the 1980s. As can be seen, this pattern of ageing is closer to that of the United Kingdom (which established a trend that would become typical for north-western Europe) than that of Latin America or other developing regions. Since ageing began sooner and was more rapid in Argentina than in neighbouring countries, it contained a disproportionately high number of elderly by the 1990s.

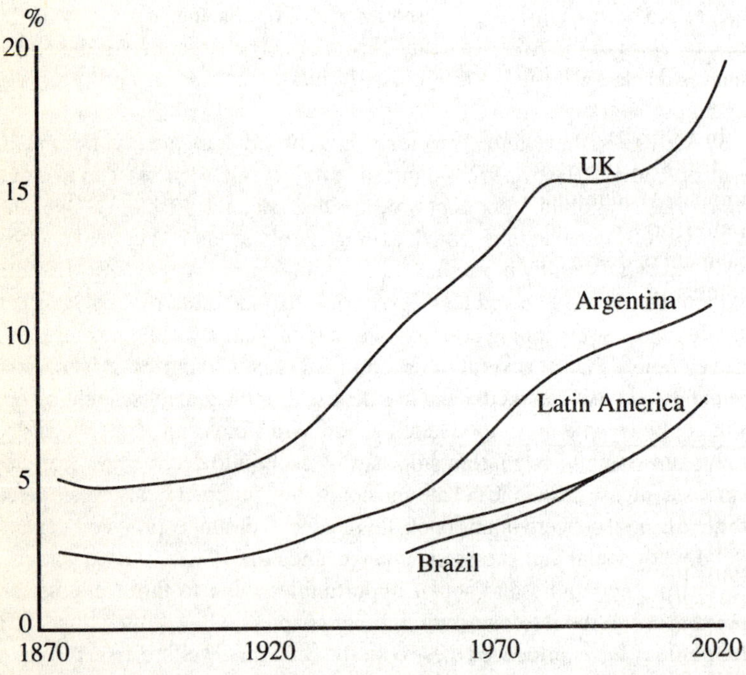

Sources: Mitchell, 1962: 12–13; UN, 1991a:244, 310, 332, 586; Schkolnik, 1975:71.

Figure 2.1 Percentage of population aged 65 or over, 1870–2020

As explained in Chapter 1, population ageing results from a combination of factors, including reduced fertility and increased adult life expectancy. The limited data available for Argentina (Table 2.1 and Figure 2.2) show that both trends were very pronounced during the period of economic prosperity and subsequently levelled out. By the 1930s these changes were having a noticeable effect on the structure of the population as a whole and the rate of demographic ageing began to accelerate. Fertility and life expectancy are, in turn, influenced by a large number of non-demographic factors, including urbanisation, standards of living and healthcare (Cochrane 1983:587–626). In the case of Argentina, particular attention must also be paid to the impact of immigration, which was the dominant demographic feature of the late nineteenth and early twentieth centuries.

Table 2.1: Average life expectancy at birth in Argentina, 1869–1948

1869–95	32.86	1959–61	66.37
1895–1914	40.04	1965–70	67.20
1913–15	48.50	1975–80	68.60
1946–8	61.08	1980–5	69.70

Sources: Lattes, 1975:40; UN, 1991a:310.

In 1880 the country's total population was estimated to have been only 2346000. Consequently, the argricultural export boom required larger amounts of additional labour than could be provided by the native workforce and efforts were made to attract foreigners. Inducements included the payment of ocean passages and the establishment of emigration offices in a number of European cities (Sanchez Albornoz, 1974:152).

Table 2.2: Net immigration to Argentina, 1861–1970

Period	Net immigration	Net immigration as % of total population
1861–70	77 000	4.2
1871–80	85 000	3.6
1881–90	638 000	17.7
1891–1900	320 000	6.8
1901–10	1 120 000	16.5
1911–20	269 000	3.0
1921–30	878 000	7.4
1931–40	73 000	0.5
1941–50	386 000	2.5
1951–60	316 000	1.5
1961–70	257 000	1.1

Sources: Germani, 1970:292; *Academia Nacional de Ciencias*, 1988.

Table 2.2 shows net immigration to Argentina in absolute terms and as a proportion of the total native population. Whilst overseas flows of labour to Argentina were very erratic, they mainly occurred between 1880 and 1930. Over this period net immigration totalled over three million and accounted for around half of the country's total population growth. Although immigration began to rise again during the 1940s, its impact relative to the total host population was much smaller than it had been before 1930.

As well as powering Argentina's dramatic economic expansion, these newcomers transformed the country's demographic structure. First, the great majority of immigrants were of working age, which initially reduced the relative proportions of children and elderly (Figure 2.1). These immigrants would, however, themselves become elderly in later decades, promoting the acceleration of ageing in the mid-twentieth century. Secondly, immigrants promoted urbanisation. Opportunities to buy farmland and settle permanently in the Pampas region were limited and so the great majority of foreigners were drawn to the main cities of the region, which served as export shipment centres. Between 1869 and 1914 the share of population living in urban areas rose from 28.6 to 52.7 per cent.[2] An additional effect of immigration, which

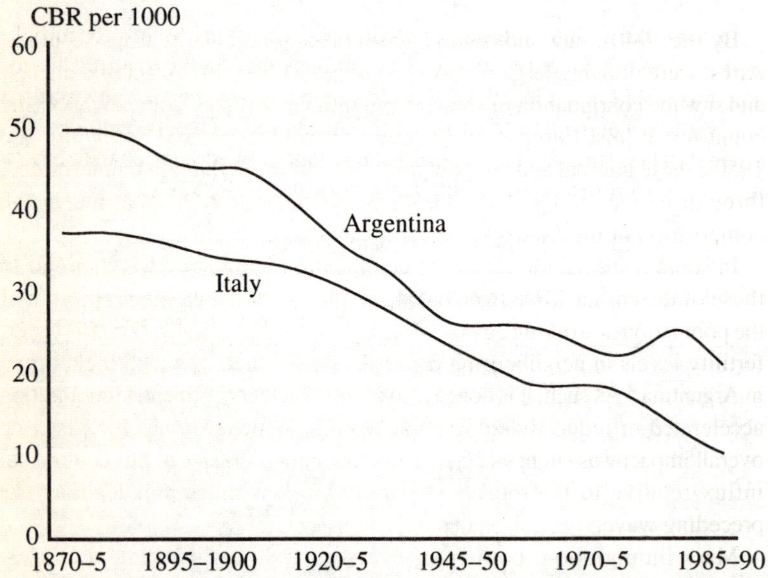

Sources: Livi Bacci, 1977:57; UN, 1991a:370, 510; Schkolnik, 1975:34.

Figure 2.2 Crude birth rate per 1000 in Argentina and Italy, 1870–1990

is often ignored, was its lowering of fertility levels in the host country. The great majority of immigrants were from southern Europe where fertility was low relative to Argentina at that time (Figure 2.2). By the second quarter of the twentieth century, low immigrant fertility was beginning to result in a noticeable rise in the proportion of elderly in the population as a whole.[3]

Table 2.3: Place of birth of the Argentine population, 1869–1991

Year	Native-born (%)	Neighbouring countries (%)	Other (%)
1869	87.9	2.4	9.7
1895	74.6	2.9	22.5
1914	69.7	2.6	27.7
1947	84.7	2.0	13.3
1960	87.0	2.3	10.7
1970	91.0	2.0	7.0
1980	93.0	2.0	7.0
1991	95.0	3.0	2.0

Sources: Argentine Republic, *Consejo Federal de Inversiones*, 1973; Torrado 1992:77; INDEC 1993:55.

By the 1940s, new industrial opportunities, particularly around Buenos Aires, were drawing large numbers of migrants from the Argentine interior and saw the continuation of small but significant influxes from neighbouring countries. Whilst European immigration had again petered out by the late 1950s, these internal and continental flows continued, largely uninterrupted, through to the 1970s. This was reflected in long-term changes in the composition of the resident population, as shown in Table 2.3.

In some respects, the effects of continental immigration were similar to those of the earlier wave from overseas. It both increased the proportion of the population at working age and encouraged further urbanisation. However, fertility levels in neighbouring countries were generally much higher than in Argentina.[4] As such, it is not easy to assess whether continental immigration accelerated or reduced demographic ageing. Whichever was the case, the overall impact was slight since, as Table 2.3 shows, the size of this continental influx relative to the total host population was much smaller than the preceding wave.

Mass immigration, both from overseas and neighbouring countries, occurred at the same time as there were dramatic improvements in general living conditions and as the initial steps were taken to develop effective healthcare, education and welfare systems.[5] All of these factors combined to reduce fertility and encourage population ageing. Nevertheless, it is possible to separate the impact of immigration from these more general changes by comparing the age structures of the foreign and native-born populations. Table 2.4 shows that the proportion of native-born Argentines aged 65 or more in 1960 (3.2 per cent) was significantly lower than that for the total population (5.5 per cent). Thus, had no immigration occurred, Argentina's population would have been only marginally more aged than countries such as Brazil (2.9 per cent aged 65 or more in 1960). It can be concluded, then, that although general improvements in welfare may well have contributed to the ageing of both native and foreign-born residents, immigration accounted for most of the difference between Argentina and other major Latin American countries.[6]

Public policy had encouraged immigration and was, therefore, indirectly responsible for the fertility decline and population ageing. However, in the first half of the twentieth century most Argentine governments and academics considered their country underpopulated and consequently saw neither of these developments as desirable. In 1940 Alejandro Bunge, a leading Argentine economist, urged: 'with all our vigour, our patriotism and a selfless Christian spirit, we should seek to restore the acceptability of large families and the idea that children are a blessing' (Rock, 1991:36). These concerns were embodied in the implementation of a pro-natal family allowance scheme from 1957. Nevertheless, by as early as 1955, Gino Germani, another prestigious academic figure, was able to foresee the complex ramifications that demographic ageing would bring:

> It is very important that the transition to larger proportions of elderly occurs as gradually as possible...Faced with a burgeoning elderly population, it is not just necessary that we develop as broad and as solid a system of welfare, pensions and insurance as can be done, along with adequate modifications in the structure of social assistance and healthcare. We must also bring about a major shift in public attitudes towards old age, including the attitudes of the elderly themselves. It will be necessary to modify much of our behaviour in order to rationally adapt to a change in our demographic structure which has never before been witnessed.
>
> (Germani, 1955:32)

The responses of policy-makers to some of these challenges are examined in Chapter 3.

Argentina's mid-century surge in population ageing was, then, largely the consequence of population flows and socio-economic changes which had occurred before the 1930s. Over the following decades these effects were compounded by the continued upgrading of healthcare, the expansion of social welfare and living standards which until recently remained far higher than those in Latin America as a whole.[7] The impact of the first wave of overseas immigration had passed by the 1970s, since the majority of first generation immigrants were no longer living. This may explain the levelling off of ageing from that time. The slight acceleration of ageing projected for the start of the next century will reflect both the impact of second generation immigrants and that of the smaller, post-war waves.

Table 2.4: Age structure by place of birth (%), 1895–1991

Age	1895	1914	1947	1960	1970	1980	1991
Total							
0–14	41.3	40.1	30.9	30.7	29.1	30.3	30.6
15–64	56.6	57.6	65.2	63.8	63.7	61.5	60.5
65+	2.1	2.3	3.9	5.5	7.2	8.2	8.9
Native							
0–14	50.9	52.8	36.1	34.6	31.9	32.2	32.0
15–64	47.2	45.6	61.9	62.2	63.3	61.2	60.2
65+	1.9	1.6	2.0	3.2	4.8	6.6	7.8
Foreign							
0–14	12.7	10.1	1.8	5.5	3.3	4.5	4.7
15–64	84.6	86.0	83.7	73.6	66.9	65.2	67.1
65+	2.7	3.9	14.5	20.9	29.8	30.3	28.2

Source: INDEC, 1993:52.

Table 2.5: Population of Greater Buenos Aires, 1869–1991

Year	Total population	Population aged 65 or over (%)*
1869	229 000	2.0
1895	782 000	1.8
1914	2 034 000	2.3
1947	4 722 000	4.7
1960	6 739 000	6.9
1970	8 435 000	8.2
1980	9 766 000	9.6
1991	10 935 000	10.5

*Data for Federal Capital and Province of Buenos Aires.
Sources: Recchini de Lattes, 1975:124; 'Apendice' in Recchini de Lattes and Lattes, 1975:201, 205; INDEC, 1993.

Table 2.5 and Figure 2.3 show the pattern of ageing in Greater Buenos Aires.[8] Not surprisingly, the Federal Capital district experienced more pronounced demographic ageing than Argentina as a whole. This resulted from numerous effects. First, the city was the most popular destination for European immigrants and from the 1930s was also receiving very large numbers from the Argentine interior. Table 2.6 shows that these flows continued to account for the bulk of the city's growth through to the 1970s. Secondly, Greater Buenos Aires has traditionally enjoyed healthcare and other social welfare services far superior to those found in the Argentine interior. For example, in 1969 the Federal Capital district contained 7.8 hospital beds per 1000 inhabitants, compared to a national average of 5.6.[9] Whilst no regionally disaggregated data for living standards (such as per capita income) are available for before 1980, indirect indicators show that levels in the city were significantly higher than in most other parts of the country (INDEC, 1981b:220–3, 276–81). These disparities served both to attract migrants and to accelerate the ageing of the existing population.

As can be seen in Figure 2.3, the Province of Buenos Aires contains a much smaller proportion of elderly than does the Federal Capital district.

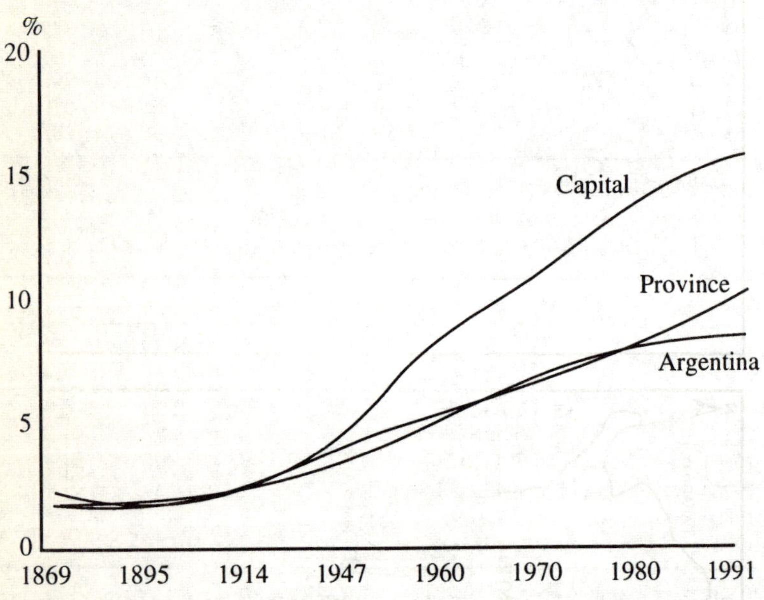

Sources: 'Apendice' in Recchini de Lattes and A. Lattes, eds, 1975:201; INDEC, 1991a:52.

Figure 2.3 Population aged 65 and over in Argentina and Buenos Aires, 1869–1991

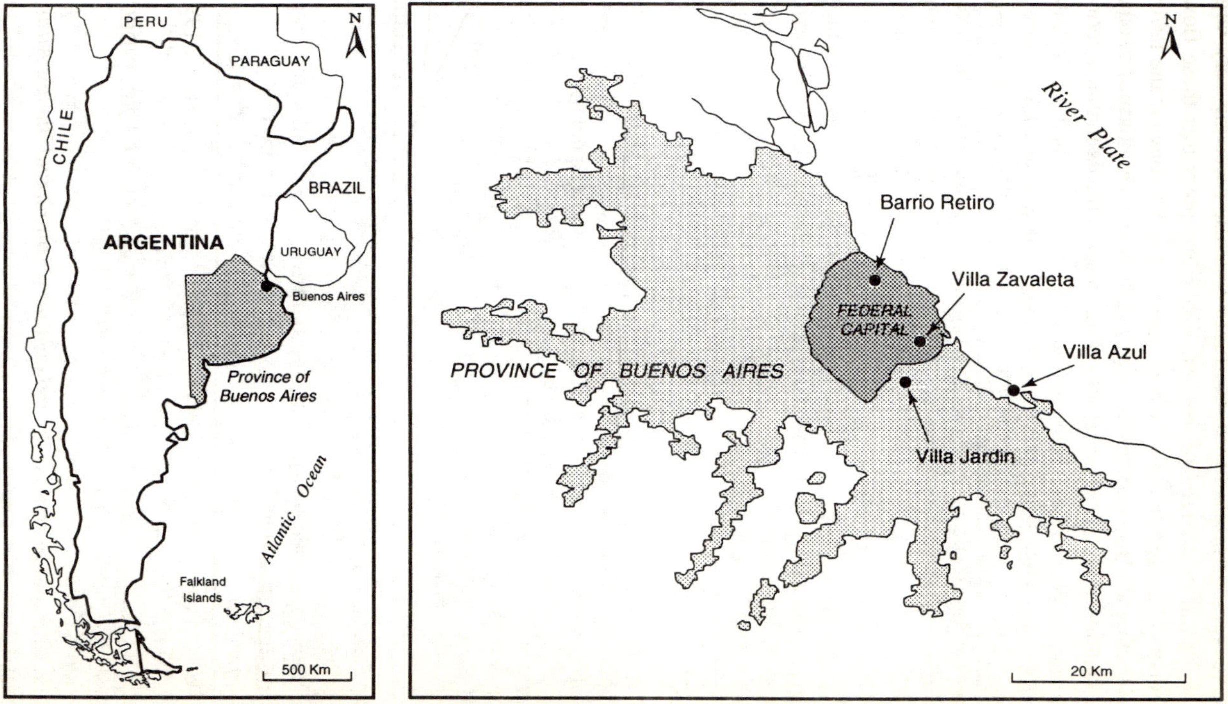

Map 2.1 Greater Buenos Aires

Unfortunately, disaggregated data for those sections of the Province which form a part of Greater Buenos Aires are unavailable. For the same reasons given above, it is probable that these sections contain a larger share of elderly than the surrounding countryside. However, since these areas themselves account for two-thirds of the Province's total population, it would seem that the proportion of elderly in these outlying parts of the city is substantially lower than in the central Federal Capital district.

Table 2.6: Components of demographic growth in Greater Buenos Aires (%), 1855–1970

Period	Natural increase	Internal migration	Immigration	Residual
1855–70	15.1	12.9	95.7	–23.7
1885–95	30.7	12.3	68.2	–11.2
1905–15	38.5	6.4	70.2	–15.1
1915–35	49.7	22.6	45.9	–18.2
1935–45	35.3	57.9	22.6	–15.8
1945–60	26.0	44.0	30.0	0.0
1960–70	46.9	47.2	5.9	0.0

Source: Recchini de Lattes, 1975:131.

Table 2.7: Place of birth of population resident in Buenos Aires, 1947

Place of birth	Resident of Federal Capital (%)	Resident of Province of Buenos Aires (PBA) (%)
Capital or PBA	67.0	75.1
Elsewhere in Argentina	2.8	4.2
Elsewhere in Americas	2.2	1.3
Beyond the Americas	28.0	19.4

Source: Calculated from Argentine Republic, 1956a:38–9, 44–5.

Differences in demographic ageing between the Federal Capital and outlying districts mainly reflect the periods during which each experienced surges in their population growth. In the Federal Capital this occurred between 1870 and 1940, since when the district has seen a gradual but steady population decline. Conversely, the population of the outlying districts roughly trebled between 1947 and 1960 and consequently this area contained a much higher share of migrants from the Argentine interior (Table 2.7). These tended to have relatively high fertility levels and were less likely to have reached old age by the 1980s.[10] Thus, although Greater Buenos Aires contained a larger proportion of elderly than did Argentina as a whole, there were marked variations between more central and more outlying districts.

CHANGES IN THE ARGENTINE LABOUR MARKET SINCE 1900

It is logical that the real incomes and occupations held by individuals during their prime working years have a considerable influence on their propensity to save, make pension contributions and to accumulate assets for later life. It follows that the economic condition of elderly in Argentina in the 1990s depended to some extent on the performance of the economy and the configuration of the labour market during the preceding decades.

Although Argentina has never since been able to recapture its economic success of the 'boom' period, the national labour market continued to expand. Between 1900 and 1980 the economically active population increased from approximately two million (68 per cent of the total population at that time) to over ten million (36 per cent) (CEPAL,1959:37; ILO, 1986c:79). It is possible to identify a number of phases in Argentina's development and employment structure since the start of the twentieth century. Initially, with the economy dominated by the export of primary produce, agriculture accounted for the largest share of employment (see Table 2.8). Nevertheless, urbanisation and the wealth generated by rapid growth had also enabled the formation of a substantial tertiary sector. Industrial employment was relatively limited and was not particularly prominent in Greater Buenos Aires.[11]

Table 2.8: Sectoral composition of the labour force, 1900–80 (1000 workers)

	Agriculture	Manufacturing*	Services	Construction**
1900–4	783	396	723	94
1925–9	1 539	890	1 647	212
1947	1 646	1 497	2 801	304
1960	1 457	2 014	3 549	459
1970	1 411	2 095	4 579	766
1980	1 306	2 270	5 347	1 067

* Data from 1947 include mine workers.
** Data up to 1929 exclude mine workers.
Sources: Calculated from CEPAL, 1959:37–9; Torrado, 1992:125.

Table 2.8 shows that the economically active population more than doubled between 1900 and 1930, with both manufacturing and services slightly increasing in relative importance. However, it was between 1930 and 1955 that both sectors experienced their most impressive expansion. In this second period industrial growth mainly consisted of production for the domestic market and was stimulated by tariffs and a range of other import-substituting policies (Diaz Alejandro, 1970:106–26; Lewis, 1990:79–98, 184–88). Much of this new industry consisted of labour-intensive, light consumer manufacturing and was highly concentrated in and around Greater Buenos Aires.[12] The equally rapid expansion of the service sector was in large part due to a three-fold increase in public employment.[13]

Although employment in both services and manufacturing continued to grow quickly after the mid-1950s, this belied important changes in the pattern of development. New policies began to emphasise high-tech, capital-intensive activities and afforded a greater role to foreign firms and investment (Alschuler, 1987:46–63). Thus, whereas manufacturing output rose by 123 per cent between 1950 and 1969, employment in the sector only increased by 32 per cent, 1946 to 1973 (ECLAC, 1969:141–2; Torrado, 1992:217). Limited opportunities for industrial employment and acute cyclical recessions partly explain the persistence of a small but significant urban informal sector (Table 2.9).

Table 2.9: Composition of the urban labour force, 1950–92 (%)

	Urban informal sector	Domestic service	Other
1950	13.2	7.9	78.9
1960	11.3	7.0	81.7
1970	11.6	7.5	80.9
1980	20.4	6.0	73.6
1985	22.9	6.5	70.6
1990	24.7	7.9	67.4
1992	25.9	7.8	66.3

Note: 1950–70 = share of urban employment; 1980–92 = share of non-agricultural employment.
Sources: PREALC, 1982:34; 1993:4.

A combination of economic bottlenecks and political unrest caused Argentine industrial growth to falter by the late 1960s (Mallon and Sourrouille 1975:29–34). As a result of deepening crises and, at times, intentional policies the sector declined in both relative and absolute terms during the 1970s and 1980s. Between 1960 and 1980 industry's share of total urban employment fell from 20.2 to 14.6 per cent (Torrado, 1992:207). Since this decline was not off-set by substantial rises in formal employment, either in agriculture or services, it led to the expansion of the informal sector (Table 2.9).

The vagaries of Argentina's economic performance and changes in the configuration of its labour markets increase the probability that a high proportion of those who had reached old age by the 1990s may have worked in a variety of activities, including urban and rural, formal and informal. At the same time, the general economic instability of this period was reflected in repeated cycles of recruitment and dismissal of industrial labour. Thus, urban workers were frequently forced to change employer and faced the threat of periodic unemployment. The rise and fall of the industrial sector was also reflected in the performance of real wages. Figure 2.4 shows that during the 1940s and early 1950s the real earnings of industrial workers rose spectacularly; they fluctuated sharply up to the mid-1970s, since when they have gone into a pronounced decline. Given that remuneration in Argentina's growing urban informal sector is generally much lower than for factory workers, the overall effect has been a very sharp fall in per capita earnings from the mid-1970s.

Faltering economic growth, deindustrialisation and the expansion of informal activities all contributed to significant increases in urban poverty from the mid-1970s. As shown in Figure 2.5, in 1970 (the first year for which data are available) 5 per cent of urban households were classified as below the official poverty line. By mid-1980s this had risen to more than 20 per cent. Several studies observe that the majority of Argentina's 'new poor' are of middle-class origins, whereas there has been little change in the number of those experiencing more extreme and permanent forms of poverty (Minujin,

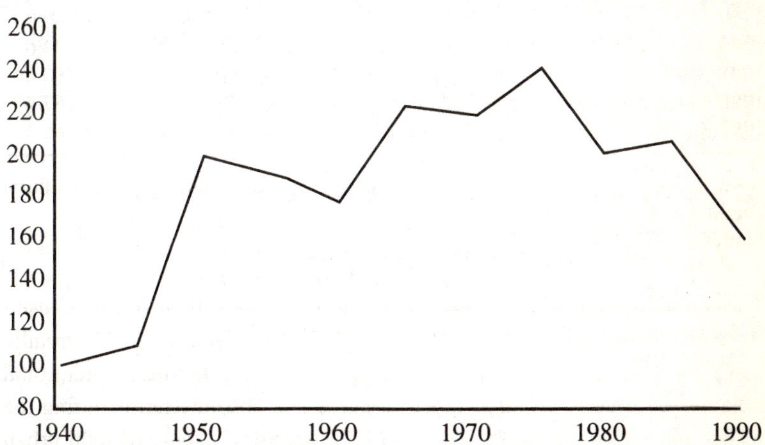

Sources: Roxborough, 1993:104–5; Lo Vuolo 1995:137.

Figure 2.4 Index of real industrial wages in Argentina, 1940–90

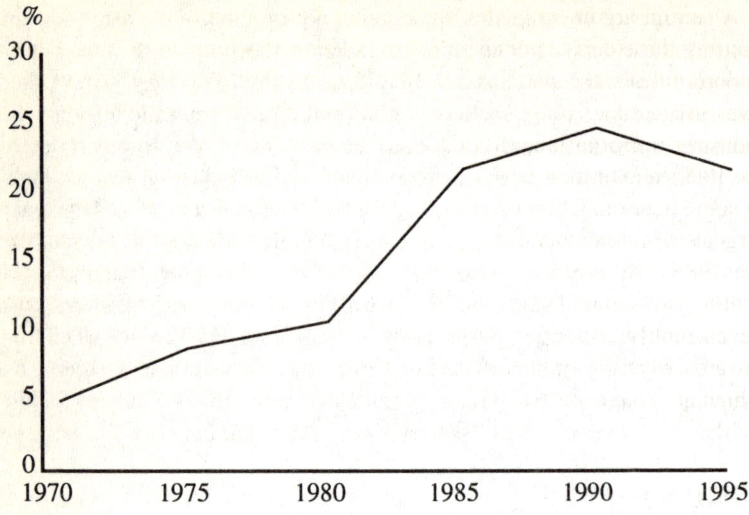

Sources: Lloyd-Sherlock, 1996b; Republic of Argentina, 1995:45.

Figure 2.5 Households below poverty line in Greater Buenos Aires, 1970–95 (%)

1992). This suggests that recent labour market trends may have been less significant for social groups likely to inhabit districts such as shanty towns than they have been for other sections of the population. Nevertheless, it has also been demonstrated that changes in the labour market caused Argentina to become a much less egalitarian society than in the past. Table 2.10 shows that between 1974 and 1994 the share of total income received by the poorest 20 per cent of households fell from 8.1 to only 4.6 per cent. It is, therefore, to be expected that the economic welfare of the poorest groups in cities such as Buenos Aires has deteriorated markedly.

Table 2.10: Estimated per capita secondary income distribution in Greater Buenos Aires, 1974–94

Year/income quintile	1–20%	21–40%	41–60%	61–80%	81–100%
1974	8.1	11.7	17.2	22.6	40.4
1980	6.5	10.8	15.7	21.8	45.1
1985	5.5	10.2	14.6	21.9	47.6
1990	4.8	9.2	13.2	20.3	52.5
1994	4.6	8.6	13.0	20.4	53.3

Source: Lloyd-Sherlock, 1996a:23.

A central argument of this book is that the economic welfare of groups such as the elderly cannot be fully understood without reference to the opportunities and constraints which they faced during earlier stages of their lives. Argentina's long-term economic decline and the rise and fall of the industrial sector influenced the material conditions of both elderly living in the 1990s and of their families and households. These effects are examined in some detail in Chapters 4 and 5. Clearly, the prosperity which underlay Argentina's premature demographic transition was no longer in evidence by the 1980s. As a result, a country which has a 'European' demographic profile had begun to face social and economic problems more typical of the developing world. In this respect, the Argentine experience may point towards what the future holds for a number of other developing countries which are now experiencing ageing.

SHANTY TOWNS AND OLD AGE IN BUENOS AIRES.

Table 2.11 summarises available data for the growth of shanty towns in Greater Buenos Aires. These data are both patchy and, at times, misleading. Indeed, most academics recognise that shanty towns (known locally as *villas miserias*) were found in Buenos Aires well before the 1940s.[14] Nevertheless, two important conclusions can be drawn from Table 2.11. First, it is clear that the population of *villas miserias* in the city as a whole expanded markedly between the mid-1940s and the 1980s.[15] This no doubt partly resulted from Argentina's poor economic performance over the period. Secondly, it should be stressed that, whilst not being insignificant, the proportion of Buenos Aires' total population living in *villas* (4.7 per cent in 1970) was far smaller than for other large Latin American cities at that time.[16] There are a number of explanations for this, including relative prosperity and an egalitarian distribution of wealth (at least up to the 1970s), as well as slower rates of city growth than elsewhere in the region. As can be seen, the socio-economic changes of the 1980s led to a substantial rise in the shanty town population in outlying districts, although this still remains less prominent than in other Latin American cities.

In the context of Buenos Aires, shanty towns may therefore be characterised as relatively limited 'pockets' of urban poverty. Nevertheless, if current trends persist, they may eventually contain large sections of the city's population. As such, conditions in these neighbourhoods may be more representative of poorer Third World cities (where such housing is much more prevalent) and future developments in Buenos Aires than they are of the city today.

Table 2.11: Selected estimates of the shanty town population of Greater Buenos Aires, 1947–91

Year	Federal Capital	Outlying districts
1947	0	0
1960	22 700	72 000
1970	127 800	265 200
1980/81	40 500	290 100
1991	65 000	485 000

Source: Lloyd-Sherlock, 1996b:25; *Microsemanario*, 1996.

The origin and nature of *villas miserias* influenced both the number of elderly living there and their economic condition. Given that their principal period of expansion was after the 1950s, it follows that these neighbourhoods were mainly populated by non-European migrants from the interior or neighbouring countries. The relatively high fertility levels of these groups would have increased the proportion of children and reduced the proportion of elderly in the *villas*. Also, numerous surveys stress poor levels of hygiene and inadequate healthcare facilities in the shanty towns, which would have reduced life expectancy and hence the number of elderly (Provincia de Buenos Aires, 1981). The desire of many residents to move to a more secure neighbourhood once they had sufficient savings was also significant. In more prosperous periods, newcomers would generally be younger than the upwardly mobile *villa* residents they replaced and only the most unsuccessful would remain in the shanty town until old age. The rapid rise in poverty and fall in wages in Buenos Aires from the 1970s reduced the likelihood that residents could save enough to purchase a plot of land outside the *villa* and consequently promoted ageing in the locale. Thus, whilst high fertility and low life-expectancy served to depress the relative weight of the elderly in *villas*, reduced opportunities for escape had the opposite effect. Any overall change in the age structure of the *villas miserias* depended upon the relative importance of these two effects.

Very little data exist for the age structures of shanty town populations in Greater Buenos Aires, particularly for before the 1980s. The only general survey of *villas* which includes data on residents' ages was the 1981 census conducted in Buenos Aires Province but which excluded the Federal Capital district (Table 2.12). This found that *villas miserias* in the Province contained a much lower proportion of elderly than did the Province as whole. This was also the case in the districts of Lanús and Avellaneda, which are locations for two of the case-studies detailed in Chapters 4 and 5. Unfortunately, no comparable studies were carried out for shanty towns in the Federal Capital, which as a whole contains much higher proportions of elderly. Nor do data exist for changes in the age structure of *villas* over time. As such, it is impossible to assess the impact of any changes in fertility and life expectancy, as well as opportunities for 'escape' on the age structures of the city's *villas*.

Table 2.12: Population aged 60 or over in villas *in selected districts of Buenos Aires Province, 1981*

District	Total aged 60+	60+ as % of total population
Buenos Aires Province (BAP)	1 293 000	11.9
Villas in BAP	8 271	2.9
Villas in Lanús district	1 618	3.6
Villas in Avellaneda district	802	3.4

Sources: INDEC, 1981a; Provincia de Buenos Aires, 1981.

The absence of data on ageing in shanty towns is part of a broader problem. Whilst demographic information is available at various levels of geographical desegregation (nation-wide, provincial and by various types of city district), it is not broken down by different socio-economic groups. Consequently, it is difficult to ascertain whether population ageing has been significant among groups such as the urban poor. This is a key issue for all developing countries. The social and economic ramifications of projected population ageing will be very different if this only reflects changes in middle and upper income groups, instead of in society at large. Fragmentary information for shanty towns in São Paulo, Brazil, show a rapid acceleration in the absolute number of elderly and a more gradual convergence with other parts of the city in terms of relative numbers.[17] Chapters 4 and 5 return to this question, presenting demographic data for a small number of individual neighbourhoods.

CONCLUSIONS

The experiences of Buenos Aires both with regards to population ageing and the evolution of shanty town settlements do not conform to those of most other large Latin American cities. This mainly reflects the peculiarities of Argentina's economic and social history: the long period of growth before 1930 and the subsequent decline. Accelerated demographic ageing was largely due to the long-term impact of transatlantic immigration. This involved two effects. First, immigrants had lower fertility levels than the host population. Secondly, immigrants were mostly young adults. This caused a bulge in the national age pyramid, which gradually worked its way upward over time. By the 1930s and 1940s, these immigrant cohorts were reaching old age. The momentum of demographic ageing was subsequently sustained by relatively high levels of wealth and rapid socio-economic change. Consequently, even in the 1990s Argentina still contained a far greater proportion of aged than most other developing countries. Providing for the economic welfare of this group was a major challenge, yet from the 1930s it was becoming clear that Argentina was losing its economic dynamism. Contracting formal sector employment and falling real wages must have reduced the capacity of family members to provide the elderly economic support. Increasing poverty and hardship must have placed additional pressures on the social security system and intensified intergenerational resource conflict. These issues are dealt with in the following chapters.

3 Social Security and Other Income Strategies Available to the Elderly in Buenos Aires

INTRODUCTION

As discussed in Chapter 1, elderly economic welfare, both in developed and developing regions, has been strongly associated with the operation of formal social security programmes. Less attention has been paid to other sources of support, which are often relegated to a residual category of 'informal' support networks. This chapter outlines the range of formal and informal income maintenance strategies open to elderly living in Greater Buenos Aires. Just as it is impossible to understand the condition of elderly individuals without referring to changing economic opportunities over their lifetimes, so any analysis of contemporary welfare institutions has to be put in a clear historical perspective.

This chapter begins by looking at the evolution of formal social security programmes in Argentina, placing them in the context of the general models and philosophies of state welfare intervention outlined in Chapter 1. This leads on to a detailed review of public welfare provision for the elderly Greater Buenos Aires in the early 1990s. The chapter then goes on to examine other potential sources of economic support, which range from large-scale institutions (such as mutual aid societies, NGOs, overseas aid and private pension funds), to informal, micro-level strategies (such as community networks and household dynamics). By way of conclusion, the chapter brings together these diverse phenomena, noting interrelationships, as well as areas of overlap and complementarity.

FORMAL SOCIAL SECURITY

Chapter 1 gives a general account of the expansion of and problems confronting formal social security programmes in developing regions. It pays detailed attention to Latin America, observing that programmes in this region were relatively comprehensive and were facing particularly acute difficulties by the 1990s. The development of social security in Argentina has been quite typical of Latin America. To a certain extent this is surprising, given the distinctive economic and demographic history, which sets Argentina apart from the rest of the region, as outlined in Chapter 2. Instead, the similarities between social security programmes testify to the major role played by political factors in this process. As will be seen, many aspects of Argentina's political development closely parallel those of neighbouring countries. This section examines how these varied influences combined promote to the emergence of large-scale social security systems in Argentina, paying attention to the form these initiatives took and their impact on general welfare.

The evolution of social security in Argentina up to the 1990s

Most accounts of welfare programmes in Argentina focus on the impact of General Juan Domingo Perón, Evita Perón and the Peronist political movement. In Argentina and beyond it remains a widely held view that public sector welfare interventions were very limited before Juan Perón's political ascendance in 1944. Likewise, it is the prevailing belief that the Peronists implemented an embracing welfare state, which included insurance pension programmes and a range of assistance measures for the elderly, and that much of this remained in place through to the 1990s (Mesa-Lago, 1979:163–5; Passanante, 1987:125–33). As such, any study of contemporary welfare structures in Argentina must begin with an assessment of the Peronist welfare model.

Before Perón (c. 1890–1944)

Argentine social and economic policy in the late nineteenth and early twentieth centuries is generally considered to have been predominantly liberal, emphasising free market forces and keeping state intervention to a minimum. Nevertheless, this period saw the appearance of several occupation-specific social insurance programmes (among the first in the world) and increasing state involvement in assistance projects. By 1915 all public employees, as well as workers in private railway companies had been enrolled in public pension schemes. These were obligatory and replaced pre-existing private funds (Lewis, 1993:177–8). The apparent paradox between liberal policies and the expansion of pension funds has been explained in a number of ways. Some accounts claim that the most powerful labour unions were able to impose their demands on the state (Ross, 1989:19). Conversely, other studies argue that the state itself took the initiative and sought to co-opt sections of the labour movement (Isuani, 1988:29).

Social assistance funding was provided primarily by the *Ministerio de Asuntos Exteriores y Culto* (MAEC). Aid was channelled through a number of organisations which, whilst originating in the voluntary sector, developed increasingly close ties with the national government. According to Ross:

> The *Sociedad de Beneficencia*, despite its appearance as the major private charity organisation, was a semi-state body which received somewhere between 81 and 92 per cent of its funding between 1894 and 1903 from government grants. (Ross, 1989:134)

In 1908 this state of affairs was recognised by law, which placed the *Sociedad* formally within the jurisdiction of the MAEC. Lacking adequate financing from non-government sources, voluntary organisations had little alternative but to accept their loss of autonomy. As seen in Table 3.1, the level of government funding for social assistance increased substantially in real terms through the early twentieth century. Given, however, that only 2.3 per cent of the population were aged over 65 in 1914 and that the proportion for low-income groups was probably much lower, it is unlikely that the elderly received a significant proportion of assistance financing (Tenti Fanfani, 1989).

Table 3.1: Social assistance funding by the Ministerio de Asuntos Exteriores y Culto, *1905–42*

Year	MAEC funding MN$
1905	567 336
1910	4 055 212
1938	41 916 808
1942	64 911 763

Source: Calculated from Ross, 1989:231, 237.

Thus, the extension of state involvement in social insurance and assistance programmes was a gradual process, which was already well underway before regimes more generally considered to be welfarist had taken office. This process continued, albeit erratically, through the 1920s and 1930s. Again, the expansion of social insurance appears to have had little to do with the broader economic and social role allotted to the public sector, which varied from proto-statism in the 1920s to renewed liberalism in the mid-1930s. In 1922 pension coverage was extended to banking workers, but efforts by the same regime to set up funds for other white-collar workers were thwarted by determined political opposition (Lewis, 1993:177–85). Nevertheless, by 1939 additional occupation-specific funds had been established for financial workers, journalists and the merchant marines.

Less information is available about social assistance funding in the interwar period. Accounts of the social hardships resulting from a number of sharp economic recessions make little reference to the activities of such programmes (Lewis, 1989:104–6 and 123–5; Rock, 1993:142–3). In 1932 the state set up the *Fondo de Asistencia Social* to co-ordinate the payment of subsidies to, and activities of, a number of private charities. In 1933 the first national conference for social assistance was convened and proposed the establishment of a national programme of direct assistance. The conference made specific reference to a number of vulnerable social groups including mothers, young children, invalids and even ex-prisoners, but made no direct mention of the elderly (Argentine Republic, 1934: volume I 17–8, volume II 160–5). This constituted a failure to recognise that the elderly were, by that time, accounting for a rapidly growing proportion of the populace. In any case, most of the conference's proposals were shortly afterwards rejected, as attempts were made to channel public expenditure to the struggling rural economy (Diaz-Alejandro, 1970:97; Tenti Fanfani, 1989:72–6). This shows that, although the state was the principal funder of assistance programmes, these were nevertheless low on its list of priorities for intervention.

The first Peronist governments (1944–55)

Most political histories of Argentina still struggle to provide a clear definition of Peronism's guiding ideology, although parallels have been drawn with Mussolini, southern European fascist regimes and a number of Latin American leaders of the same period. A central element of Peronist policy was a virtuous Keynesian circle of industrialisation and increased domestic consumption. Within this strategy, social welfare policy played a key role, both as a means of bolstering demand and as a device for political control. As such, studies of state welfare policy in Argentina generally portray the first Peronist regimes of 1944 to 1955 as a crucial turning-point. Indeed, it is often claimed that this period saw the transformation of a number of disparate, limited social measures into a universal, Beveridgian welfare state. However, whilst few dispute that the broader development policies of the regime were strongly statist, recent revisionist writings have questioned whether this was reflected in significant increases in public welfare expenditure, particularly within social insurance (Lloyd-Sherlock, 1992:12–18).

The early Peronist period saw a dramatic expansion of the social insurance system. Public pension funds were set up for commercial and industrial workers in 1944 and 1946 respectively and in 1954 protection was extended, at least on paper, to self-employed and rural workers. Ross claims that the total number of insurance affiliates rose from 2771446 to 4681411 between 1947 and 1954. However, as shown in Figure 3.1, a different study concludes that evasion may have reduced real levels of affiliation to only 2129000 in 1954. This compared to a total economically active population of 7106000 in 1950. Moreover, the ratio of pensioners to affiliates in pension funds remained very low *(Review of the River Plate*, 30 December 1952). Consequently, whilst the creation of new pension funds would ultimately lead to a large increase in the number of benefits granted, this did not occur during the lifetime of early Peronist governments. Rather, accelerating inflation reduced the overall effect of social insurance on the welfare of the elderly. A 1954 survey found that retirement pension values in every fund had fallen since 1947, sometimes by as much as 52 per cent. In only one fund did average pensions exceed the minimum industrial wage of the day *(Review of the River Plate,* Buenos Aires, 20 April 1954).

Peronist social assistance policies represented a more dramatic break with the past. The increased priority afforded the welfare needs of the elderly was reflected in a number of guarantees enshrined in the new Constitution of 1949:

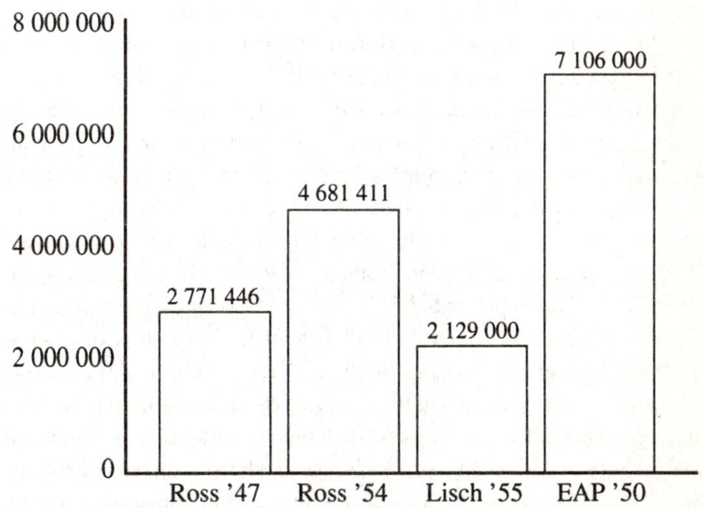

Sources: Lischinsky, 1989:5, 11; Ross, 1989:65a; ILO, 1989: volume III 79.

Figure 3.1 Alternative estimates of social insurance affiliation, 1947–55

> All the elderly have the right to full economic protection, which should be provided by their families. Where this does not occur, the State will provide such protection either directly or through institutions and foundations created to this end. The State or the above-mentioned bodies retain the right to demand that any relatives who are able to provide financial support do so.[1]

Thus, although it placed the emphasis on family support, the regime took on the responsibility of providing a universal safety net for all those elderly without insurance pensions or sufficiently prosperous relatives.

The government soon made plain its unwillingness to operate through private charities. The state cut funding to organisations such as the *Sociedad de Beneficiencia*, prohibited their use of voluntary staff and imposed unrealistic minimum wages (Ross, 1989:246). In 1948 a new welfare organisation was set up under the control of the President's wife. To many Argentines the *Fundación Eva Perón* (FEP) embodied Peronism's genuine concern for the welfare of the most disadvantaged. The FEP's high-profile activities did not, however, lead to higher levels of social assistance expenditure by the state. The bulk of its revenue came from a national lottery, a new tax on labour and donations which employers were 'encouraged' to make. Although the FEP was formally a private institution, it was largely run through the Ministry of Labour (Navarro, 1983:23–6). Indeed, it could be argued that, whilst social assistance still combined the efforts of the private and public sectors, their roles as executive and funder had been reversed.

Peronist assistance policies influenced the economic welfare of the elderly in several respects. Most importantly, they included the first large-scale non-contributory pension programmes. From 1950 the FEP began to grant benefits to unprotected over-60-year-olds who could no longer work and lacked immediate family members in employment. By 1953, official sources claim that 32000 such pensions had been granted in Greater Buenos Aires alone (Ross, 1989:345). This represented 5.5 per cent of over-60-year-olds in the city (Argentine Republic, INDEC 1948:108–10). However, even if the number of pensions granted was as large as official sources suggest, their monetary value was very small and they were devalued by inflation; by 1953 assistance pensions were worth only one sixth of the minimum industrial wage (*Review of the River Plate*, 20 April 1954; Ross, 1989:345). As with many of the activities of the FEP, this programme was implemented with the maximum publicity and self-congratulation. According to Ross: 'Many of the recipients received the pensions in public ceremonies, orchestrated in such a way as to be emotional and sentimental events widely reported in the media.'[2]

As such, the pension programme and other FEP activities provided an important precedent for the implementation of high profile, populist assistance programmes by future regimes, some of which would be of direct benefit to the elderly.

The *Fundación* continued its activities despite the death of Evita Perón in 1951. However, in September 1955, the democratically-elected government of General Juan Domingo Perón was ousted by a military coup, heralding a period of intensifying political instability which continued through to the early 1980s.

After Perón (1955–73)

The 1950s and 1960s did not see significant changes in the basic administrative and legal framework of social insurance. On one hand this reflected political considerations: the power of the unions and the desire of non-democratic regimes to co-opt the support of a range of interest groups. On the other it complemented broader development policy which remained largely statist and considered public welfare as necessary to provide a co-operative, efficient workforce (Lewis, 1993:191–5).

Whilst social insurance policy did not change dramatically, its financial position and impact on welfare did. As a growing proportion of affiliates reached retirement age, the number of insurance pensions (known as *jubilaciones*) began to increase. This was paralleled by a shift from surplus to deficit in pension fund finances (see Table 3.2).

Pension fund deficits are not an inevitable consequence of increasing numbers of benefit payments. As long as pensions are fully capitalised, fund finances should reach an equilibrium after the initial start-up period. However, Argentina's social insurance schemes rarely struck a balance between expenditure and interest accrued by contributions. Even before 1944 a number of individual funds were in debt.[3] From the late 1940s, these were being baled out by transfers from more recently established funds[4] and in 1954 the scheme as a whole shifted to a pay-as-you-go system of financing, which sought to balance annual contributions with expenditure. This merely postponed the effect of the rising ratio of pensioners to contributors.

Various factors explain why the Argentine social insurance system was not developed on a sound financial basis. These include an absence of actuarial forecasting and the dominance of short-term political agendas over longer-term economic rationalism. Sometimes this was reflected in promises of unfeasibly large benefit hikes or low retirement ages.[5] At other times it entailed the accumulation of substantial public debts to the system.[6] Moreover, the administrative structure was highly fragmented with separate funds and separate benefits for different occupation groups. This increased administrative costs and facilitated evasion and fraud.[7] Fragmentation led to the development of privileged funds for groups such as the military, the police and high-ranking functionaries. Between 1950 and 1972 average military pensions were roughly double those paid by other funds (Dieguez and Petrecolla, 1977:185–6). This was a drain on resources and reduced the credibility of the social insurance system in the eyes of the general public.

Table 3.2: Social insurance coverage, 1950–90

Year	Number over retirement age (000s)*	Pensions granted (000s)	Coverage (%) **	Fund surplus (deficit) ***
1950	1 495	188	12.59	28 880
1955	1 836	473	25.76	21 735
1960	2 236	749	33.51	5 628
1965	2 674	1 086	40.62	3 350
1970	3 123	1 390	44.52	(4 492)
1975	3 575	1 695	47.41	145
1980	4 039	2 342	58.00	(136)
1985	4 528	2 759	60.93	na
1990	4 977	3 031	60.90	(2 367 870)

*Until 1967 this was 60 years for men, 55 for women; subsequently, it became 65 and 60 years respectively.
**This figure is the total population above the retirement age divided by the total number of benefits granted. Since a proportion of pensions were granted to individuals below the retirement age and some individuals held more than one, this figure overestimates the true percentage of elderly with an insurance benefit. Unfortunately, there are insufficient data to provide a more accurate estimate.
***Data exclude provincial and municipal funds. Financial data as follows: 1950–70, 1960 pesos (000s); 1975–85, 1985 australes (000s); 1990, 1990 australes (000 000s).
Sources: Dieguez and Petrecolla, 1977; Feldman et al, 1988:103; Isuani and San Martino, 1993:19, 29.

In 1966 a military junta committed to moderately liberal economic policies seized power and began to plan a complete overhaul of the pension system. These reforms, implemented in 1967, gave rise to the administrative structure still in place in the early 1990s. Non-military occupation-specific funds were grouped into three divisions: public employees, private waged labour and self-employed workers. The range of available benefits was rationalised and the retirement age was pushed on to 65 for men and 60 for women. However, as the military regime became increasingly unpopular, it was forced to make numerous concessions to interest groups and was unable to prevent the system from generating large deficits in the 1970s (see Table 3.2).

No major innovations in social assistance took place during the 1950s and 1960s. Whilst some of the FEP's activities were continued under the aegis of a new state agency, the *Instituto Nacional de Asistencia Social,* there are no indications that significant numbers of assistance pensions were granted. Expenditure in this area remained very small, compared to insurance. Meanwhile, there was a gradual shift in emphasis away from large-scale projects to initiatives in individual neighbourhoods and by 1971 a national network of 'community development programmes' had been established. These aimed to combine the efforts of state agencies with grassroots actors and, as such, marked the beginnings of a gradual shift away from the state welfare monopoly.[8] The impact of these programmes is examined in detail in the following chapter.

Despite the system's financial problems, in 1970 a new dimension was added to state social insurance programmes, with the creation of the *Instituto Nacional de Servicios Sociales para Jubilados y Pensionados* (INSSJP). This was to offer a broad range of services for the elderly from the late 1980s, but most of its activities were originally restricted to healthcare provision,[9] including discounts for a large range of drugs and treatments.[10] Uninsured elderly aged over 70 and those in receipt of national assistance pensions were eligible for a small number of these services. The Institute was financially autonomous from the other components of the social insurance system, receiving funds from a separate scheme of workers' contributions.

Financial crisis

The extension of social insurance coverage in the immediate post-war decades was impressive but financially unsustainable. From the mid-1970s this expansion began to slow and its positive impact on the economic welfare of the elderly declined. The *Proceso de reorganisación nacional* of 1976 to 1982 sought, for the first time since the 1930s, a dramatic shift away from developmentalist to neo-liberal economic and social policies. The new military government rejected the notion of the state as a guarantor of welfare for the whole population, with brutal repression replacing co-optive, if occasionally violent, populism. All areas of social policy suffered sharp spending cuts, with the full burden of social insurance contributions passed on to the workers.[11] Whilst the number of beneficiaries continued to rise, this largely reflected official encouragement of early retirement as a means of reducing open unemployment levels and as such would not have influenced the economic welfare of the elderly (Cortes, 1990:223). Despite the political orientation of the *Proceso* regime, the level of state involvement in welfare remained far higher than during earlier periods of liberal rule. This reflected the enormous socio-economic changes which had occurred, the durability of pre-existing welfare structures and the need to maintain a modicum of political support.

Table 3.3: Value of social insurance benefits, 1971–90

Year	Average pension as % of average wage	% beneficiaries with minimum pension	Minimum pension value (A)	Minimum pension value (B)
1971*	na	22.1	70.6	na
1972	na	40.6	76.6	na
1973	na	50.2	86.9	na
1974	na	50.9	117.9	na
1975	46.6	84.4	115.1	1 061
1976	56.2	58.3	68.1	700
1977	67.4	68.1	74.8	700
1978	95.8	48.2	92.1	840
1979	73.2	50.0	82.3	819
1980	65.0	50.1	82.3	962
1981	64.0	66.1	86.6	843
1982	61.6	73.7	73.8	713
1983	58.0	74.3	80.3	663
1984	45.8	76.9	93.9	651
1985	51	79.7	76.4	733
1986	43	na	na	753
1987	45	na	na	546
1988	55	82.3	na	na
1989	42	na	na	na
1990	55	na	na	na

*Unlike other figures which are taken from the year's end, this is a January figure.
A=1985 australes
B=June 1988 australes
Sources: Feldman et al, 1988:119–22, 124; Frediani, 1989:39, 47; Isuani, 1993:30.

Whilst there is some disagreement over whether average pension values rose or fell during the 1950s and 1960s,[12] it is generally agreed that there were significant reductions from the 1970s. As Table 3.3 indicates, between January 1971 and November 1976, the proportion of insurance pensions paid at the minimum value rose from 22.1 to 58.3 per cent. Although pensions values were able to keep pace with average wages, it should be noted that the latter fell by over half between 1975 and 1992.[13]

Table 3.2 shows that, although the number of benefits granted continued to rise during the 1980s, levels of coverage remained largely the same. This resulted from a combination of population ageing and the persistence of a 'hard core' of evaders and unemployed, who remained beyond the system's scope. A survey of workers lacking insurance cover in 1988 found that 46 per cent were rural labourers, 36 per cent were employed in the urban informal sector and 11 per cent worked in domestic service (Frediani, 1989:80). Thus, even when the extreme liberalism of the *Proceso* was replaced by moderately progressive social policies, the worsening financial position of the pension funds prevented any improvement in either qualitative or quantitative coverage.

In one respect, however, the Argentine social insurance system was in a relatively healthy condition, especially compared to those of other Latin American countries. Reductions in public sector real wages since the late 1970s had led to a substantial fall in staffing costs. Between 1983 and 1986 these only represented 3.4 per cent of total expenditure, compared to 6.8 per cent in Brazil and 8.2 per cent in the newly privatised Chilean system.[14] However, the overall deficit of the Argentine system had reached such proportions that these economies had a minimal impact.

Social insurance funding reached crisis point in 1986 when the Supreme Court ruled that minimum pension values should be in line with the 82 per cent figure promised in the past. Contributions were increased, new taxes on food and telephone use were introduced and a number of direct transfers were made from the treasury (*Latin American Weekly Reports*, 20 November

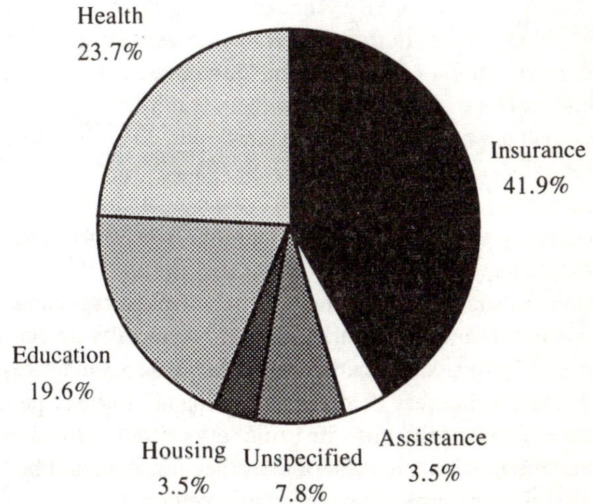

Source: Isuani '*El Estado borrado*', *Página 12*, 8 November 1992.

Figure 3.2 Composition of social spending in Argentina, 1990–2

1986). Despite these measures the pension system's deficits continued to rise. By the start of the 1990s government transfers to the system accounted for 42 per cent of total social spending: a sum equivalent to the combined budgets of the education and health sectors (see Figure 3.2).

The financial crisis prompted new debates about thorough reforms, which continued into the early 1990s.[15] Since the first occupation-specific funds had been established, affiliation had been, at least in theory, obligatory. By taking over private pension schemes, the state had effectively granted itself a monopoly of pension fund management. The reform proposals of the 1980s began to challenge this policy and in 1989 provision was made for the establishment of complementary private pension funds.

As shown in Figure 2.5 in the previous chapter, a failure to restore long-term economic growth had led to a marked increase in poverty levels from the late 1960s. This process was accelerated by the policies of the *Proceso* and a series of acute economic crises which afflicted subsequent governments. By the 1980s Argentina was no longer a country which enjoyed 'European' living standards. This both reflected the failure of the state welfare monopoly and the mounting economic crisis. In consequence, the need for effective social assistance initiatives intensified.

During the *Proceso* no new social assistance initiatives were implemented and funding for existing community-level projects was reduced. There is no evidence of projects providing non-contributory pensions or other measures of direct benefit to the elderly. Indeed, many of the community-level programmes implemented during the 1960s were actively discouraged at this time. This contrasted with subsequent democratic governments which responded to growing poverty levels with a series of food aid projects on a scale which had not occurred since the days of the FEP. These included the *Programa de Alimentación Nacional* (PAN, 1984–89) and the *Bono Nacional Solidario de Emergencia* (BNSE, 1989–91), which provided food aid to several million households. As with the FEP, no provisions were made to include private or voluntary organisations in the distribution of the aid.[16] Some studies claim that these programmes were inefficient and clientelistic and that only a small proportion of their budgets went to those households in greatest need.[17] Despite such claims and the fact that they did not specifically target the elderly, the very scale of the projects' 230 000 parcels being distributed in Greater Buenos Aires alone by 1988 (INDEC, 1989:49) suggests that they must have been of some benefit to the aged.

National assistance projects were complemented by an increasing array of initiatives implemented by provincial and municipal governments. This partly reflected the increased autonomy granted these tiers of government after the years of military rule. It also stemmed from a policy of social assistance decentralisation (FIEL 1987:189–93; Vargas de Flood, 1992:6). A number of new agencies were set up offering the elderly means-tested, non-contributory pensions and subsidies. The impact of these changes is assessed in greater detail later in this chapter.

Social security under Menem: Peronism betrayed (1989–94)?

In 1989 the Peronists returned to power, with the election of Carlos Saúl Menem to the presidency. As has been shown, previous Peronist regimes had been strongly statist in their policies and had been responsible for the public sector monopoly of insurance and assistance. The distribution of BNSE food vouchers largely through the trade unions (considered the traditional base of Peronist support) was reminiscent of previous Peronist welfare initiatives. However, the programme was discontinued in 1990 amidst allegations of corruption and mismanagement. Moreover, the general economic policies of the Menem government represented a sharp break with Peronist tradition, advocating privatisation, fiscal reforms and tighter controls on public expenditure.[18] As such, there emerged a contradiction between the traditional orientation and support base of the ruling party and its apparent conversion to neo-liberal policies.

The change of government saw no immediate shifts in insurance or assistance provision for the elderly. Benefit increases continued to lag behind inflation and pensions were not made more widely available.[19] This prompted weekly, occasionally violent, demonstrations by disaffected pensioners outside the National Congress building.[20] However, the Menem administration's initial policy inertia belied a strong commitment to radically overhaul the public welfare system. Since it accounted for the largest share of government expenditure, social insurance received particular attention. Calls to privatise the system were given additional impetus by a number of high-profile failures to resolve the problems of the insurance system from within the public sector. These included the creation in 1990 of a new state agency to bolster efficiency levels which in fact led to a doubling of administrative costs (FIEL, 1991:302–3). In 1992 it was proposed that the system be privatised along the lines of the Chilean pension programme, although with a larger number of government checks and balances. The reform was strongly resisted by the unions and main political opposition parties and suffered a number of important revisions.[21] However, in December 1993 the Congress and Senate duly voted to grant affiliates of the old system a choice between remaining where they were or switching to a private pension fund. Much was made of the supposed advantages of the private system.[22] However, by July 1994, the initial deadline for making the change, only 30 per cent of affiliates had chosen to leave the state insurance system. Nevertheless, analysts remained confident that affiliation to the private administrators would substantially increase in the following years, spurred on by high returns on fund investments.

The partial privatisation of social insurance had few implications for those who had already reached old age by the 1990s. As was the case in the mid-1940s, there will be a significant lag period until the welfare implications (unlike the fiscal and political ones) of the reform are felt. Following the reform, the financial position of the remaining public pension system continued to deteriorate. In 1994 total expenditure of the public pension system was three times higher than in 1986 and forced a series of unprogrammed cost-cutting measures in other areas of public spending. Consequently, the chances of substantial rises in benefit values appeared remote.

Summary

The evolution of social insurance in Argentina followed a pattern similar to that of several other developed and developing countries. The system drifted from an initial phase of large surpluses to increasing deficits and ultimate crisis. This was not an inevitable consequence of demographic ageing. Rather, it resulted from a failure to establish a direct relationship between contributions, interest accrued and benefit payments. This problem was compounded by a disorganised administration, evasion and the plundering of early surpluses for investment in areas which generated low, if any, rates of return. As a result, a large amount of fund resources were effectively transferred to other areas of public spending and from later generations to earlier ones. This could not be adequately compensated for by raising contributions, nor could the number of benefits granted be reduced. Thus, the final result was the devaluation of pension payments.

Government commitment to social assistance programmes was markedly inconsistent. As such, they did not provide an effective safety-net for those denied insurance pensions. Two distinct approaches can be identified. The former was low-key, small-scale, with both private and public agencies playing an active role. The latter was on a grander scale, was often politicised and made little or no provision for the participation of non-state agencies. The relative merits of these approaches are examined in greater detail below.

Table 3.4 shows that the welfare role allotted the public sector did not always reflect the general development policy (nor rhetoric) of the government of the day. From the late nineteenth century until the mid-1970s, state involvement in insurance and assistance programmes continued to increase and scope for participation by the private and voluntary sectors was very limited. The public sector monopoly of insurance and assistance which emerged should not be equated with a fully-fledged Beveridgian welfare state, since the protection it afforded was by no means universal nor sufficient. Subsequent attempts to cut back state involvement both in welfare and the economy at large were in the main unsuccessful. This reflected the size and resilience of the public sector and the lack of politically viable alternatives. Despite this, the real impact of state pension schemes was undermined by the system's financial collapse. This, coupled with a surge in poverty levels, increased the need for participation by the private and voluntary sectors.

Table 3.4: Periodisation of development and welfare policy

	General development philosophy/rhetoric	State welfare role
19th century to 1930s	Traditional liberal	Gradual rise in state intervention and growing voluntary sector.
1940s to 1955	Strongly statist	State monopoly of insurance and assistance. No other actors allowed.
1955–76	Moderately statist	State remains dominant. Small but gradually increasing role for voluntary sector.
1976–82	Neo-liberal	Reduction in state involvement but it remains the dominant actor.
1983–90	Moderately statist/ neo-structuralist	Large-scale state assistance programmes. Increasing participation of voluntary sector. First involvement of private sector.
1991–4	Strongly neo-liberal	Small-scale, decentralised assistance. Major role for private sector in insurance.

PUBLIC WELFARE FOR THE ELDERLY IN GREATER BUENOS AIRES (GBA) IN THE EARLY 1990s

The evolution of social security in Argentina was a complex process, reflecting political horse-trading and economic restrictions rather more than it did the changing welfare needs of the population. It is impossible to make sense of the resulting institutional arrangements without understanding this process. Whilst welfare provision across the population was highly uneven and administrative structures were very fragmented, distinctions between insurance and assistance programmes remained very clear. Thus, Argentine social security remained very much a two-tier system.

This section provides a more detailed analysis of public welfare programmes for the elderly functioning in Greater Buenos Aires in the early 1990s. These include contributory pension programmes, the various services offered by the INSSJP and a range of small-scale assistance schemes. Particular attention is paid to the quantitative and qualitative coverage these schemes offer.

*Table 3.5: Geographical social insurance coverage in selected areas, 1970–90**

	1970	1975	1980	1983	1990
Argentina	42.7	45.2	53.3	54.6	9.30
Federal Capital***	65.3	66.9	72.8	73.1	21.42
Province of Buenos Aires	44.4	47.9	56.9	58.1	10.41
Formosa**	6.5	8.3	13.7	15.7	1.49

*The 1970–83 figures for national coverage are smaller than those cited in Table 3.1. Both are taken from the *Secretaría de Seguridad Social*, but the former defines the eligible population as all those aged over 60 years old. This should, in fact, lead to a higher coverage. The reasons why it does not are not apparent. The 1990 figure does not take eligibility into account, simply dividing the total benefits granted by the total population.
**The province with lowest coverage in 1970.
***The province with the highest coverage in 1970.
Source: Argentine Republic, *Ministerio de Trabajo y Seguridad Social*, 1990:38; Isuani and San Martino, 1993:31.

To understand the impact of social security in Greater Buenos Aires it is helpful to draw comparisons with other parts of Argentina. Table 3.5 shows that large differences in insurance coverage existed amongst provinces, although these had been slightly reduced since the 1970s. This reduction may have reflected an expansion of public sector employment in the poorer provinces, which continued until the late 1980s.[23] Throughout this period coverage was higher in Greater Buenos Aires than in Argentina as a whole (although roughly a quarter of those over the retirement age still lacked pensions). Conversely, disparities between the Federal Capital and Buenos Aires Province became more pronounced. These differences cannot be explained by variations in relative proportions of elderly since the figures up to 1983 are themselves based on age. Some studies have sought to explain geographical variations of insurance coverage in terms of urbanisation (Mesa-Lago, 1979:186), yet 94.5 per cent of the population of Buenos Aires Province was defined as urban in 1990 (Argentine Republic, INDEC, 1993:47). An alternative explanation is that the Province contained larger concentrations of types of employment with high evasion propensities than in the Capital. However, the 1980 National Census revealed few significant differences in the areas' respective employment structures.[24] High insurance coverage in the Capital may also have reflected ease of access to centrally-located social security offices and higher levels of political mobilisation. Whatever the cause, the exceptionally high level of coverage in the Federal Capital district and, to a lesser extent, in the surrounding Province suggest that poor elderly in these areas received more economic support than did those living in poorer parts of the country. This issue is returned to in Chapters 4 and 5.

Data for the value of insurance benefits are not available for individual provinces. As mentioned above, pensions and real wages suffered significant reductions from the 1970s. A number of developments in the late 1980s and early 1990s served to accelerate this process. The state was unable provide benefits at the level stipulated in the 1986 Supreme Court ruling and from late 1991 began to transfer its accumulated debt into public bonds. These were held by pensioners but were only cashable in exceptional circumstances.[25] The broader economic climate reduced the real buying power of benefits, particularly during the hyperinflationary crises of 1989 and 1990, since they were not effectively indexed. From early 1991 a policy of tying the Argentine peso to the US dollar was able to reduce inflation but both salaries and pensions continued to lag behind the cost of living as the gap that opened during the early phase of the stabilisation programme was not corrected.[26] As a result, in September 1992 minimum insurance pensions were equivalent to only 12 per cent of the cost of a basic monthly basket of household goods.[27]

Table 3.6: Variations in pension payments by fund, June 1991

Monthly value (pesos*)	Total	Public	Self-employed	Industry/commerce
under 120	64.6	16.7	97.7	59.8
120–160	16.0	22.7	1.9	24.1
160–200	8.3	28.0	0.3	6.0
over 200	11.1	32.6	0.0	10.1

*A 1991 peso is worth exactly one US dollar.
Source: *Previsión Social*, April 1991:115–17.

Table 3.6 shows that there were substantial differences in pension values in 1991. Whilst the majority of beneficiaries received the minimum payment of 120 pesos, the proportion varied from almost 98 per cent of the self-employed to under 17 per cent of public sector workers. Thus, previous occupation had an important effect on benefit values. Since provinces in the interior generally contained larger numbers of self-employed and fewer public sector workers, it is probable that average values here were lower than those in Greater Buenos Aires. As such, there were differences in both qualitative and quantitative coverage between Greater Buenos Aires and elsewhere in Argentina.

Table 3.6 only provides data for the three most important national funds. A significant proportion of public sector workers were provided for by separate agencies. The military, police, politicians and high-ranking functionaries had individual funds which received large state subsidies and paid benefits far in excess of those provided by the main system.[28] Provincial and municipal government workers were also covered by separate schemes. In 1992 these accounted for 9 per cent of total affiliations and paid average benefits of over 500 pesos (Vargas de Flood, 1992:3; Isuani and San Martino, 1993:23, 34). Although the rapid increase in provincial public sector employment had sustained the ratio of contributors to beneficiaries, by the 1990s the majority of funds were in financial difficulties comparable to those of the national system. In 1993 the Federal Capital and PBA pension funds generated deficits of roughly 200 million pesos[29] and it was projected that provincial fund deficits would treble by the end of the century (World Bank, 1993:132–3).

From the mid-1980s the INSSJP began to broaden its range of activities within the *Programa de Atención Médica Integral* (PAMI) to include economic support as well as healthcare discounts. In 1984 a number of special grants to cover basic needs and the costs of family care were proposed but there is no evidence that these were implemented on a large scale.[30] In 1992 PAMI launched the *Programa Social Integral* which included a less ambitious package of financial assistance, including a means-tested supplement to those in receipt of the minimum pension.[31] By April 1993 it was claimed that 16312 such supplements, worth between 50 and 100 pesos a month, were being paid to members in 'extreme need'.[32] The source of funding for these supplements was unclear.[33]

From the 1970s PAMI encouraged the formation of pensioners' day centres (*Centros de jubilados*) and from the 1980s provided them with financial support. By the early 1990s several hundred of these day centres had been established within GBA.[34] These provided a range of services including recreation and legal advice for obtaining benefits. Day centre members benefited from heavily subsidised day trips and holidays. However, over-60-year-olds without contributory pensions were denied effective participation in the centres and were excluded from most of their activities.[35] In 1992 PAMI launched the *'Programa Pro-Bienestar'* which sought to provide members with emergency food aid. This was to be distributed through communal kitchens operating out of recognised day centres. By April 1993 it was claimed that 320 kitchens had been set up and it was planned that 112000 elderly would be benefiting from the scheme by the end of the year.[36]

Thus, 1992 saw two large-scale initiatives that were designed to provide economic benefit to PAMI members (insured elderly). Their timing may have partly reflected political factors. Discussions of pension fund privatisation, weekly pensioner protest marches and a series of economically-motivated pensioner suicides had been attracting a considerable amount of public attention.[37] The PAMI measures were subsequently incorporated into a broader government initiative, the *Plan Social*, which sought to reduce general levels of social discontent and reassert the national government's Peronist pedigree.[38] The initiatives may have also reflected the INSSJP's president's apparent success in restructuring the organisation and putting its finances in order.[39] However, it should be stressed that the programmes only included a fraction of pensioners with the minimum benefit and excluded most of those without insurance cover. As such they may have served to increase the marginalisation of the poorest elderly. Whilst the new PAMI programmes entailed a broadening in the range of services offered to insured elderly, the low values of basic insurance pensions meant that the overall level of protection afforded this group remained very low.

What state protection existed for elderly living in Greater Buenos Aires who did not have insurance pensions and were thus excluded from the majority of services offered by PAMI? Argentine national law stipulated the provision of monthly means-tested assistance pensions for all over-65-year-olds and people with serious physical disabilities.[40] At the national level, two agencies were charged with providing such benefits: the *Administración Nacional de Seguridad Social* (ANSES) and the *Dirección Nacional de la Ancianidad* (DNA).

ANSES, part of the Ministry of Labour and Social Security, provided means-tested pensions for over-65-year-olds, invalids and a number of other, unspecified contingencies. Applicants were initially dealt with by social workers operating at the level of individual municipalities who would interview them at home. This information would then be vetted by the central ANSES office in the Federal Capital. Eligibility criteria were rigorous, including proof that no immediate family members had sufficient income to offer economic support.[41] Nevertheless, Table 3.7 shows that the total number of benefits granted by ANSES rose steadily between 1985 and 1992.[42] In 1992 average ANSES monthly pension values were 124 pesos, slightly lower than the minimum contributory benefit at that time.

Table 3.7: Non-contributory pensions granted by ANSES and the National Congress, 1985–92

	ANSES*	Honorary Congressional Pensions (HCPs)	HCPs funded from general revenues**
1985	60 583	72 505	5 961
1986	69 787	96 377	13 295
1987	73 058	124 242	25 455
1988	76 428	142 601	31 942
1989	81 941	188 901	51 767
1990	84 011	219 114	65 814
1991***	86 446	222 220	66 157
1992	94 484	na	98 026

*Pensions paid by the *Administración Nacional de Seguridad Social*, covering old age, invalidity and general assistance.
**Funded from general revenues. It is unclear how the remaining honorary pensions were financed.
***Data for first quarter only.
Source: Argentine Republic, INPS, 1991:125; Argentine Republic, *Secretaría de Seguridad Social*, 1993 (unpaginated).

The DNA, part of the Ministry of Health and Social Action (MHSA), was established in 1949 to provide sheltered housing for poor elderly in Greater Buenos Aires. Over the following 40 years it implemented a number of small-scale, low-budget projects for the elderly, including day centres.[43] In 1989 the DNA began to grant small grants for elderly in Argentina as a whole. A pilot scheme involving 15 pensioners had grown to 6000 by 1992. The grants were considered a cheaper alternative to putting the elderly into sheltered homes and differed from the ANSES pensions in a number of respects. First, they were not an acquired right: the DNA was under no legal obligation to make regular payments of a given value. The aim of the grant was to provide short-term relief for over-60-year-olds suffering acute hardship. Applications would have to be filed by the claimant or a relative at the DNA office in the Federal Capital. Following this a social worker would interview the claimant at home. The director of the DNA suggested that successful applications would typically be elderly whose contributory pension claims had been delayed.[44] In late 1992 average DNA subsidies were worth 100 pesos and were paid approximately two months out of every three. However, following the creation of the *Secretaría de la Tercera Edad* (STE) (see below) the DNA's future became uncertain and grant funding was terminated.

Argentine national law also makes provision for the granting of 'honorary' pensions by the National Congress, in accordance with the prescriptions of the national budget (FIEL, 1991:299). Table 3.7 shows that the number of congressional pensions awarded in the early 1990s was far in excess of the combined efforts of ANSES and the DNA. However, it is unlikely that the majority of these were awarded to the elderly.[45] Honorary pensions were financed by fixed sums allotted to individual politicians who made awards according to 'merit' rather than general eligibility criteria.[46] Whilst there were no restrictions on the value of benefits, in 1992 the average monthly payment was 146 pesos: almost the same as the minimum insurance pension at that time.

The combined actions of ANSES and the DNA amounted to a total of roughly 100000 assistance benefits in 1992, some of which may not have been for the elderly. This compares to a total population of 1946000 above the retirement age in 1990 who were not in receipt of an insurance benefit.[47] Although ANSES and DNA benefits were both means-tested, there are indications that they did not systematically target those elderly in greatest need. Both organisations received fixed budgets from their respective ministries which could not be increased according to demand. This probably explained why both benefits were given little publicity: this would have taken a share of existing funding and created demands which could not have been met.[48] Information about the benefits was largely spread by word of mouth and thus targeted the better-informed rather than the most needy. Budget restrictions may also explain why no efforts were made to facilitate the arduous application procedures for both benefits. This was particularly apparent with claims for the DNA subsidy which could only be initiated in a single location. Neither agency took an active role in seeking out the most deserving cases.

After the BNSE was discontinued in 1990, there were no national food aid programmes until PAMI initiated the *Pro-Bienestar* project in 1992. Thus, of the total number of uninsured elderly, only those who had obtained membership of PAMI were eligible for food aid from a national programme. This shift away from large-scale food aid was not due to a significant reduction in poverty levels. Rather, it reflected the high cost of such initiatives and the criticisms of corruption and administrative inefficiency mentioned earlier. It may also have reflected a desire to decentralise food aid administration to provincial and municipal authorities. The local government response to this is outlined below.

In October 1992 the *Secretaría de la Tercera Edad* was created to provide assistance for uninsured elderly. It was proposed that the *Secretaría* be funded by the MHSA, the national lottery and the social insurance system.[49]

However, there was no mention of specific initiatives and, by mid-1993, none were forthcoming.[50] Indeed, the principal effect of the new agency was to throw into doubt the roles played by existing ones, particularly PAMI and the DNA.[51] An investigation by government auditors into the expenditure of the MHSA found that 80 per cent of its 1993 budget for the elderly had not been used.[52] This testifies to the failure to develop effective assistance projects for the uninsured and to publicise the availability of services.

Thus, at the national level, the only significant source of social assistance for uninsured elderly were the benefits granted by the DNA and ANSES, but the former had been discontinued by 1993. These elderly were denied PAMI pension supplements and, for the most part, participation in PAMI soup kitchens. This may have reflected a lack of political mobilisation and media concern for this group, which was reflected in the tendency of newspaper reports to use the term '*jubilado*' (person in receipt of an insurance pension) when referring to the elderly in general[53] and an apparent lack of participation of the uninsured in the pensioner demonstrations mentioned earlier.

Figure 3.3 shows that whilst municipal spending on social assistance only fluctuated between 0.1 and 0.2 per cent of GDP, provincial spending rose almost five-fold from 1980 to 1993. This suggests that some elements of social assistance may have been decentralised. Following 1990 both the Buenos Aires Province and the Federal Capital established food aid programmes: the *Programa Alimentario Integral Solidario* (PAIS) and the *Programa de Alimentación de la Municipalidad de la Ciudad de Buenos Aires* (PAMBA). By 1992 it was claimed that PAIS was supporting 770 000 people in Buenos Aires Province. However, the programme targeted mothers, the unemployed and young children rather than the elderly (Golbert, 1993:45–7, 59–60). The PAMBA scheme made more provision for the elderly, distributing food parcels through day centres.[54]

Provincial governments also granted a number of non-contributory pensions. The PBA established such a programme in 1986 and was granting 4000 new benefits a year by 1993. These were targeted at uninsured over-65-year-olds and were fixed at 70 per cent of the value of the minimum insurance pension. Claimants were means-tested and cross-checked with registers of national and municipal pensions. As with ANSES and the DNA, the programme's annual budget was fixed and could only provide for a fraction of potentially eligible claims. Again little effort was made to publicise the service or to facilitate applications. Claimants were initially required to visit the central office in the city of La Plata, 40 miles south of central Buenos Aires. Despite this, by May 1993, 35 000 successful applicants were on a waiting lists for benefits for which there was no funding.[55] This suggests that the sharp rise in provincial assistance expenditure had little direct benefit for uninsured elderly.

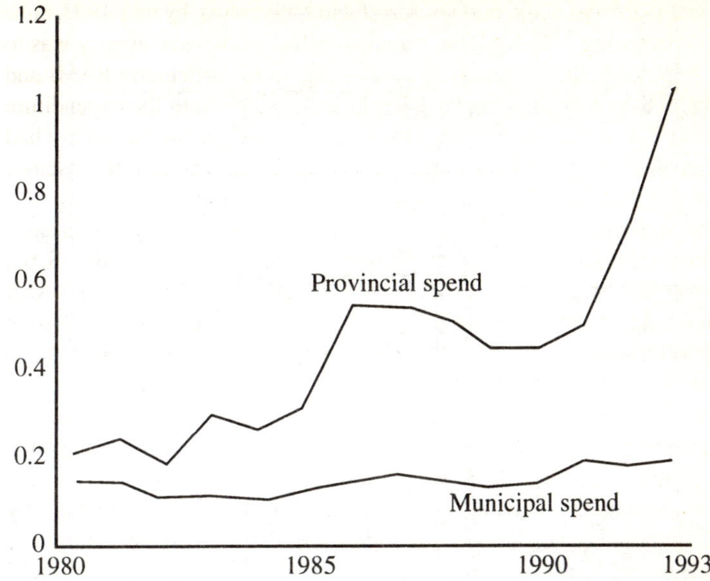

Source: Vargas de Flood, 1992:6.

Figure 3.3 Social assistance expenditure by provincial and municipal governments as a percentage of gross national product, 1980–93

Figure 3.3 shows that at the level of municipal government there were no increases in assistance expenditure. Individual municipalities were free to develop their own range of assistance programmes, prioritising different social groups. Rather than briefly outline the activities of each of the 21 municipalities in city, it is sufficient to examine an individual case. Figure 3.4 is a matrix of social assistance and insurance agencies operating within the municipality of Lanús. Those operating at the national and provincial levels have already been discussed. They were complemented by the activities of the *Dirección Municipal de la Tercera Edad* (DMTA) which was providing 300 assistance pensions a year in the early 1990s. These were of a similar value to the ANSES pensions. In addition, the DMTA offered a small number of grants for elderly with outstanding needs.

Figure 3.4 indicates that co-ordination between the various assistance programmes was scant. The DNA preferred to deal directly with local organisations or needy individuals rather than work through local government. Likewise, the local social workers employed by ANSES had little contact with the municipal authorities.[56] Despite sharing funding from Buenos Aires

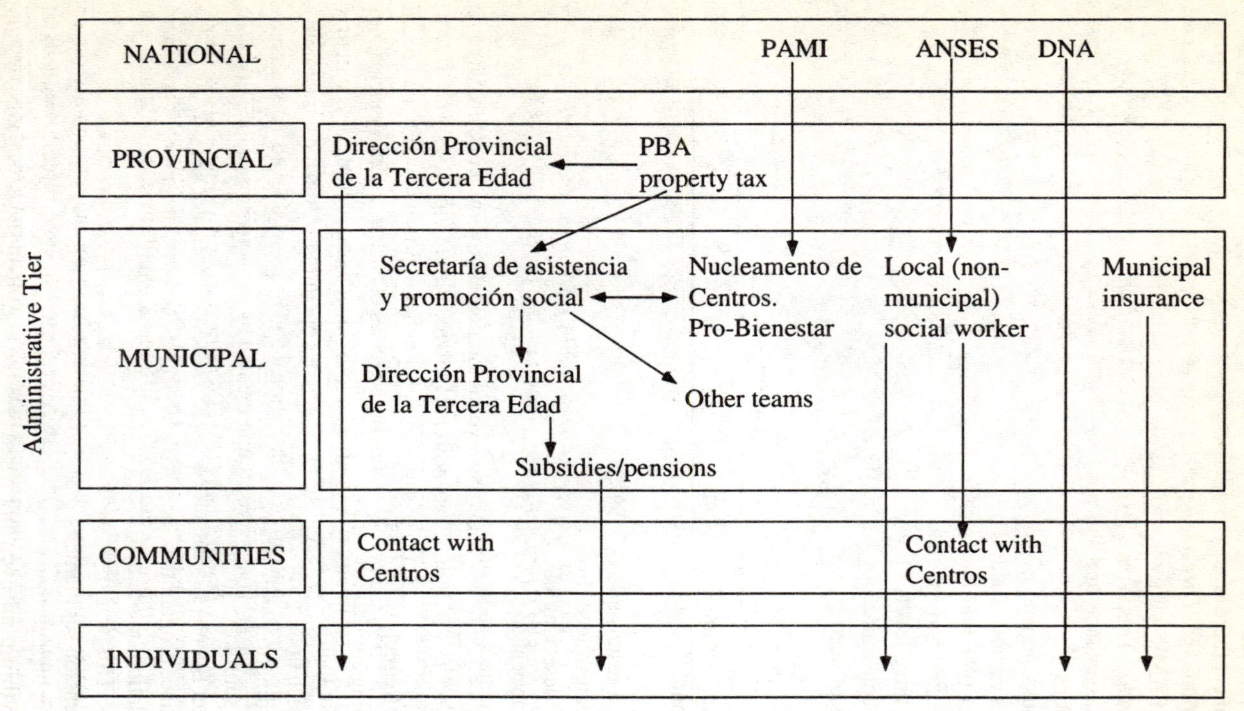

Figure 3.4 Social provision for the elderly in the municipality of Lanús

Province, there was no evidence of communication between the provincial and municipal *Direcciones*. The strongest external ties of the DMTA were with PAMI, with whom it jointly organised meetings at local *Centros de Jubilados*. This is paradoxical given that the former was primarily concerned with assistance and the latter with those already in receipt of insurance pensions.

Thus, uninsured elderly living in Lanús could seek financial assistance from a variety of state agencies operating largely independently of each other. Rather than facilitate access to benefits, these multiple channels served to create confusion and increase bureaucracy. The assistance agencies operating at all three levels of government shared a number of weaknesses. First, all were constrained by small, fixed annual budgets, which did not reflect real levels of need.[57] According to the head of the DMTA:

> Yes, there is a tendency to decentralise social policy decisions...but this a long-term, drawn-out process...I believe that everybody's budgets are being 'rationalised'[58] a little...Today you have to watch every penny you spend.[59]

As a result, no agencies took a proactive role, seeking out those elderly in greatest need. Instead, they relied on individuals or local associations to bring deserving cases to their attention.[60] Furthermore, unlike PAMI, no assistance agencies made efforts to publicise their services. This led to a highly fragmented, underfunded and inaccessible system of social assistance, which might have been avoided if funding had been concentrated in a single agency. The failure to do so reflected the piecemeal creation of agencies, which was more frequently motivated by political considerations – a need to be seen to be doing something – than a desire to improve the welfare of the uninsured. Similar matrices could be drawn for the other municipalities of the city, most of which undertook some form of assistance aimed at the elderly and lacked co-ordination with other levels of action.[61]

In summary, the pattern of social insurance and assistance coverage in Greater Buenos Aires in the early 1990s was extremely complex. Whilst social insurance programmes included a large part, but by no means all, of the elderly population, the benefits they provided usually fell far short of subsistence needs. This was only partly compensated for by PAMI initiatives such as the pension supplements and *Pro-Bienestar* programme. Despite having far smaller budgets than social insurance funds, assistance agencies suffered from, if anything, an even higher degree of fragmentation and bureaucratic confusion. Assistance programmes did not provide an effective safety net for the uninsured elderly, with national schemes only providing pensions for roughly 5 per cent of this group. Local initiatives were fragmented, poorly co-ordinated and underfinanced. In every case assistance pensions were worth less than the minimum insurance benefit and thus fell even further short of providing for subsistence needs.

It is not easy to locate state initiatives for the elderly in Greater Buenos Aires within the general policy typology outlined in the first section of the chapter. On the one hand, the complex array of public assistance agencies and their lack of contact with private organisations suggests a statist orientation. On the other, the lack of funding and the limited economic impact of their initiatives is more typical of the neo-liberal approach. This apparent contradiction reflected an incomplete shift towards neo-liberalism. Funding was reduced whilst pre-existing agencies were allowed to continue their operations and new 'ghost' organisations such as the STE were created. The maintenance of at least the facade of a complicated welfare structure served to obfuscate the real failure of the system to meet the economic needs of the majority of the elderly. Plans to privatise insurance and to further decentralise assistance will have accelerated this shift towards liberal welfare policies.

NON-STATE ACTION

Non-state income maintenance strategies are very diverse, ranging from the actions of international organisations to decisions taken by individuals. For the sake of clarity, this section groups these phenomena into two loose categories: large-scale formal arrangements and micro-institutional strategies. Particular attention is paid to the level of cover these activities afford poor urban elderly and the degree of co-ordination with state agencies.

Formal institutional strategies

As shown in Table 3.4, private and voluntary sector actors were afforded very little significance in welfare provision in Argentina for most of the twentieth century. Consequently, the following analysis of large-scale organisations focuses on two specific periods: (1) the years before the statist welfare monopoly and (2) the gradual reversion to a more pluralistic approach.

Mutual aid societies

The early expansion of social insurance schemes in Greater Buenos Aires was a very gradual process which only catered for a minority of the urban workforce until the mid-twentieth century. This was by no means compensated for by comprehensive assistance programmes. Consequently, the majority of the population had to provide for its own welfare needs. One means by which this was accomplished this was through the expansion of mutual aid societies. These organisations were usually established along ethnic lines, reflecting the immigrant origins of urban workers (Baily, 1982:485–514; Devoto and Fernández, 1990:136–41). In some cases, however, they were established by occupational grouping as part of the expanding union movement or by the Catholic Church as 'workers' circles' (Recalde, 1991:32–8; Badoza, 1992:72–90; Ivereigh, 1995:64–5).

Although the first mutual aid society did not appear until the 1850s, they numbered 214 in the Federal Capital alone by 1914 (Argentine Republic, 1917a:92). These organisations provided a broad range of social and welfare functions, including hospitals, insurance against accidents and sickness and burial expenses (Passanante, 1987:75–80; Fogarty, 1989). Three mutual aid societies specialised in providing pensions. The most important of these was the *Caja Internacional Mutua de Pensiones*, which was established in the Federal Capital in 1901 and contained 72835 members by 1916 (Argentine Republic, 1917a:100–3).

Table 3.8: Membership of welfare organisations in the Federal Capital, 1914

Contributory pension funds	76 056
Union funds	13 420*
Catholic organisations	23 920
Military funds	368
Mutual aid societies	300 000**

* This was dominated by the railway workers' fund, which contained 8378 members.
** This is a rough calculation made by A. Bunge.
Source: Bunge, 1917:128–33.

Table 3.8 shows that on the eve of the First World War, mutual aid societies dominated welfare insurance in Buenos Aires, containing roughly 300000 affiliates. This represented 29 per cent of the total population of working age and, when taking into account that the coverage of individuals usually extended to their immediate family members, demonstrates that a substantial proportion of the population participated in collective welfare organisations.[62]

There are indications that mutual aid societies began to suffer increasing financial difficulties following the First World War. This resulted from rising demands for benefits from their ageing memberships, falling contributions due to the recession of 1914–19 and administrative fragmentation

(Baily, 1982:492). These problems might have served as a warning to future social security policy-makers. Despite these set-backs, mutual aid societies' memberships continued to expand, with some estimates gauging their national affiliation to be around two million in 1943 (roughly one fifth of the total population of working age).[63] This reflected the rapid increase in urban, industrial employment and the expansion of trade unions.[64] Figure 3.5 shows that the bulk of the societies' expenditure was concentrated on healthcare. Nevertheless, services largely targeting the elderly, such as pensions and funerals, accounted for over a fifth of outgoings.

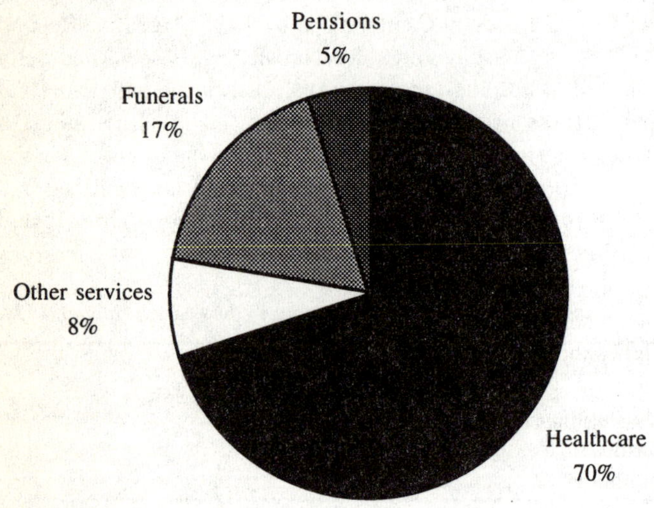

Source: Juárez, 1947:128.

Figure 3.5 Mutual aid society expenditure in 1943

The important role played by mutual aid societies was recognised in the preamble to a government decree law in 1945:

> In this country mutualism currently constitutes a powerful force for worker solidarity, reaching a hitherto unimaginable scale and dimension...the development of private initiatives by these institutions has been of benefit to the country's labourforce, thus erasing problems of impoverishment.[65]

Yet the same decree law took steps to impose state authority over virtually all areas of the mutual aid societies' activities:

> the State cannot remain indifferent and must stimulate this social activity, co-ordinating its action...state intervention will guarantee the seriousness and efficiency of mutual aid societies, preventing abuses and the exploitation of the economically weakest sectors of the populace.
>
> (*Revista de Trabajo y Previsión* 1945:742)

All mutual aid societies were immediately put under the jurisdiction of the newly formed *Dirección de Mutualidades* and were obliged to comply with a bewildering array of regulations. These included stipulations that staff could only work on a voluntary basis, that all members pay a fixed minimum contribution rate of 10 centavos and, with reference to the societies' ethnic origins, that statute books be written in Spanish only. The *Dirección* did nothing to hide its ultimate objectives:

> Mutualism should move without delay from being simply the loaning of services offering protection and assistance; it must become integrated with the various elements of social provision...closer to a system of social insurance... (Mensa, 1946:83)

Within a short period the societies lost their individual welfare functions; their pension schemes were incorporated into the new social insurance funds, whilst their healthcare functions formed the basis of the semi-public medical system.[66]

Thus, during the 1940s mutual aid societies met the same fate as state-funded charities such as the *Sociedad de Beneficencia*. This gave the Argentine state a monopoly of large-scale institutional initiatives for the elderly, although, as has already been shown, this did not mean that all Greater Buenos Aires' elderly received adequate protection. The rapid expansion of social insurance affiliation which brought with it prospects of early retirement and relatively generous pension payments reduced the perceived need for large-scale private institutional action. This was also discouraged by the mood of statism which predominated from the 1940s to 1960s.

Non-governmental organisations

Non-governmental organisations (NGOs) are extremely heterogeneous in both form and function and can only be loosely defined as:

> private, non-profit organisations that are publicly registered (i.e., have legal status), whose principal function is to implement development projects favouring the popular sectors, and which receive financial support.
>
> (Padrón, 1986)

Given the breadth of this definition, it is helpful to group NGOs into a number of distinct categories. One way in which this can be done is to look at international NGOs, national NGOs and smaller-scale grassroots organisations. The term 'NGO' itself was coined during the 1960s, at which time both international and domestic organisations began to develop significant roles in Latin America and most other developing regions (Fernández,1987; Landim, 1987:31–5, 39–49).

The emergence of NGOs in Argentina paralleled the gradual deterioration of state welfare programmes from the late 1950s. This coincided with a shift in the emphasis of welfare planning throughout Latin America. The new thinking stressed the role of 'community development programmes', which aimed to encourage the poor to participate more actively in their own welfare through mutual support, co-operatives and a combination of grassroots organisation and top-down planning (Tenti Fanfani, 1989:83–90). However, a series of repressive regimes tended to stifle rather than encourage popular participation. Thus, church organisations and political militants from the traditional left became aware of the need and opportunities for non-state actors to play a significant role in small-scale, grassroots development projects (Landim, 1987; Hall, 1993:422–3). Much of this activity was conducted informally by small groups of individuals in poor urban and rural neighbourhoods (Pastrana, 1980:135–40). However, in some cases formal NGOs emerged, some of which were still operating in the 1990s.[67] These NGOs sought to nurture their own versions of community development through the promotion of local grassroots associations. As such, it was possible to distinguish between formal NGOs consisting of interested but essentially 'external' parties and grassroots organisations formed *in situ* by those with more direct interests at stake. Whilst these two forms of organisation were often very closely articulated, this distinction is essential for any understanding of NGOs both in Argentina and Latin America as a whole.

Table 3.9: Period of foundation of NGOs still operational by June 1992

1960:	6	1970:	17	1980:	56	1990:	162
1965:	13	1975:	33	1985:	104	1992:	168

Source: GADIS, 1992:209.

Table 3.9 shows that the number of formal NGOs in Argentina grew steadily during the 1960s and 1970s and at a faster rate during the 1980s.[68] This reflected worsening poverty, the diffusion of the NGO concept and, from the 1980s, increased opportunities due to redemocratisation. The growth of formal NGOs was closely associated with a sudden blossoming of grassroots organisations, particularly in poor urban neighbourhoods. In the *villas miserias* the initial impetus to local organisation was provided by draconian demolition policies of the military government.[69] However, the scope of concerns voiced by grassroots *villa* organisations was soon extended to a much larger range of political and economic demands.

It has been widely observed that the scale and significance of these grassroots organisations reached its peak during the mid-1980s and that they subsequently went into decline (Cavarozzi and Palermo 1995:34–9). The rise and fall of grassroots organisations has been linked to the process of democratic transition in Argentina; indeed there are strong similarities with the experiences of other Latin American countries in the 1980s. It has been argued that the return to party politics served both to reduce the perceived need for informal political organisations and to increase the incidence of clientelism and co-optation, thus undermining the legitimacy of community leaders. Despite the apparent demise of grassroots movements, Table 3.9 shows that the number of formal NGOs being established increased markedly through the late 1980s and early 1990s. This suggests that the presence of these organisations was more a reflection of increased social hardship than the short-term euphoria of redemocratisation.

There has been some controversy about the capacity of poorer urban groups to autonomously develop their own grassroots organisations. During the 1960s it was widely held that the condition of poverty in itself reduces social cohesion and the capacity to organise (Lewis, 1959, 1969). However, subsequent research has tended to support the view that poverty and disadvantage can in fact serve to promote solidarity and mutual support.[70] One study of poor households in Greater Buenos Aires, whilst not making specific reference to the elderly, postulates that:

> in such conditions [of poverty] poor and marginal groups – excluded from effective forms of institutionalised social security – create their own social solidarity and mutual aid as a spontaneous response to a socio-economic situation which imposes severe restrictions upon them. The actors, confronting a situation of chronic economic insecurity, become aware of the need to create their own social network of mutual support as a means of adaptation. (Ramos, 1981:19–20)

Whilst this view is probably over-optimistic, it would seem to have been partly borne out by the prominent role played by the *villas* and slum areas in the re-emergence of new social movements in the 1980s. To date, no research has examined the welfare implications of the emergence and demise of these phenomena for groups such as the elderly. These issues are examined in considerable detail in Chapter 4.

International NGOs have been less visible in Argentina than in most other Latin American countries. There are a number of reasons for this tendency. Both these NGOs and their own sources of funding (such as the Overseas Development Administration (ODA) and the European Commission, not to mention the general public) consider Argentina to be a 'middle income country', whose social problems are less acute than many other developing countries. According to the Latin American projects officer of one such NGO:

> [Our] trustees, who are on the international operations committee...some of them do have objections to funding in Argentina and I can't say that we would now be able to increase our work there again...It's to do with making comparisons with poorer countries...If we really felt we had real reason to expand the programme again, we would have to have a debate in that forum and find out what the real objections were...If we do, they might cut funding altogether.[71]

At the same time, groups such as the elderly were afforded a low priority in international development funding, greatly restricting the activities of NGOs in this field. According to the same projects officer:

> It has taken a while to get on board the issues that elderly people face and why they are important in the development process...There are definite trends in the development world and ageing and older people certainly wasn't one of them...It is beginning to change but it's still difficult to get...money or support for the kind of programmes that we have.[72]

The combination of low priorities afforded Argentina as a country and the elderly as a group indicate that international NGOs have played a relatively minor role in this field. It is less easy to assess the impact of local NGOs and grassroots organisations. Of the 172 formal NGOs listed in the *Grupo de análisis y desarrollo institucional y social* (GADIS) register, 15 claimed to run programmes specifically directed at the needs of the elderly, of which 13 were located in Greater Buenos Aires (GADIS, 1992:220). Two of these provided direct financial support, nine provided advice and training, two promoted healthcare and two were concerned with academic investigation. Seven of these NGOs provided data on their annual budgets, which amounted to a total of US$ 1 167 000 for 1992. Thus, the information provided by GADIS suggests that NGOs concerned with the economic needs of the elderly were too few in number and too restricted in their budgets to play a significant role in filling gaps in state social insurance and assistance.

Nevertheless, it is conceivable that NGOs had a more important effect on elderly welfare than the GADIS register suggests. The survey was far from complete, excluding several of the formal NGOs referred to below, not to mention those smaller grassroots organisations which were still functioning by the 1990s.[73] Moreover, a number of the NGOs listed in the register as not providing services specifically for the elderly did in fact offer a number of direct and indirect benefits to this group. The most notable example of this was Caritas, described in detail below. Finally, it should be stressed that the aim of most NGOs was not to distribute direct welfare benefits, but to provide advice and training to grassroots initiatives among deprived social groups (Landim, 1987:33–5). Consequently, the relationship between the size of their budgets and their impact on elderly welfare was less clear-cut.

The limited number of studies of NGOs in Argentina identify various problems common to these organisations. One area of general difficulty is the expansion of NGOs from individual small-scale projects to larger regional or national organisations. This poses several challenges, including the need to develop effective administrative structures while maintaining flexibility and the organisation's original ethos (Anis, 1987 and Martínez Norgueira, 1987). The process may be hindered by erratic flows of funds, particularly when these are derived from overseas. However, the most serious challenge to growth is the nature of the relationships between NGOs and the state. As shown above, earlier voluntary sector organisations had suffered from a high level of reliance on government funding and, as a result, lost their independence. By contrast, through the 1970s and 1980s voluntary organisations received little if any funding from the state. Since most early NGOs were established during authoritarian regimes, relations between them and the state must at best have been mutually suspicious. Subsequent redemocratisation and the devolution of some social welfare functions to local governments presented NGOs with both opportunities and dilemmas. By 1989 a small number of government loans and subsidies were being made available to NGOs and several public agencies had expressed interest in joint projects. By the late 1980s, most NGOs had obtained official registration as non-profit making entities, which exempted them from paying taxes and, in some cases, may have facilitated access to state resources.[74] Nevertheless, a 1988 conference on relations between the Argentine state and NGOs identified the following problems:

1. The heterogeneity of state agencies, each with their own agendas, which can lead to conflicting and contradictory alliances.

2. The risk of compromising the NGOs' political autonomy.
3. Differences between NGOs and state agencies in the scale of projects and attitudes towards participation (Thompson, 1989:27–8).

Recent studies of relations between Argentine NGOs and government agencies provide strongly contrasting views. Some stress the inherent dangers of these ties, whilst others point to relatively successful instances of collaboration.[75] The way in which NGOs concerned with elderly welfare confronted these challenges is considered in the descriptions of individual agencies which follow.

Help Age International (HAI). HAI was established in London in the early 1980s as a network of age-care NGOs based in both developed and developing countries. By 1993 40 such organisations participated in the network, either as full or associate members. The former had direct involvement in HAI's strategic decisions, whilst the latter were allowed to participate in regional fora and conferences. The network contained several Latin American NGOs, including three full members[76] and five associates.[77] This both attested to HAI's interest in the region and the degree of participation afforded to organisations from developing countries.

Nevertheless, the activities of HAI in Argentina were restricted by a number of factors. The first of these was the low priority afforded Latin America as a whole. HAI funded a large number of projects across the developing world. Some of these consisted of 'operational programmes', which involved the direct participation of HAI workers in the field. However, the preferred *modus operandi* for Latin America was the indirect funding of projects initiated by local organisations. It was argued that this reflected a higher degree of social organisation and voluntary activity in the continent. Indirect funding may also have been due to the smaller budget allocated to Latin America as compared to Asia or Africa. This reflected HAI's particular concern for elderly refugees and victims of large-scale natural hazards (both relatively uncommon in Latin America) and the preference of major external funding agencies, mentioned above.

These restrictions partly explain why HAI involvement in Argentina was reduced from five to just two projects between 1992 and 1993. Detailed descriptions of a project which maintained funding and one which lost it are given below in separate sections.[78] According to HAI, the process of selection favoured local organisations with a specialist interest in the elderly, rather than ones with broader development objectives. The scaling-down of operations reduced what was already a marginal role in promoting the economic welfare of needy elderly in GBA as a whole and is indicative of the problems facing other international NGOs operating in this field.

El Centro de Promoción y Estudios de la Vejez (CEPEV).[79] CEPEV was formed in 1987 by a number of PAMI social workers and academics. One of these, having conducted a detailed study of old age and poverty in the poor urban neighbourhood of La Boca, proposed the implementation of a pilot project there (Redondo, 1990). Through contacts with internationally recognised academics, CEPEV was able to obtain funding from the Inter-American Foundation (IAF), an organisation based in the USA. The La Boca project aimed to

> form an association of elderly people in an area of poverty, given that these groupings do not develop spontaneously in pockets of poverty, and facilitate the access of these poor elderly people to private and public benefits or resources which other groups are able to obtain thanks to their better relative positions, their better experiences of life, their greater capacity to exploit such resources.[80]

This objective contains the implicit assumption that the PAMI *Centros de Jubilados* programme was less easily established in poor neighbourhoods whose residents often lacked organisational experience. Furthermore, CEPEV considered such day centres less appropriate to the needs of poor elderly, many of whom lacked insurance pensions and were therefore denied PAMI membership. These issues are considered further in Chapter 4.

The project in La Boca proved a success and by 1991 the resultant elderly organisation contained 250 members. CEPEV played a purely consultative role in La Boca and by 1990 most of the day-to-day decisions were being taken and executed by elderly locals. By grouping together, the elderly of La Boca were able to obtain a number of PAMI benefits, including medical aid and subsidised day-trips. The organisation distributed food parcels obtained through the PAMBA programme and provided general advice about applications for contributory and assistance pensions (Thompson, 1991). As a result, it was decided to set up a second project in a shanty town outside the Federal Capital, Villa Jardín. This is examined in detail in Chapter 4.

Whilst CEPEV took pains to preserve its autonomy, it had a large number of contacts with state agencies. Indeed, its executive director remained a senior official in PAMI. As is shown in Chapter 4, CEPEV used these personal contacts to great effect in obtaining welfare benefits for elderly in the two projects. This approach did not go so far as favouring participation in joint projects with state agencies and received no government funding. Indeed agencies such as PAMI and the STE may have been more inclined to regard CEPEV as a rival organisation, given its commitment to establish elderly organisations with no formal ties to the state.

CEPEV achieved a number of successes in the first years of its life, but ambitions to expand activities beyond two urban neighbourhoods were thwarted. This failure was due to changes in funding largely beyond the organisation's control. By 1991 it was receiving funds from Help Age International (HAI) and CONICET (an Argentine research institute), in addition to support from IAF, giving a total of US$ 60000 per annum (GADIS, 1992:55). However, during the following two years the IAF funding was discontinued and HAI's aid was frozen. This forced CEPEV to reduce its staff from three full and two part-time workers to just one part-time and to give up its small rented office. Thus, by 1992 it activities were reduced to just maintaining occasional contact with the Villa Jardín project. Attempts to develop contacts with other local NGOs concerned with the elderly, such as FOC (see below), were not reciprocated. By early 1993 the prospects of obtaining additional funding appeared slim and so CEPEV's activities seemed destined to remain pilot projects with very localised impacts.

The experiences of CEPEV illustrate the problems that NGOs face if they are not prepared to develop close relations with state agencies. Despite the evident success of its two pilot programmes, CEPEV remained dependent on a small number of funding agencies who discontinued their support, threatening its eventual collapse.

La Fundación de Organización Comunitaria (FOC).[81] Whilst FOC's activities did not extend to any of the neighbourhoods studied in this book, it provides a useful comparison with the experiences of CEPEV. FOC was established in 1981, at the end of the *Proceso* period, by a group of women living in shanty towns around Lomas de Zamora in Province of Buenos Aires, rather than by social workers and academics. They sought to improve healthcare and hygiene by establishing womens' groups and providing basic medical training (FOC, 1981). FOC's slow initial growth and informal origins were reflected in the fact that it did not obtain legal recognition until 1989.[82]

By 1992 FOC had been transformed into one of the largest development NGOs in the city. Its activities had been broadened to include communal kitchens, kindergartens, micro-enterprises, housing improvements and a number of services for the elderly. FOC was receiving funding from a wide range of sources, including UNICEF Argentina, *La Fundación Antorchas* (a local trust), the Dutch Embassy and Help Age International. In early 1993

FOC moved to larger well-equipped premises in the centre of Lomas de Zamora. Thus, at first sight, FOC would appear to provide a clear example of successful NGO expansion.

The rapid transformation of FOC from a number of informal projects to a large organisation reflected the close relationship it was able to develop with the municipality of Lomas de Zamora. Its legal recognition and rapid expansion were linked to the election of a new mayor in 1989. This was followed by the appointment of a founder member of FOC as municipal minister of social assistance and by 1992 several other members of FOC were employed by the ministry.[83] These officials proposed to extend the successful experiences of FOC to other parts of the municipality as part of a state programme for the establishment of 'Centres of Community Organisation' (*Subsecretaría de Acción Social,* 1992). Thus, rather than simply establishing joint projects, municipal and FOC activities and personnel were being integrated to the extent that it was difficult to separate the two organisations. This contrasts sharply with the relation between CEPEV and state agencies. Whilst there was no clear evidence that FOC received direct subsidies from the municipality, their close ties made this quite likely.

It is not clear whether FOC's expansion was the cause or result of its strong municipal ties. Given that FOC personnel were appointed to the municipality rather than vice versa, it would appear that the relation was more NGO penetration of a state agency than the reverse. Nevertheless, the relation carried the risk of comprising FOC's development objectives with political ones and posed serious administrative challenges. Moreover, the relation was extremely sensitive to any future change in municipal office-holders.

There are indications that the expansion of FOC's activities occurred more in breadth than in depth. Its services for the elderly stressed the importance of forming local day centres and workshops. By November 1991 two of these had been established, with a total membership of 45 elderly women. A third centre was set up in conjunction with a PAMI *Centro de Jubilados* and contained 50 active members (FOC, 1990; 1991). These groups had a wide range of objectives including providing advice for pension applications, gymnasia classes for the elderly and healthcare education. However, by early 1993 there was little evidence that these had evolved beyond informal discussion groups and funding from Help Age International was discontinued. Several factors may account for this failure. The shanty towns around Lomas de Zamora contained far smaller numbers of elderly than the neighbourhoods in which CEPEV worked and thus the creation of large groups was more difficult.[84] Moreover, FOC admitted that its central concern was the plight of mothers and young children, rather than the elderly.[85] Most members had more experience of working with mothers' groups and childcare than of the special needs of the elderly. None were aware of the range of potentially available pensions or benefits and few efforts were made to directly involve the elderly in group decision-making.

The experiences of FOC illustrate some of the potential difficulties faced by NGOs as they seek to expand their activities beyond a small number of pilot projects. Growth can lead to the development of new activities beyond the range of experience of existing members. FOC was far less successful in its dealings with the elderly than it was in areas closer to its original remit. As was seen in the elderly day centres, NGO expansion may reduce the scope for grassroots participation. It also increases the temptation to develop strong ties with organisations, be they funding agencies or government organs, whose objectives may not coincide with those of the NGO. Whilst they pose new challenges, none of these developments are necessarily detrimental to the success of NGOs. Indeed, FOC's links with the municipality could be a valuable source of experience and training for members, enabling them to develop more effective programmes for the elderly in the future.

Caritas Argentina. The Catholic Church played a central role in the provision of social assistance in Argentina in the nineteenth and early twentieth centuries, through charitable organisations similar to the *Sociedad de Beneficencia*. Whilst these generally focused on the needs of mothers and young children as opposed to the elderly, the encouragement of 'workers circles' contributed to general expansion of mutual aid societies' pension coverage. As mentioned earlier, these assistance and insurance initiatives came into conflict with the welfare monopoly imposed during Peronist rule and largely disappeared. The overthrow of Perón gave the church more scope for action and in 1956, a year after the dissolution of the *Fundación Eva Perón*, Caritas Argentina was formally established (GADIS, 1992:27).

Caritas Argentina stated its central objective as:

> To encourage and co-ordinate the official charitable activities of the catholic church, as part of its broader pastoral mission, through practices reflecting circumstances and experiences, in order to attain a more integrated development for all men, especially the most marginalised people and communities. (*Comisión Nacional de Caritas,* Argentina 1991).

Caritas is part of an international hierarchy, paralleling the organisation of the Catholic Church. This ranges from the global headquarters in Rome, to the Latin American secretariat in Bogotá, to the national centre, to individual bishoprics and dioceses. These tiers of organisation are presided over by the corresponding priests, bishops and archbishops. Thus, Caritas activities are closely connected to the broader structure of the Catholic Church. As will be seen, the individual components of this hierarchy enjoy considerable autonomy, although they may be called upon to fund other areas of Caritas at times of crisis.

Caritas activities expanded steadily through the 1960s and 1970s, reflecting the growth of the NGO sector as a whole. This expansion occurred despite the conservative orientation of the Argentine Church.[86] Caritas was of particular significance during the *Proceso* period, since it was largely exempt from government repression and interference.[87] Indeed, several Caritas branches in Buenos Aires formed the focus of popular opposition to the eradication of shanty towns in the late 1970s (Bellardi and de Paula, 1986:63–77). The economic crises of the 1980s saw a dramatic expansion in the scope of Caritas activities, including emergency food aid programmes (*Comisión Nacional de Caritas Argentina,* 1991:10–13). At the same time, there was a shift in policy away from pure assistance to employment training workshops and micro-enterprises.[88]

A full evaluation of the impact Caritas activities on the welfare of the elderly in GBA is not easy, since each individual parish establishes its own priorities and runs its own assistance programmes. The cases of three individual parishes are examined in detail in the next chapter. Nationally, Caritas activities tended to prioritise the needs of poor northern provinces rather than those of GBA.[89] This might havc reflected the particular lack of social insurance and state assistance in these regions (see Table 3.5). Publications at the national and bishopric level, made more reference to groups such as children, flood victims and unemployed men than the elderly. The only programme run at the national level directly targeting the elderly was the establishment of a small number of rest homes, which benefited a maximum number of 2363 individuals across the country.[90] It is difficult to estimate the proportion of elderly who benefited from more general assistance programmes, such as emergency food aid. However, it is possible that the shift in emphasis away from assistance to productive ventures could have favoured social groups who are more capable of work.

Caritas did not suffer from many of the limitations common to NGOs. Through the Catholic Church, it had a secure base of funding which could be increased at times of crisis by support from overseas branches. In the early 1990s, Caritas Argentina was receiving significant levels of financial assistance from its German, Spanish and Italian counterparts. Its large size and prestige also enabled it to attract funding from a range of private businesses and run joint projects with organisations such as UNICEF. Financing was also facilitated by flexible arrangements between national bishoprics. For example, during the inflationary crisis of 1989 the Federal

Capital district provided funding for food aid in more peripheral parts of the city.

Relations between Caritas and state agencies differed from the case of most NGOs in as much as Caritas Argentina was often the larger member of the partnership. Thus, there was less danger that its objectives would be hijacked or modified. Nevertheless, Caritas Argentina was wary of involvement in projects which might be of party political inspiration.[91] Co-operation with state agencies increased through the 1980s and early 1990s. By late 1992 Caritas was developing links with PAMI and the STE to establish a new assistance programme aimed at the elderly, although no details of the project had been agreed by mid-1993 (*Comisión Nacional de Caritas Argentina*, 1991:11–31).

Caritas Argentina was successful in implementing a wide range of assistance projects of benefit to disadvantaged groups, including the elderly. However, it should not be considered an adequate safety-net for the shortcomings of state action. In 1992 the national headquarters only contained 13 full-time staff and just one computer (GADIS, 1991:27). Moreover, its dual objectives of social assistance and furthering the Catholic faith might not necessarily be compatible.[92] This raised the question of whether assistance should be dependent upon religious and moral compliance to catholicism.[93] Again, these issues are examined in more detail in the next chapter.

As has been seen, it is more meaningful to stress the great diversity of NGO activities in GBA rather than generalise about their significance and performance. This diversity encompasses all aspects of NGOs, including their origins, objectives, structure, scale and relations with other organisations. However, it is likely that their impact on the economic welfare of poor elderly was very limited, compared to the actions of large state programmes. It is possible that development NGOs evolved more slowly in Argentina than in other parts of Latin America due to the country's relatively high living standards and the large welfare role played by the public sector. Clearly, they were not able to provide an alternative to nor a safety-net for public sector failure. Most NGOs and external sources of funding did not afford the elderly the same priority as other social groups. Small, unreliable budgets reduced the scale of their operations and tempted them to submit their particular objectives to those of more powerful organisations.

The role of NGOs was also limited by a lack of close co-operation amongst them. In the early 1990s a number of general conferences were held and a register of NGO activities was published (Thompson, 1989:27; GADIS, 1991). However, the continued absence of communication between the various GBA NGOs funded by HAI indicated that the impact of these initiatives must have been minimal. Whilst co-operation between NGOs was hindered by their very diversity, it would have enabled them to redress the imbalance of power with state agencies and to exert more influence over general welfare policy. Financial co-operation may have also enabled NGOs to overcome some of their budgetary limitations.

Direct overseas assistance

As well as providing funds for local NGOs, some European governments sought to offer more direct forms of social security for citizens residing in Argentina. Given the timing of European immigrations, it was probable that a high proportion of second generation or post-war immigrants had reached old age by the 1990s. The intervention of European governments reflected international recognition of the failings of the Argentine welfare system and fears that large numbers of impoverished pensioners would return to their countries of origin in order to obtain assistance. No comparable services were offered by Latin American governments, despite high levels of emigration to Argentina. This was probably because Argentine welfare programmes were generally considered superior to those elsewhere in the continent.

The most important form of overseas welfare intervention was the provision of retirement pensions. A 1991 Labour Ministry report estimated that overseas pensions accounted for 2 per cent of total affiliation to social security (Scipione et al, 1992:36). These included 65 000 *Titulari di beneficio previdenziale*, which had been awarded by the Italian government since the signing of an international treaty in 1961. *Titulari* consisted of regular monthly pension payments, worth 400 pesos in early 1993. Until the early 1990s eligibility for these benefits required proof of Italian citizenship, one year's work and military service in Italy and at least 15 years of pension contributions within the Argentine system. Eligibility criteria were subsequently tightened, stipulating at least five years' work in Italy. This change reflected the mounting financial difficulties of the social security system back in Italy.[94]

The Italian government offered its citizens a number of other benefits in addition to the *titulari*. These included 5000 non-contributory military veterans' pensions worth 200 pesos a month in 1993. During the economic crisis of 1989 and 1990 large amounts of emergency food aid and medical drugs were made available.[95] Emergency financial assistance remained important after the crisis: 2500 such grants, worth up to 400 pesos, were being distributed in the Federal Capital and PBA in 1993.[96] These employed similar means-tests to state assistance pensions and information about them was spread by word of mouth rather than by formal publicity.[97] Finally, some Italian government assistance was channelled through local Italian clubs, several of which had their roots in the old mutual aid societies. These clubs sometimes liased with the consulates over individual claims for social assistance and provided members information about both Italian and Argentine benefits.

In contrast with the Italian government, direct Spanish assistance was upgraded in 1993. Beforehand, the principal form of assistance had consisted of 10000 quarterly grants based on similar legibility criteria to the *titulari* (Scipione et al, 1992:36). In 1993 a new assistance package was developed, consisting of monthly grants for any Spanish citizens aged over 65 with incomes below 202 pesos a month (the equivalent minimum payment in Spain). According to Spain's labour attaché, these benefits sought to target those elderly who received minimum pensions from the self-employed workers' fund. The Spanish consulate predicted that around 15000 grants would be granted by the end of 1993.[98]

The activities of the Italian and Spanish governments reflected growing international recognition of the shortcomings of Argentina's public welfare system. Whilst the new criteria for *titulari* would have reduced the number of contributory benefits granted, both governments maintained or even increased expenditure on means-tested support. This meant that the impact of direct overseas intervention on the poorest elderly was of growing significance.

Private pension funds

The 1914 national census alludes to the existence of a number of private pension funds but does not undertake a full survey of them. Instead, it provides an account of one typical example, *La Unión Popular*, which contained 37000 members by this date (Argentine Republic, 1917a:93). No further information is available about these funds or their evolution up to the 1940s, although it is highly probable that they subsequently met a similar fate to that of the mutual aid societies. Indeed, through much of the second half of the twentieth century private companies were expressly forbidden from offering any form of retirement pension scheme. This attitude reflected the belief that private pensions were superfluous to and would interfere with the operations of the state system. However, as the social insurance system plunged deeper into crisis in the 1980s, some provision was made to afford the private sector a limited role in this area of welfare (*Latin American Weekly Report*, 20 November 1986).

In 1987 the first private pension funds were established. These were to provide optional schemes, which would complement rather than substitute the public programme (Peluffo, 1991). As such, no provision was made for opting out of the state system. Table 3.10 shows that after a slow beginning, affiliation to private insurance rose rapidly in the early 1990s, accounting for approximately 3 per cent of the total economically active population by mid-1992. However, the impact of private insurance on those who had already reached old age was very limited, since virtually no affiliates had as yet retired.

Table 3.10: Affiliation to private insurance schemes, 1988–92

Year	Trimester	Individual	Collective	Total
1988	4	5 252	569	5 821
1989	1	8 795	714	9 509
	2	15 584	1 331	16 915
	3	38 269	2 956	41 225
	4	67 534	41 048	108 582
1990	1	79 801	28 412	108 213
	2	82 698	28 818	111 516
	3	96 020	30 941	126 961
	4	99 180	37 932	137 112
1991	1	96 952	37 867	134 819
	2	75 273	40 510	115,783
	3	74 546	41 417	115 963
	4	83 199	204 326*	287 525
1992	1	83 484	223 191	306 675
	2	84 420	259 531	343 951
	3	85 067	286 877	371 944

*This sudden rise was due to the affiliation of all members of the commercial workers' union.
Source: Argentine Republic, *Secretaría de Economía, Superintendencia de Seguros de la Nación,* from 12 November 1991 to 26 February 1993.

The role afforded the private sector in social insurance was dramatically increased with the passing of a far-ranging reform bill in September 1993.[99] This enabled private insurance companies to participate directly in a mixed, obligatory insurance system, albeit with a large number of state controls and guarantees. By the end of 1993 a large number of local and overseas firms were preparing to take advantage of the reform.[100] However, its effect on those already retired had yet to be felt during the period research was undertaken.

Micro-level strategies

The preceding sections have explained the failure of large-scale institutions, be they state or non-state, to meet all the income needs of the elderly. As a result many elderly remained dependent on a number of other income sources, such as employment, family support and savings. These strategies have generally received less official and academic attention than the operations of large organisations and thus the available data are often incomplete and highly fragmented.

The household, family and friends

This section looks at the structure of urban households, families and friendship networks, the role the elderly play in them and the degree of economic support they obtain. Before proceeding, it should be emphasised that 'family' and 'household' are not synonymous terms, especially in Latin American societies.[101] The former are based on kinship, whilst the latter involve an element of shared residence and may include non-kin. Frequently, distinctions between immediate kin, household members and more distant relatives are extremely blurred.

Earlier in this chapter it was shown that the Argentine National Constitution puts the responsibility of providing for the economic needs of the elderly squarely on the shoulders of their immediate family members. This was reflected in the criteria applied by the various means-tested benefits for the aged. The capacity of families and households to provide economic support for the elderly is influenced to some degree by changes in their size or composition. The only sources of data for such changes are the national censuses and occasional surveys. Both of these suffer from a number of weaknesses. National censuses do not always include data on households and do not always present them in a standard format, thus hindering comparison. Surveys are often based on samples too small to be statistically significant and are restricted to particular cities or neighbourhoods.

Table 3.11: Proportion of total and elderly population living alone, 1947–91

Year	Number living alone (a)	(a) as % of total pop.	65+s living alone (b)	(b) as % of total 65+s
1947	648 829	4.1	na	na
1960	302 539*	1.5	na	na
1970	615 900	2.6	na	na
1980	749 600	2.7	268 977	12.0
1991	1 206 541	3.7	491 267	17.5

* This figure is most probably a miscalculation by the census authorities.
Source: INDEC, 1961:105; 1970:2; 1973:48; 1983:119; 1993a:130.

Table 3.12: Changes in the structure of Argentine households, 1970–91 (as % of total households)[102]

Year	Unipersonal	Nuclear	Extended	Composite
1970	10.2	58.5	24.7	6.7
1980	10.4	58.2	24.0	7.4
1991	13.3	64.1	19.3	2.2

Source: INDEC, 1961:105; 1970:2; 1973:48; 1983:119; 1993a:130.

Table 3.13: Comparison of household structure between Federal Capital and Argentina and between over-65-year-olds and the total population (%)

		Unipersonal	Nuclear	Extended	Composite
1980	Argen.	2.7	56.0	31.5	9.9
	Arg 65+	12.0	35.7	43.1	9.3
	Capital	5.6	59.0	28.5	6.9
	Cap 65+	na	na	na	na
1990	Argen.	3.7	66.4	25.7	4.1
	Arg 65+	17.5	44.0	34.4	4.2
	Capital	8.2	66.5	21.4	3.9
	Cap 65+	22.7	44.2	29.6	3.4

Source: INDEC, 1961:105; 1970:2; 1973:48; 1983:119; 1993a:130.

Tables 3.11, 3.12 and 3.13 summarise census information about household structures. They show that only a small minority of the total population lived alone, but that this had increased substantially between 1980 and 1991. As seen in Table 3.12, the growth of unipersonal households was part of a broader shift away from larger, extended units to smaller, nuclear ones. This trend has been observed in many urbanised, western societies and has been ascribed to a number of factors including falling fertility, improved access to housing and rising divorce rates (Cotts Watkins, 1986:420–49; United Kingdom, Central Statistical Office, 1994:33–42).

Table 3.13 shows that the proportion of elderly living alone was substantially higher than that for the total population, accounting for almost a quarter of over-65-year-olds in the Federal Capital. This reflected the relatively low probability of an elderly individual having young children or a living partner. The latter was especially important for elderly women, who, due to their longer life expectancy, were much more likely to outlive their partners than the reverse. Consequently, elderly women were more likely to be living alone (29.3 per cent in the Federal Capital) than were elderly men (11.4 per cent) (INDEC, 1993b:85).

Whilst the great majority of elderly lived in multi-person households, this had experienced a significant fall during the 1980s. Unfortunately, it is not possible to disaggregate the census data to examine whether elderly with different socio-economic characteristics (such as *jubilados* or uninsured *villeros*) were more or less likely to live in a certain type of household. Nor is it possible to establish whether nuclear households containing over-65-year-olds just comprised an elderly couple or whether they also contained adult children. This could affect the capacity of the household to provide economic support. These issues are returned to in Chapter 5.

Some light is shed on these issues by smaller-scale surveys of the elderly living conditions, two of which are summarised in Table 3.14. The Gallup data are based on a sample of 2000 people in receipt of a retirement or widow's pension living in the Federal Capital and a number of provincial capitals, whilst the La Boca survey comprises of 223 elderly individuals living in a low income neighbourhood in the Federal Capital. Both surveys indicate that approximately a third of the elderly were living just with their spouses. As a result, less than half were parts of households containing non-elderly members.

3.14 Individual survey data c. 1990: the structure of households containing elderly in provincial capitals and La Boca (%)

	Capitals	La Boca
Alone	20.7*	27.8
With spouse	35.4	33.2
With spouse and children	12.5	10.3
With children	22.2	13.9
With other relatives	7.1	14.8**
With others	2.2	–

*The corresponding figure for the Federal Capital was 28.1 per cent (unfortunately, no other geographically disaggregated data were presented).
**This also includes the 'with others' category.
Source: Redondo, 1990:201; Scipione et al, 1992:72.

It is interesting to compare the results of the two surveys since the former was designed to represent the total urban elderly population, whilst the latter relates specifically to a low income neighbourhood. The proportions of elderly living alone or in a couple are similar, but a higher proportion of elderly in La Boca live with people other than their children. This indicates that nuclear household structures are less frequent in poor districts than elsewhere in large cities.

The structure of elderly families and households reflects a large number of factors, including demographic change, individual and cultural preferences, the availability of housing and the economic positions of their members.[103] These effects are often contradictory or difficult to disentangle. Consequently, it is not easy to support the census and survey data with intuitive deductions. For example, the greater frequency of households containing non-kin in La Boca may have been because larger homes afford greater security, especially when individual incomes are erratic. However, Redondo concludes that the majority of elderly surveyed in La Boca expressed a preference for living alone or in couples. According to Redondo, it was their increasing frailty and a generalised housing shortage in Greater Buenos Aires which forced many elderly into other arrangements (Pantelides, 1988; Kaplan and Redondo, 1992:116).

Nor should it be assumed that there is a direct link between the composition of households containing elderly and the pattern of economic interaction between aged individuals and other household or family members. An elderly person may live alone but still receive substantial support from nearby relatives.[104] Likewise, it should not be assumed that economic relations between elderly and other household members can be reduced to the degree of economic assistance which the former receive from the latter. The reality may be more complex, especially in extended households and the elderly may themselves make a number of direct economic contributions. The *Centro Latinoamericano de Demografia* (CELADE) survey found that 72.3 per cent of over-60-year-olds were owner-occupiers and another 16.2 per cent had handed over the ownership of their residence to other family members (CELADE, 1989:110). During the early 1990s the proportion of household expenditure taken up by accommodation costs rose sharply.[105] Consequently, free lodging was an important economic benefit to other people sharing the residence (assuming there was no rental agreement).[106] Likewise, Table 3.15 indicates that the daily domestic activities of elderly men and women should not be reduced to the passive receipt of economic support. Housework and childcare (for which, unfortunately, CELADE provide no data) may enable other household members to participate more fully in waged employment.[107] Finally, the elderly may contribute through the sharing of their salaries and benefits with the household as a whole. The latter, whilst small, may provide a guaranteed, monthly source of income which may reduce the impact of variations in earnings characteristic of the informal sector.

Unfortunately, most surveys which examine economic relations between the elderly and the household characterise this process as passive and unidirectional. Moreover, as shown in Table 3.16, there are large discrepancies between the findings of such studies. These may partly be explained by the specific wording of the questionnaires: the Gallup questionnaire was concerned with levels of satisfaction with family support, whereas the others stressed its economic significance.[108] Taken together, the surveys imply that, although the elderly were not generally dissatisfied with family support, it was only of direct economic benefit to a small minority, even in low income urban districts.[109] These findings contrast with studies of other countries which emphasise the importance of family support (Contreras de Lehr, 1992:215–23).

Table 3.15: Daily activities of population aged 60 or over, 1989 (%)

	Men	Women	Total
Go shopping	81.4	80.8	81.0
Sew, knit, darn	5.0	69.4	42.9
Housework	91.1	87.5	89.0

Source: CELADE, 1989:179, 184.

Table 3.16: Degree of economic support/autonomy from other household or family members, c.1989 (%)

Support	Autonomy	Capitals (Gallup)	CELADE	La Boca
Much		62.3		
	None		1.5	na
Enough		24.1		
	Some		8.7	na
Little		8.0		
	Complete		89.7	87.6
None		4.3		
NA		1.3		

Sources: CELADE, 1989:189; Redondo, 1990:203; Scipione et al, 1992:75.

The survey results may underestimate the true importance of the household, due to the non-quantifiable nature of some forms of assistance and the difficulty of 'capturing' them in a short questionnaire. Also, respondents may have been reluctant to admit the true extent of their economic dependence on relatives. Nevertheless, the limited available data suggest that direct economic support is generally insignificant and does not compensate for the gaps in the protection offered by larger institutions. This may partly be attributable to the failure of state agencies, such as PAMI, to develop large-scale programmes encouraging family support (see above). It may also reflect the general impact of increasing poverty in the 1980s on the ability of family members to help out. Chapter 5 ascertains whether the survey results were reflected in patterns of economic relations in *villas*.

As the census data demonstrate, it is difficult to blame the limited role of the family on a preponderance of nuclear households and the residential isolation of the elderly. Whilst over half of the elderly live with other family members, only one out of ten obtains significant support from them. This may reflect two scenarios: (1) an absence of income pooling between household members; or (2) economic relations between members which do not entail a large 'net gain' for the elderly. Although available survey data shed no light on the relative importance of these potential scenarios, general studies of poor urban households in Latin America stress the importance of income pooling, suggesting that the second explanation carries more weight (Lomnitz, 1977:117–22; Ramos, 1981:51–7).

Less information is available about economic support received by the elderly from family members and friends beyond the household. The small number of personal testimonies collected by M. Oddone suggest that shared residence is not necessarily an important factor.[110] However, this contradicts the conventional wisdom that the intensity of economic relations between kin is reduced by geographical distance (MacEwan, 1974:197–226; Lomnitz, 1977:133–4). Given that direct financial support from household members is scant, it is unlikely that friends or other family members make an important contribution. Whatever the case, this relationship should be tested empirically, not just accepted intuitively.

As has been demonstrated, existing data about relations between the elderly and other household members are ambivalent and leave many questions unanswered. It is important to understand why an increasing proportion of elderly, especially women, were living alone and to assess what economic effects this may produce. Similarly, it is essential to follow up inconclusive indications that the majority of elderly in multi-person households did not obtain economic support from kin. This must involve a more sophisticated approach, taking into account the complexity of the micro-economic dynamics of households and families. The weakness of the data here contrasts with the wealth of material concerning the structure and impact of public sector agencies. Chapter 5 attempts to correct this imbalance by giving detailed accounts of interhousehold relations in three shanty town districts.

Employment

To understand the continued employment of elderly beyond officially-designated retirement ages, it is necessary to examine changes in the labour market as a whole. Chapter 2 has already provided some general background about the evolution of the Argentine economy and employment trends. This showed that the absolute size of the workforce expanded rapidly over the twentieth century. However, this did not occur at the same rate as the total population growth. As a result, the economically active proportion of the total population fell continuously between 1950 and 1990 (Table 3.17). Several factors account for this decline, including a shift from labour to capital intensive industrial and agricultural processes and the country's poor overall economic performance. Social factors, such as an increased tendency to pursue further education and opt for early retirement, were also significant.[111]

Table 3.17: Rates of economic activity in Argentina, 1950–90 (%)

Age/sex	1950	1960	1970	1980	1990*
Total population	41.45	39.35	38.95	36.50	35.10
Total 60–64	45.70	38.70	33.40	29.65	27.55
Total 65+	30.85	21.60	16.10	9.70	7.20
Men 60–64	78.40	66.40	57.20	52.00	49.40
Men 65+	56.20	38.60	29.10	18.00	14.10
Women 60–64	8.10	9.00	10.50	9.70	8.20
Women 65+	6.60	5.20	4.70	3.20	2.10

* Projected figures.
Source: ILO, 1986b:79–81.

Official data for economic activity may fail to register the full extent of employment in the informal sector as well as part-time and occasional labour.[112] These emerging forms of employment generally received less complete insurance protection than did formal occupations and often paid lower or less reliable wages.[113] Thus, there was a reduction in both the proportion of the total population in employment and in the quality of jobs which were available to them.

Table 3.17 shows that the decline in economic activity of the elderly population between 1950 and 1990 was considerably more rapid than that for the total population. The decline was particularly pronounced among over-65-year-olds, for whom activity rates fell from 30.85 to 7.2 per cent. Differences between age groups reflected the large increase in the number of elderly receiving pensions, which continued up to the 1980s. Likewise, gender differences may partly be explained by the lower retirement age for women. However, it should not be assumed that there is a direct correlation between the expansion of pension coverage and declining employment. The Gallup survey of pensioners found that 11.4 per cent admitted to remaining in gainful employment in order to supplement their benefits (Scipione et al, 1992:35). Conversely, the number of economically active elderly was lower than the number excluded from insurance provision (see Table 3.2), indicating that some elderly without benefits remained out of formal employment.

CELADE provides information about the types of economic activity the elderly were most likely to be engaged in. This shows that larger proportions were self-employed commercial or construction workers: activities which generally entail a high degree of informality.[114] CELADE also identifies a tendency for industrial workers to switch to self-employment or informal activities as they reach old age (CELADE, 1989:164–7). Similarly, the Gallup pensioner survey found that 58.3 per cent of those in employment worked less than six hours a day (Scipione et al, 1992:109). Neither the CELADE or Gallup surveys provide information about wage levels. However, a census of elderly *villeros* in the Province of Buenos Aires in 1981 found that elderly heads of household who remained in employment earned on average less than other age groups (Argentine Republic, *Ministerio de Trabajo y Seguridad Social,* 1987:70).

The high level of informality among the elderly may have resulted from a number of causes. It is useful to divide the working elderly into those with and those without insurance benefits. The former sought to supplement the value of their benefits but no longer continued in full-time employment or in their original occupations. This was partly because they were no longer capable (or were not considered so by employers) to hold on to permanent, regular occupations. Also, legal restrictions, though frequently ignored, may have discouraged both insured elderly from seeking such work and employers from taking them on. As such, the elderly would be the first to feel the effects of reduced opportunities in the formal sector as a whole. Insured elderly were often left with little option but to pursue part-time, informal employment in activities which did not entail entry high barriers (capital, skills, and so forth). In some cases, formal sector workers sought to delay retirement in order to maintain their existing levels of income (Oddone, 1994:21).

Given the low coverage rates of assistance benefits, it was unlikely that non-insured elderly would have a state pension. As such, they were not legally prevented from working. They would have been less affected by the contraction of the formal labour market and would be more likely to remain in the same occupation. Without pensions, the need for this group to continue working full-time would be higher than was the case for insured elderly.[115] Indeed, their working practices would only change as a result of physical and mental frailty.

Little evidence exists to either corroborate or disprove the two scenarios outlined in the preceding paragraphs. Chapter 5 will return to these issues and assess whether the above characterisations held for elderly *villeros*.

The fall in elderly economic activity rates can be interpreted as evidence of the success of insurance and assistance schemes in providing for their economic needs. However, it could also have resulted from a reduction of access and opportunities for gainful employment. As mentioned above, a number of elderly had access to neither insurance benefits nor employment. CELADE found that 40.1 per cent of over-60-year-olds felt an economic need to continue working, but only 16.5 per cent were able to do so (CELADE, 1989:154, 161). The high proportion of elderly working in informal activities, where incomes were generally lower and less reliable than in the formal sector, also reflects their difficulties in obtaining work elsewhere. Finally, the general fall in real wages will have reduced the value of continued employment (UN, 1992:32).

Other sources of income

Savings comprise an important source of income for the elderly in many countries (Johnson and Falkingham, 1992:59–60), but their importance in Argentina has been limited by a number of factors. Economic instability, high inflation and government manipulation of private deposits served as strong disincentives for savings in domestic banks (Escudé and Guerberoff, 1990:25–73; Bouzas, 1993:9–13). Monthly interest rates consistently failed to keep pace with inflation during much of the 1980s (ECLAC, 1989:150; 1993b:34). At the same time, significant falls in real wages reduced the capacity for individual savings (see Figure 2.4).

The CELADE survey provides no information about elderly savings, implying that these were not a significant source of income. This is reflected in Table 3.18 which shows that only a very small proportion of pensioners received income from savings and corresponds with the finding of Redondo's La Boca survey that the majority of elderly complained that their savings had been significantly devalued by inflation (Kaplan and Redondo, 1992:115).

Table 3.18 also includes information about income from other, non-specified sources. These provide support for a slightly larger number of cases than do savings. Given that a high proportion of elderly were property owners, it is probable that a large part of this category was accounted for by rents. However, a number of other potential sources of income exist, including subsistence production, scavenging and begging. The opportunities for the former were limited in urban areas such as Greater Buenos Aires. A survey of household incomes in three low-income neighbourhoods located in the outskirts of the city (where there was more available land for plots and small-holdings) found that subsistence accounted for less than 3 per cent of total income (Aguirre, 1990). Scavenging and begging were clearly strategies of last resort, not to be pursued unless income from any other source was insufficient to meet the elderly individual's basic needs. No reference is made to such activities either in academic investigations, official surveys, NGO reports or the local press. Chapter 5 provides detailed survey data for specific shanty towns and considers whether any elderly residents were forced into such desperate straits.

Table 3.18: Additional sources of income (other than benefits, family or employment) for pensioners (%)

	Total	Retirement pension	Widow's pension
Dollar savings	0.9	1.3	1.2
Short-term deposits	1.2	1.4	0.8
Interest on savings	3.5	4.5	1.8
Other	4.2	4.9	2.9

Source: Scipione et al, 1992:35.

OVERVIEW AND CONCLUSIONS

The confused, fragmented structure of institutional economic support for the elderly living in Greater Buenos Aires in the early 1990s can only be understood in the light of its complex historical evolution. This can be divided into three approximate phases. The first, occurring from the late nineteenth to mid-twentieth century, involved considerable pluralism with the expansion of public programmes and organisations such as mutual aid societies. Throughout this period, there was a general labour shortage, enabling a large proportion of elderly to support themselves by remaining in employment. This was followed by the imposition of a state welfare monopoly and extended, though far from universal, protection which coincided with a sudden increase in the size of the elderly population. As a result, the elderly became increasingly dependent on state initiatives. This, along with an emerging labour surplus, led to a sharp falls in activity rates for the elderly. By the 1980s, the reduced capacity of the public sector to meet the welfare needs of the majority of the elderly and an ideological shift away from statism led to the gradual re-emergence of a more pluralistic structure. Rather than encourage the simplification of the state welfare apparatus, however, this process was accompanied by further public sector fragmentation. This partly reflected the resilience of such agencies and partly resulted from the state's failure to match the readiness with which it set up new programmes with the provision of adequate funding. Opportunities in the labour market remained limited, with many elderly resorting to informal employment.

It is not possible to obtain historical information about all aspects of elderly income maintenance. The most important missing link in the above schema is the role played by households and family members. These have been shown to provide the elderly its most significant source of income in many countries. Nevertheless, the expansion of state provision may have reduced the role of family members in providing support to the elderly. The corollary of this would be that family support increased as the quality of state provision fell, yet the limited available evidence indicates that the elderly received scant assistance from household members.

Even with these historical insights, the general pattern of income maintenance strategies in the early 1990s does not, at first sight, make complete sense. First, it shows that the dominant role of the state in elderly welfare provision masked large gaps in the population's insurance coverage and the inadequacy of benefits. These failings had only been partly compensated for by the expansion of PAMI's activities and the establishment of numerous assistance agencies. Secondly, it shows that large non-state institutions provided economic support for only a very small number of elderly, due to the small budgets of NGOs and the recent establishment of private pension programmes. Following this, it shows that direct economic support from household members and opportunities for well-remunerated employment were very limited. Finally, other income strategies, ranging from saving to scavenging are shown to have been largely insignificant.

As such, it could be concluded that neither macro- nor micro-scale strategies were enough to compensate for the shortcomings of state protection. Were this the case it would be expected that a large proportion of elderly would be left in a condition of poverty. Despite this, Table 3.19 shows that levels of poverty among the elderly, whilst not being negligible, were low compared to other age groups. This indicates that the elderly were relatively successful in obtaining income and may account for the lack of economic support they receive from other, less favoured, household members. Rather than indicating that income levels for the elderly were satisfactory, the data in Table 3.19 reveal that the incomes of other groups fell even further short of their requirements. This had been a consequence of falling real wages and the contraction of formal labour markets. Moreover, social insurance and assistance programmes made little provision for groups such as the unemployed and single-parent families.[116] Another possible explanation is that higher income groups enjoyed a greater life expectancy than the poor and thus accounted for a disproportionate share of the total elderly population. As was seen in Chapter 2, the limited available data would seem to suggest this trend. Whether those elderly from less-privileged socio-economic strata were better or worse off than younger individuals from the same background is a very different matter, which is considered in the next two chapters.

Table 3.19: Age and poverty among household heads in Greater Buenos Aires, 1980 and 1987 (%)

Age/status		Under 60	60 or over
Not poor	1980	66.9	33.1
	1987	66.4	33.6
Below poverty line*	1980	68.7	31.3
	1987	71.0	29.0
Basic needs unsatisfied**	1980	89.5	10.5
	1987	84.8	15.2
Both	1980	90.9	9.1
	1987	91.1	8.9

* Poverty as defined by household income alone.
** Poverty as defined by basic need satisfaction. These include a range of indicators such as accommodation, sanitation and access to primary education. A detailed explanation is provided in INDEC, 1984:9–17.
Source: Minujin and Vinocur, 1992:398.

In most cases no single source of income was enough to satisfy the basic economic needs of an elderly individual. Consequently, many elderly had to resort to combining income from a number of different sources in order to survive. This is illustrated by Gallup's finding that 61 per cent of pensioners received income from other sources (Scipione et al, 1992:35). Unfortunately, there are no other available data which cross-reference income sources. Figure 3.6 provides a tentative schema of the ways in which the various types of income at the disposal of the elderly might be combined. It divides the elderly into two groups: those who had previously made insurance contributions and those who had not. This did more than influence their subsequent access to contributory pensions. Insured elderly had full membership of PAMI but were theoretically excluded from assistance pensions and formal employment. It was unlikely that insured elderly needed to resort to scavenging for economic survival. Conversely, it was probable that NGOs focused their efforts on the uninsured. Finally, the schema posits that those elderly who made pension contributions in the past were also more likely to have accumulated savings and acquired properties. This may have resulted from both higher levels of disposable income and a tendency to defer consumption. Unfortunately, there are no available data to corroborate this assumption.

If the pattern of income strategies displayed in Figure 3.6 is correct it could be concluded that a strong economic dualism existed between the insured and more marginalised elderly. It would be interesting to consider whether this dualism coincided with the condition of society as a whole. Studies of poverty in Argentina often distinguish between the 'pauperised' (formerly middle-class families whose income dips below the poverty line) and the 'structurally poor' (families who spend more protracted periods in poverty and who suffer from unsatisfied basic needs). The former might be characterised as retired formal sector workers whose insurance benefits fell short of previous earnings. Conversely, the likelihood that structurally poor elderly individuals would be eligible for an insurance benefit would be much reduced. Available official data do not shed any light on the extent of this dualism, which raises the need for detailed micro-scale surveys.

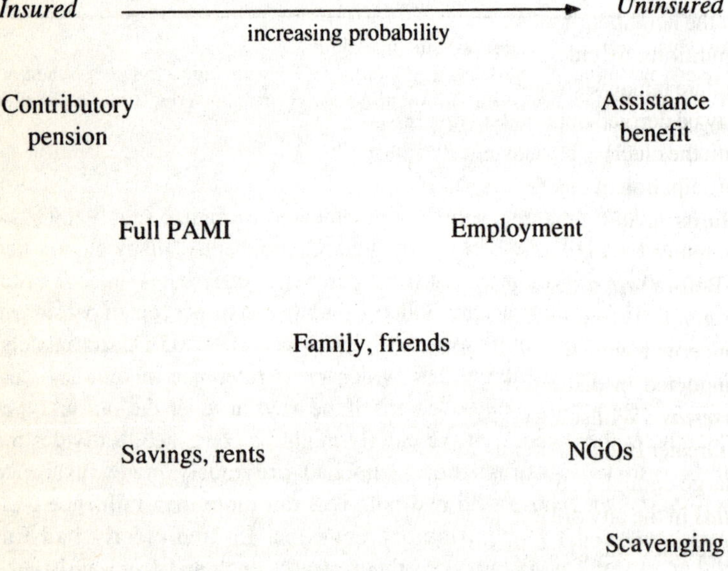

Figure 3.6 Combined income sources for the elderly

4 The Case-studies: General Features and Local Initiatives for the Elderly

INTRODUCTION

This and the following chapter move the emphasis away from the macro or national level to patterns of elderly income maintenance in specific neighbourhoods. Rather than treating these neighbourhoods in isolation, reference is made to the institutional structures outlined above. Whilst studies of macro-structures are clearly incomplete unless consideration is given to their effects at the local level, little sense can be made of micro-surveys if they are not placed within a broader context.

This chapter has two main goals. First, it provides the general background for the neighbourhoods surveyed, paying particular attention to the economic conditions of elderly residents. Secondly, it explores the effect of local welfare initiatives, considering the obstacles to and the potential benefits which may be derived obtained from effective organisations specifically concerned with the elderly. This is done by examining how patterns of organisation and participation of elderly in each location changed over time. The final section returns to the general themes discussed at the start of the chapter and compares the experiences of the neighbourhoods surveyed.

Before looking at the case-studies themselves, some explanation should be given for the choice of neighbourhoods. Since this book is primarily concerned with the plight of *poor* urban elderly, case-studies were only conducted in districts with high overall levels of poverty, namely *villas miserias*.[1] Whilst it was desirable to select *villas* which were typical of those in Greater Buenos Aires as a whole, it was necessary to study areas containing a large enough number of elderly to provide a representative sample. Many *villas* in the city did not meet this criterion and were consequently excluded. Preference was given to *villas* with distinctive patterns of local organisation and socio-economic characteristics, to reflect the diversity occurring in the city as a whole and so that the effect of these variables might be examined. Finally, consideration was also given to the level of safety which could be guaranteed to the investigator: in several shanty towns the likelihood of robbery and assault restricted the ability of the researcher to gather material.

Some data about levels of poverty and the numbers of elderly in different parts of Greater Buenos Aires are available from the 1980 survey carried out by the *Instituto Nacional de Estadística y Censos* (INDEC, 1984). However, establishing contacts and gaining acceptance in shanty towns is often a very drawn-out and complicated process. Inevitably then, the selection of shanty towns involved a degree of chance. Several neighbourhoods selected for a preliminary survey were subsequently found to be inappropriate according to the above criteria and were therefore discarded.[2]

LOCAL INITIATIVES FOR THE ELDERLY: GENERAL CONSIDERATIONS

It is to be expected that the economic welfare of elderly individuals will be strongly influenced by their immediate living environments. One way in which this may occur is through the development of 'social infrastructure' (community organisations, informal self-help groups and the like), which serve to provide new income opportunities and reduce economic vulnerability (Moser, 1995:1–15). Chapter 1 noted the importance ascribed to these phenomena in regions such as sub-Saharan Africa and Chapter 3 referred to a general flourishing of grassroots organisations and NGOs in Latin America since the 1970s. This section considers the capacity of poor elderly in Greater Buenos Aires to develop and sustain local-level organisations and the ways in which such activities may be of potential economic benefit to them.

The organisation of the poor and underprivileged is the subject of a number of broad-ranging and unresolved debates. On the one hand, it has been argued that the necessities of poverty and a common set of experiences and interests may promote solidarity. As an extension, it might be posited that the condition of poverty can impose elements of a somewhat 'less modern' form of living on its victims. This could conceivably facilitate community organisation and cushion the elderly from any negative effects associated with modernisation. In the case of *villas* in Greater Buenos Aires, this process might be reflected in a number of ways. Limited accommodation might be expected to promote larger household sizes and decrease the likelihood of elderly living alone. Moreover, the crowding together of small and often flimsily-built homes might forment social interaction and reduce the isolation of separate households. A survey of *villas* in Greater Buenos Aires in 1980 found that only 43 per cent of homes were built primarily of brick and that 28.5 per cent contained six or more people (Province of Buenos Aires, 1981). The effect may be reinforced if the majority of new arrivals at the *villa* are originally from environments which are in some respects less modern than the city (for example, isolated rural districts).

On the other hand, poverty and a lack of modernity may equally serve to reduce the capacity of groups such as elderly *villeros* to develop grassroots organisations. Whilst theories referring to general 'cultures' of marginality or deviancy have been strongly refuted since the 1970s, it is important to consider other aspects of marginality, such as exclusion from political processes and the denial of access to public goods. It has been repeatedly demonstrated that shanty towns were palpably marginalised within Greater Buenos Aires as a whole, in terms of their physical infrastructures, access to services and so forth (Pastrana, 1980:124–42; Grassi, 1991:45–56). The marginality of *villeros* was also evident in more general socio-economic terms. For example, a survey of *villas* in the provincial section of Greater Buenos Aires in 1981 found that 13.8 per cent of those aged over 14 years could neither read nor write, compared to a national illiteracy rate of 6.1 per cent (Table 4.1).[3] A study of grassroots organisations in Rosario, Argentina's second city, found that:

> only rarely have neighbourhood organisations included villa residents in their activities...Lacking legal representation, the villas also find themselves lacking social or political representation. (Martínez Norgueira, 1995:52)

As such, although it is conceivable that conditions in *villas* might promote neighbourhood solidarity and informal social networks, factors such a low literacy and political exclusion may also serve to obstruct the development of more formal organisational structures.

Table 4.1: Levels of illiteracy in villas *and Argentina as a whole, 1980 (%)*

	Villas in provincial GBA (aged 14+)	National average (aged 15+)
Total	13.8	6.1
Total men	11.8	5.7
Total women	15.7	6.4

Sources: Argentine Republic, *Ministerio de Trabajo y Seguridad Social*, 1987:5–11; UNESCO, 1991:1–23.

There are also indications that the elderly residents of *villas* were marginalised *vis-à-vis* these neighbourhoods as a whole. Chapter 2 showed that although the relative and absolute numbers of elderly *villeros* may have increased in recent years, they still comprised a smaller proportion of the population of shanty towns than in other districts. The fact that old age was a very recent phenomenon in most shanty towns meant that, as a group, the elderly had a lower profile in such neighbourhoods than in other parts of the city. According to Silvia Simone of CEPEV:

> Old age is a modern phenomenon for which these groups of people were unprepared – they almost don't notice it themselves. Old age surprises them. They didn't see their parents grow old...The old person remains hidden inside the home. They scarcely consider themselves as old. One may ask 'Are there many old people around here?' and they tell you 'No, not very many.'...the problems of mothers, children, youths, out of work adults come first. And really these are the groups who have suffered most in the crisis. But old people have their problems too and their ability to occupy a social position so that people recognise their needs...doesn't occur spontaneously in any of these neighbourhoods. (Silvia Simone, CEPEV, May 1993)

Table 4.2: Attendance of villeros *at educational establishments, 1980*

Age	Currently attending (%)	Attended in past (%)	Never attended (%)
15–24	12.64	83.56	8.43
25–49	4.25	87.51	7.71
50+	3.10	75.69	20.18

Source: calculated from Argentine Republic, *Ministerio de Trabajo y Seguridad Social*, 1987:15.

Secondly, as shown by the data in Table 4.2, educational levels were particularly poor among elderly *villeros*. In the Province of Buenos Aires in 1980 it was roughly three times as likely that *villa* residents aged over 50 had not attended schools than was the case for those aged between 25 and 49 years old. Hence it is possible that elderly *villeros* suffered from two distinct forms of marginality: that of the slum and that of old age. This chapter examines the extent to which these occurred in the neighbourhoods studied, by assessing the capacity of elderly *villeros* to organise themselves spontaneously, as well as ways in which such local initiatives may serve to reduce the elderly's doubly marginal status.

Many studies of the organisation of poor urban groups stress the importance of outside actors (Gilbert and Ward, 1985:174–240; Assies 1990:84–5; Foweraker, 1995:61–89). This chapter looks at the particular objectives of these external agents and the extent to which they facilitated autonomous action by elderly *villeros* themselves. It asks whether the role of outside actors reflects the marginal status of elderly *villeros* and whether they serve to reduce or even promote it. Such actors can perform two separate functions. On one hand, they may provide the initial impetus and organisational know-how for *villeros* to form an association. On the other, they may control the material resources for which *villeros* group together to obtain. In some cases, such as when the local government is involved, the same external agent may perform both roles. Some controversy exists regarding the desirability of external actors participating in the establishment of local organisations. It has been argued that this involvement usually constitutes external political control, which subverts the real interests of the poor to the dominant outside order (Castells, 1983:190–4; Gilbert and Ward, 1985:175–7, 237–9). Conversely, it has also been claimed that the passivity and lack of associative experience of those suffering extreme poverty renders them incapable of organising without external support (Tenti, 1992:142–6). Clearly, this was the view taken by non-state organisations such as CEPEV, as outlined in Chapter 3.

As well as examining the prospects of developing successful local initiatives for elderly *villeros*, this chapter considers the potential economic impact such organisations may have. To this end, it is useful to distinguish between the different activities which may be undertaken. The first of these, *direct economic assistance*, includes monetary hand-outs and a wide variety of other goods, such as food aid (parcels, vouchers and feeding centres), the provision of medicines, accommodation or clothing. These goods may be provided free, subsidised or on loan.

Some organisations provide *advice on obtaining benefits*. As explained in Chapter 3, in Greater Buenos Aires a complicated array of contributory and non-contributory benefits were available for the elderly. Legal entitlements, eligibility criteria and modes of application for these services were equally complex. It was therefore important to provide clear information on which benefits might be available and how to obtain them. When the state agencies involved failed to do this, other organisations sometimes opted to take on the task.

Organisations may also assist members by providing *'strength through numbers'*. This does not simply refer to direct lobbying, through demonstrations, petitions and so forth. For a combination of practical and political reasons, some state services for groups such as the elderly were not granted directly to individuals but were instead managed through officially recognised local associations. Consequently, the absence of such organisations in a neighbourhood automatically excluded its residents from these state services. Again, according to Silvia Simone of CEPEV:

> There is no other way systematically to obtain public resources without being included in official registers [of local organisations]. It is through these lists that official organs distribute their resources.
>
> (Silvia Simone, CEPEV, May 1993)

Finally, local initiatives may offer a range of *social activities*, such as subsidised holidays or literacy classes. Their contribution to the economic well-being of the elderly is less obvious than that of other activities. Reducing an individual's sense of isolation and increasing their confidence may, however, empower them to seek solutions to their own economic problems. It may also raise their collective awareness and thus increase their political significance.

Attention must be paid to the depth as well as to the range of services provided by local associations in *villas*. On one hand, identifying a single objective may allow the concentration of resources and prevent unrealistic expectations. On the other, it may result in a narrow base of participation, leading to the collapse of the organisation once this objective is wholly or partially realised. Indeed several scholars argue that local organisations generally experience cyclical phases of activity and decline, as they attain their initial objectives (Kimberly, 1980:1–14; Tenti, 1992: 132–6). This argument may not necessarily apply to organisations concerned with the needs of elderly *villeros*, since their problematic is an ongoing one, which is not usually resolved by the acquisition of a single good or service. However, elderly organisations are likely to suffer more frequent changes of personnel due to infirmity or death. The mobilisation and subsequent loss of key participants may, for different reasons, lead to similar cycles of activity and decline.

Throughout the following sections reference will be made to these general themes, including the types of assistance offered by local initiatives and their impact on the status of the elderly both within and outside the *villas*. This will be placed within the broader hierarchy of income maintenance opportunities for the elderly. By examining the failures and successes of different initiatives, the chapter seeks to develop a model for bridging the gap between formal welfare programmes and micro-level survival strategies.

GENERAL PROFILES OF THREE *VILLAS MISERIAS*

Before examining the experiences of specific local-level elderly organisations, it is useful to provide some more general information about the neighbourhoods where they were located. This information also provides background context for the experiences of individual elderly *villeros*, which are dealt with in the next chapter.

Villa Jardín: the setting

Villa Jardín is located just beyond the administrative boundary of the Federal Capital, in the municipality of Lanús (see Map 4.1). On one side it is bounded by the highly-polluted Riachuelo River; another is lined with factories, most of which are now abandoned and crumbling (see Map 4.2).

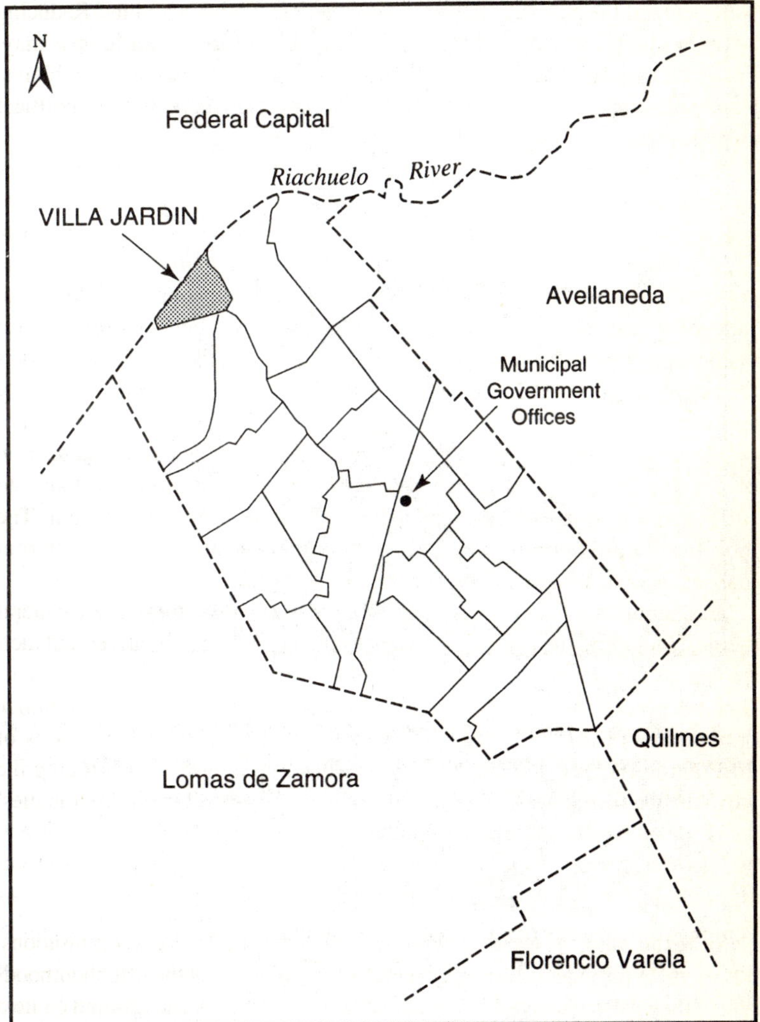

Map 4.1 Lanús Municipal District

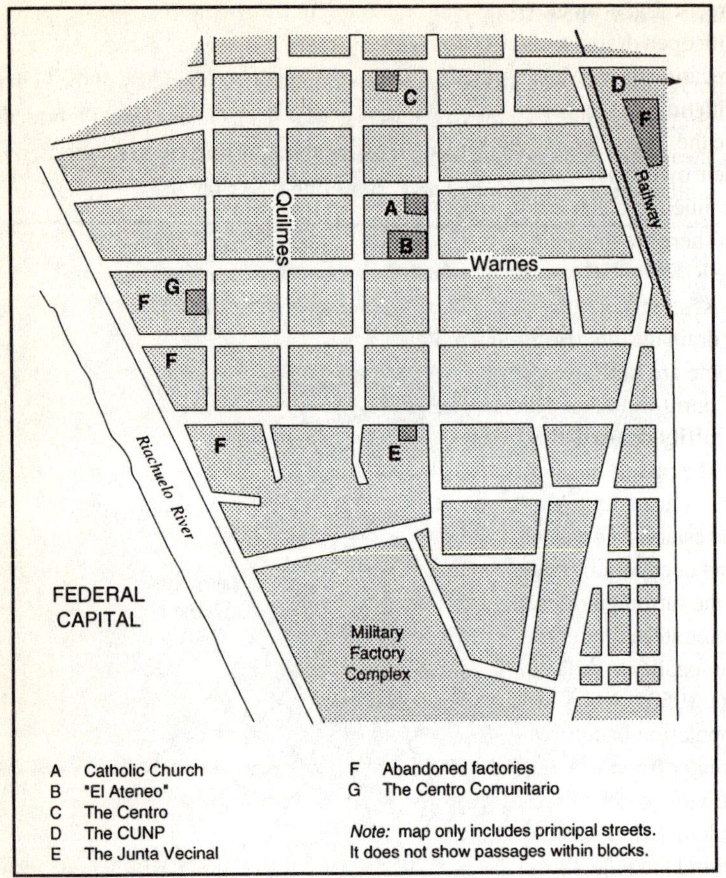

Map 4.2 Villa Jardín

At first sight much of the *villa* bears more resemblance to a run-down working-class neighbourhood than a shanty town. Houses are typically of brick, with corrugated roofs and reasonably well-maintained. Indeed, some large, detached homes suggest a number of middle-class households live in the district. Many of the principal roads are surfaced. The most important thoroughfare, Calle Warnes, is dotted with a variety of shops and businesses, ranging from grocers to video rentals. Villa Jardín is well-served by a number of bus services running to various parts of the city, including the Federal Capital.

An important difference between Villa Jardín and other typical working-class neighbourhoods is that the vast majority of homes do not front on to streets. Each block of housing contains mazes of narrow passages lined with open drainage ditches and housing at varying stages of dilapidation and precariousness. Most typically houses are small, two or three room structures with tin roofs and cement floors. An important feature of these passageways are the '*quioscos*': residents selling convenience goods through windows in their own front rooms. Neighbours would often visit these informal stores as much to catch up on local gossip as to make purchases.

There are indications that the southern end of the *villa* and areas alongside the Riacheulo River are significantly poorer than the rest of the district. Here most streets are unsurfaced and are often subject to flooding from the river or drainage ditches. Street-front houses are smaller and less well-maintained. Some are built of wood and scrap metal. There is more litter and a number of burnt-out cars. The streets are patrolled by scrawny dogs and gangs of scruffily dressed children.

The mix of housing in Villa Jardín may reflect the fact that it did not began life as a shanty town. In the early 1930s European immigrants bought land and established a small village there. It was not until the late 1940s that illegal land occupations began and clusters of precarious housing started to appear in the surrounding swampland (Lezcano, 1982:19–25). Most of the newcomers were internal migrants, drawn by the prospects of industrial employment in the locality.[4] Villa Jardín expanded in a rapid, haphazard fashion until the late 1950s, when all the available land had been occupied. By 1956 its population had grown to 24 000, making it by far the largest shanty town in Greater Buenos Aires (CNV, 1956:76). Although the land was very marshy, the *villa* was centrally located and had fairly good transport links into the Federal Capital. Nevertheless, improvements to infrastructure tended to lag behind the *villa*'s growth: the first water pipes were only installed in the late 1950s and land drainage was not completed until the 1970s. As will be seen, these developments reflected the degree of solidarity and level of organisation among local residents, as well as the external economic and political environment.

Table 4.3: Elderly population in Villa Jardín, 1980 and 1991

	Total population	Population aged 60+	Population aged 60+ (%)
1980	14 554	694	4.8
1991	16 996	1 221	7.2

Sources: *Provincia de Buenos Aires*, 1981; INDEC, 1993c:246.

Data about the demographic composition of Villa Jardín are available in the 1991 national census and a survey carried out by the Province of Buenos Aires in 1980 (Table 4.3). These show that between 1956 and 1980 the total population had fallen by almost half, followed by a slight recovery during the 1980s. The initial fall is somewhat surprising, given that the total number of *villeros* in provincial Buenos Aires had more than trebled since the mid-1950s (Table 2.11). Rather than resulting from a reduction of the physical extent of the *villa* or the abandonment of housing, the decline reflected falling population densities. In the 1950s Villa Jardín had been one of the most densely populated parts of Buenos Aires, with roughly a thousand people to a block (Rojo, 1976:48). Whilst some sections of the *villa* were still highly crowded in the early 1990s, they contained fewer residents than previously. In those parts of the *villa* containing better housing, accommodation had been considerably upgraded over time, causing both an increase in the size of homes and a reduction in the average number of people per room. This fall in population density indicates that conditions in the *villa* had improved significantly over time and that many residents had been able to move away. As such, it suggests that, for much of its history, Villa Jardín conformed more closely to the characterisation of an up-and-coming neighbourhood rather than a 'slum of despair'.[5]

The fact that Villa Jardín's total population increased by 17 per cent between 1980 and 1991 is also worthy of note, especially since the population of Lanús district as a whole fell slightly over the same period. This renewed growth was probably the result of falling real wages and increased poverty in Greater Buenos Aires, which both reduced opportunities for escape from the *villa* and may have forced additional people to take up residence there.

As can be seen in Table 4.3, the number of over-60-year-olds living in Villa Jardín increased dramatically between 1980 and 1991 (from 694 to 1221). Even in 1980 the proportion of elderly in Villa Jardín (4.8 per cent) was markedly higher than for *villas* in Lanús district as a whole. The relatively high proportion of elderly in Villa Jardín reflected its early foundation. Migrants drawn to the *villa* during the 1950s were largely in their twenties and would therefore have been reaching old age by the 1980s. In more recently formed *villas* there had not been sufficient time for this ageing process to occur. It is then to be expected, all things being equal, that the sudden ageing of Villa Jardín will be emulated by other *villas* in the future.

Table 4.4 provides additional information abut the age structure of Villa Jardín's population in 1991. The *villa* contained more than twice as many people aged 60 to 69 as it did aged 70 or more. This is in line with the sudden increase in over-60-year-olds recorded over the preceding decade. More interestingly, the size of the cohorts aged 50–59 suggests that Villa Jardín will continue to experience population ageing during the 1990s.

Table 4.4: Population structure of Villa Jardín, 1991

Age group	Total	Share total population (%)	Never attended school (%)
0–5	2035	12.0	na
6–49	12464	73.3	2.7
50–59	1249	7.3	6.6
60–64	481	2.8	8.7
65–69	337	2.0	16.6
70–74	184	1.1	21.7
75–79	135	0.8	26.7
80–84	58	0.3	13.8
85+	26	0.2	26.9

Source: INDEC, 1993c:246.

A limited amount of socio-economic data about the *villa* is provided by official censuses and surveys. The 1980 survey shows that the vast majority (88 per cent) of the *villa*'s population were Argentine nationals and that 48 per cent were born in Greater Buenos Aires. This is not surprising, since most settlers after the 1930s were themselves Argentine. It should also be noted that legal entitlement to social security benefits would be higher in a *villa* with a large proportion of long-established Argentine citizens than in one containing mainly foreigners.

The 1980 national census also contains information about basic need satisfaction and housing quality. Unfortunately, these were are not yet available for the 1991 census. Table 4.5 shows that in 1980 the district contained a strikingly high concentration of poverty compared to Argentina as a whole. Even so, the fact that 39.4 per cent of housing was deemed up to standard and 31.2 per cent of households had their basic needs satisfied again indicates a degree of socio-economic heterogeneity. The position of those aged over 60 was marginally less severe, particularly compared with that of young children. This corresponds with the results of a number of other surveys conducted in Buenos Aires during the 1980s (Table 3.19). However, as mentioned in Chapter 3, the rapid deterioration in the real values of pensions since 1989 may have worsened the relative position of the elderly in Villa Jardín.

Although it provides no data on poverty, the 1991 census does include some information about educational attainment. Table 4.4 shows that older *villeros* were much less likely to have ever attended a school than were the young. It is to be expected that levels of illiteracy were significantly higher than non-attendance figures and as such it is very probable that illiteracy was widespread among the elderly of Villa Jardín.

Table 4.5: Poverty indicators[6] for Villa Jardín (VJ) and Argentina, 1980

	% households lacking basic needs	% sub-standard housing
Argentina	22.3	8.7
Villa Jardín	68.8	60.6
Population 60+ in VJ	59.2	no data
Population under 2 in VJ	80.6	no data

Source: INDEC, 1984:66, 125.

Grassroots organisation in Villa Jardín

The challenge of settling inhospitable swamplands and a common threat of eviction helped to forge strong bonds of solidarity between the *villa*'s early inhabitants. Many residents were active in unions and other Peronist organisations during the 1950s. However, as will be seen, there were also elements of conflict and fragmentation: most notably between property owners (*propietarios*) and illegal squatters (*intrusos*).

Villa Jardín's first local organisation ('*El Sociedad de Fomento*') was formed by *propietarios* of European origin in 1952 and excluded the recent arrivals. The *Sociedad* was primarily concerned with to improving the physical fabric of the *villa*, although the overthrow of Perón in 1955 prompted some members to participate in violent anti-government demonstrations. This year also saw *intrusos* make their first attempt to band together in a rival neighbourhood council (*Junta Vecinal*).[7] There are signs that the authorities encouraged the development of the *Junta* at the expense of the more politically active *Sociedad*. A report made by the *Comisión Nacional de la Vivienda* in 1956 claims that, 'the activities of this junta should be taken seriously, since it alone is an indicator of the high moral calibre of the population' (CNV, 1956:225), but makes no reference to the presence of the *Sociedad de Fomento*. The good relations between the *Junta* and the authorities bore fruit in 1962, when, thanks to the passage of a national law forbidding evictions, the *intrusos* succeeded in securing tenureship rights. This encouraged *intrusos* to consider the settlement as a permanent residence and to take more interest in infrastructural improvements.

During the 1960s both the *Junta* and the *Sociedad* were active in improving the local infrastructure and continued to represent the respective interests of *intrusos* and *propietarios*. At the same time, several new organisations emerged, including Church initiatives and grassroots political associations. By the 1970s, however, heightened political conflict at the national level was echoed in the community life of Villa Jardín. By 1973 the *Sociedad*'s committee had been taken over by radical elements of a Peronist youth movement and became largely a political organisation. Following the military coup of 1976, the *Sociedad*'s committee was purged and it was forced to become a virtual appendage of the authorities. The *Junta Vecinal* was disbanded shortly afterwards and several prominent members of the community were either killed or forced to flee. In May 1978 the army occupied Villa Jardín, terrorising local residents. According to one *villero*:

> They used to shoot people on the rubbish tip every night, unless it was raining, between 1.30 am and 3.30 am. The rubbish scavengers used to find two or three corpses a day, young people, in nylon sacks. Someone who worked in the military steel plant told me that they used to take 200 litre drums full of corpses and throw them into the blast furnace. They took them away in trucks in the early morning. Along the streets the smell made you want to vomit. (Lezcano, 1982:120)

Only the Catholic Church was allowed to continue working in the *villa*. As a result, the Church was able to expand substantially its role in the community and took initiatives specifically directed at socio-economic issues, rather than infrastructural problems. Military oppression had a long-lasting effect on the *villa* and local activity only regained its earlier diversity and depth by the late 1980s. This partly explains why many of the initiatives for the elderly operating in 1992 were of recent origin (see below). Nevertheless, the repressive actions of the *Proceso* period did not appear to have reduced factionalism. A survey conducted in 1990 found considerable fragmentation both among community associations and grassroots political groups, although it did not specify whether these divisions occurred along traditional lines (*intrusos* versus *propietarios*) or new ones (CEPEV, 1990:14).

Despite changes in the political and economic environment, Villa Jardín contained a variety of local associations for most of its history. Whilst the majority of these were primarily concerned with the area's physical infrastructure, this study is more directly concerned with organisations that promote the economic well-being of residents, especially elderly ones. These are examined in detail later in the chapter.

Villa Azul: the setting

Villa Azul straddles the municipalities of Avellaneda and Quilmes, approximately 30 kilometres from the Federal Capital. This distance is partly compensated by it's location alongside the principal road and main railway line into the city from the south east (see Map 4.3). One side of the *villa* is flanked by an area of pleasant middle-class housing, one by factories and the remaining two by major roads. Just across the *Acceso Sudeste* motorway lies a larger shanty town, Villa Itatí.[8]

Villa Azul had a very different appearance from the other two neighbourhoods studied. There was less evidence of socio-economic variety

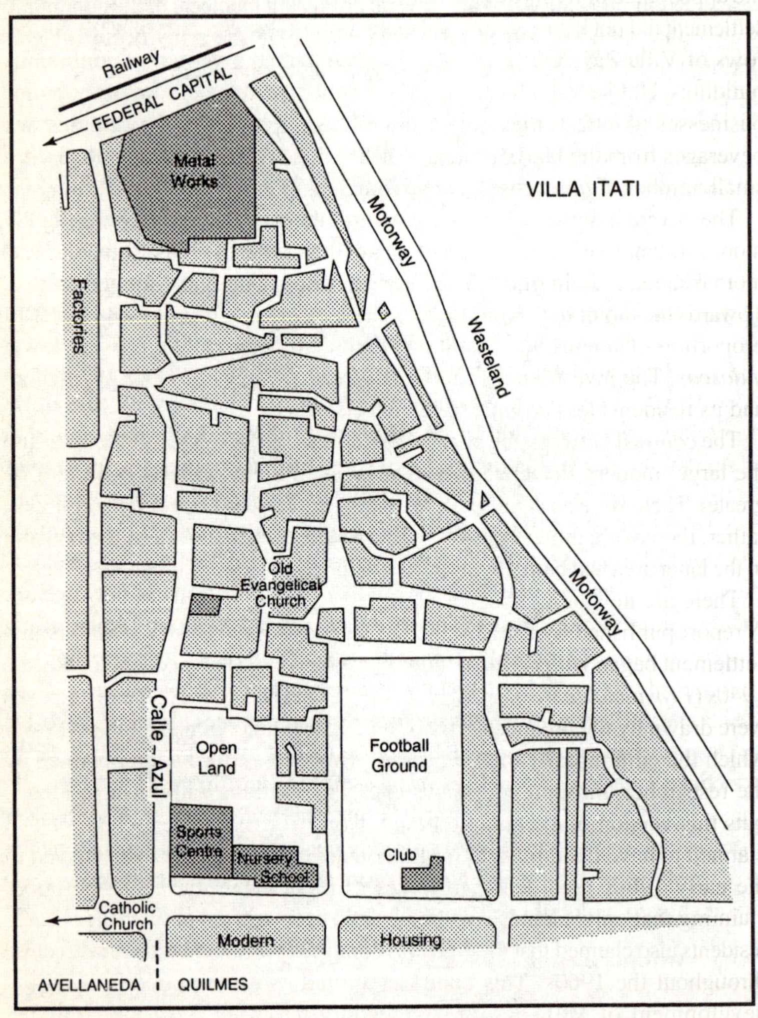

Map 4.3 Villa Azul

than in Villa Jardín: virtually all its housing consisted of small brick or wood structures with corrugated iron roofs. In some cases the walls were also of corrugated iron or odd pieces of waste material. None of the roads were surfaced and the open sewers were often blocked, causing flooding. A small proportion of homes still lacked running water and there were frequent interruptions in the electricity supply. There was more open space and greenery than in *villas* closer to the Capital, which gave the neighbourhood the appearance of a run-down village, rather than an urban slum. Whilst the settlement did not have an obvious centre, it was more compact than the narrow rows of Villa Zavaleta (see below) and contained a variety of community buildings. Unlike Villa Jardín, it did not contain a range of formal shops and businesses. Along Calle Azul a few residents sold fruit, vegetables and beverages from the land in front of their homes. In other parts of the *villa* a small number of *quioscos* could be found.

There were indications that some parts of the neighbourhood were slightly more affluent than others. Housing on the Avellaneda side of the *villa* was more frequently built of brick and the passageways were better maintained. Towards the motorway, which was flanked by a steep embankment, a greater proportion of homes were built of wood and metal and there were fewer *quioscos*. The investigator found this section of the *villa* more threatening and its residents less co-operative than elsewhere.

The contrast between the alleys and tumble-down housing of the *villa* and the large, modern detached homes of neighbouring districts could not be greater. There were no signs of social mixing between the two neighbourhoods; rather, there were indications of mutual distrust. Virtually all of the housing in the latter area had barred windows behind which guard-dogs could be heard.

There are no studies specifically referring to Villa Azul's early history. A report published by the Province of Buenos Aires in 1985 mentions that settlement began with illegal occupations of privately owned land in the late 1940s (*Provincia de Buenos Aires*, 1985). The report states that early arrivals were drawn by the prospect of employment in a neighbouring factory, from which the *villa* initially took its name.[9] However, information obtained by the researcher, through interviews and conversations with local residents, puts this version of events into doubt. None of the 55 elderly interviewed claimed to have lived in Azul for more than 35 years. Those who arrived in the early 1960s regarded themselves as pioneers in the neighbourhood, claiming that only a handful of homes had been erected at that stage. Early residents also claimed that the *villa* was completely without basic infrastructure throughout the 1960s. This contrasts abruptly with the rapid growth and development of Villa Jardín, suggesting that Villa Azul was founded somewhat later and that its early expansion was somehow restricted. One resident mentioned that during the 1960s most of the Quilmes side of the *villa* had been taken up by a large pit and motorway construction works. Following the 1960s the *villa* began to experience steady growth, initially occupying land alongside Calle Azul. According to one resident, the settlement was only a quarter of its present size in 1973. With the completion of the motorway, adjacent land became available and the *villa* began to spread south into Quilmes. At the same time, the land was bought from its private owners by the Ministry of Transport. This was followed by an acceleration in growth until all the available land was occupied in the mid-1980s. The gradual expansion towards the *Acceso Sudeste* may have led to a greater concentration of older residents and more established community associations on the Avellaneda side of the *villa*.

Thus, Villa Azul was a much less mature neighbourhood than Villa Jardín, a fact reflected in the origins of its early settlers, the majority of whom came from poor northern provinces and, subsequently, neighbouring countries, particularly Paraguay. Unlike Villa Jardín there was no indication that European immigrants played any part in its early history.

As in the other *villas* studied, the neighbourhood experienced a rapid turnover of population. One early arrival claimed that during the 1960s and early 1970s the bulk of its residents were able to buy plots of land elsewhere and move out. She added that this had become much rarer in recent years due to sharp increases in land values. This suggests that, as with Villa Jardín, population ageing was more due to reduced opportunities for escape than to the time which had elapsed since the foundation of the settlement. It is possible that a decline in fertility also contributed to the ageing of Villa Azul. A census carried out in 1990 found that the average number of children born to women aged between 15 and 49 was almost identical to national rates.[10] Whilst historical data do not exist for the *villa*, there is a strong likelihood that the level of fertility in 1990 reflected a sharp fall since its foundation in the 1960s.

Roughly one quarter of Villa Azul lay within Avellaneda municipality, with the rest in Quilmes. This makes it impossible to extract information from the INDEC analysis of the 1980 national census. Likewise, the 1981 survey of *villas* conducted by the Province of Buenos Aires is of little use since it only refers to those within a single municipality. Consequently, none of the *villas* it covered correspond with Azul.[11] Nevertheless, it is possible to obtain some information from other studies specifically relating to Villa Azul. These include a preliminary survey conducted in 1985 by the provincial government (*Provincia de Buenos Aires*, 1985) and a 1990 report published by the United Nations Children's Fund (UNICEF) (López, 1992). Also, the local *Sociedad de Fomento* has conducted various surveys of the *villa's* residents, although these do not include data for the section which lies inside Avellaneda.

The government and UNICEF reports give various estimates for the total population (Table 4.6). According to residents, the *villa* did not experience a period of rapid growth between 1981 and 1985, nor did its population noticeably drop between 1985 and 1987. Consequently, the first two figures can be discounted.[12] The final two figures appear to be more reliable since they correspond with each other and with the general opinion that the *villa*'s population had been stable in the past decade.

Table 4.6: Population estimates for Villa Azul

Year	Estimate	Source
1981	1 039	Province of Buenos Aires
1985	4 800	*Programa Nacional de Alimentación*
1985	3 174	Province of Buenos Aires
1990	3 446	UNICEF

Sources: *Provincia de Buenos Aires*, 1981, 1985; López, 1992:12.

Table 4.7: Age and sex structure of Villa Azul, 1990

Age	Men	%	Women	%	Total	%
Below 60	1 539	96.6	1 436	96.2	3 002	96.4
60–64	22	1.4	21	1.4	43	1.4
65–69	10	0.6	14	0.9	24	0.8
70–74	12	0.8	11	0.7	23	0.7
75+	9	0.6	12	0.8	21	0.7
Total 60+	53	3.4	58	3.8	111	3.6
Total	1 592	100.0	1 521	100.0	3 113*	100.0

*This figure does not include 333 residents, for whom no information was obtained.
Source: López, 1992:14.

The UNICEF survey provides a full breakdown of the age and sex of Villa Azul's occupants (Table 4.7), finding that 68 (2.2 per cent) were aged 65 or more in 1990. This compares with 53 (1.7 per cent) found within the same age category in the 1985 survey, indicating that the *villa* had experienced a slight rise in the proportion of elderly residents in recent years.[13] Nevertheless, the proportion of elderly was still much lower than in either Villa Jardín or Villa Zavaleta. The low proportion of elderly in the *villa* may have increased their marginal status by limiting their opportunities to organise and the interest taken by outside actors in their condition.

The 1985 survey contains various indicators of levels of hardship in Villa Azul. For example, it shows that 62 per cent of houses were built precariously and 42 per cent vulnerable to flooding. These both correspond with basic needs criteria used by INDEC in its 1984 report. The survey finds that 63 per cent of the economically active population were labourers, domestic servants or odd-jobbers and that 24 per cent of families declared a total income below the minimum monthly wage. The high level of informality partly reflected reduced opportunities for employment in neighbouring factories following the closure of a large sheet metal plant in the late 1970s. The 1990 UNICEF survey shows that problems of employment and income generation remained serious. For example, it observed that 5 per cent of under-14-year-olds were in full-time employment, usually assisting in litter scavenging trips.

A certain amount of information relating specifically to the welfare of the elderly can be gleaned from the UNICEF report. First, it can be seen that rates of economic activity among the elderly in the *villa* were substantially higher than for Argentina as a whole (Table 4.8). Unfortunately, no indications about the types of activity engaged in are provided. It is likely high rates of elderly activity reflect a scarcity of income opportunities rather than privileged access to continued formal sector employment.

Table 4.8: Rates of economic activity in Villa Azul and Argentina as a whole, 1990 (%)

	Argentina	Villa Azul
Total population	35.10	41.50
Aged 60–64	27.55	62.80
Aged 65+	7.20	17.70

Sources: López, 1992:19; Table 3.17.

From information provided in the survey, it is possible to calculate the proportion of elderly men and women who were defined as household heads. This is a subjective judgement and is usually left to the household in question. Although it carries no hard and fast connotations, the label does give a general impression of the role and prestige enjoyed by elderly individuals in their families. Table 4.9 shows that 90.9 per cent of elderly men aged between 60 and 64 were household heads, as were more than half those aged 65 or over. This indicates that males retained a position of importance in households, regardless of age. For elderly women, rates of headship were significantly lower. Nevertheless, they were far in excess of those found for women aged between 20 and 59 years old, which averaged 16.3 per cent. This most probably reflects the greater probability of widowhood for women aged over 60. These issues are returned to in Chapter 5, which analyses the results of a separate questionnaire survey.

Table 4.9: Proportion of elderly men and women in Villa Azul defined as household heads (%)

	Men	Women
Aged 60–64	90.9	47.6
Aged 65+	61.3	32.4

Source: López, 1992:41.

Grassroots organisations in Villa Azul

During the 1960s, with the exception of a football club, there were few attempts at forming local associations in Villa Azul, nor did interviewees have any recollection of grassroots party political activity. Nevertheless, in 1969 a small group of residents formed a *Junta Vecinal*, which achieved some success in improving the local water supply and passageway surfaces. The *Junta* continued to make improvements to the *villa* until the mid-1970s and received a donation of more water pipes from the newly installed Peronist provincial government. However, these successes came to an abrupt halt in 1974, when:

> a group of bad people took it [the *Junta*] over and everything came to an end. They took everything that was there – silly little things...wooden benches...the cooker...They were from the *villa* but had arrived from outside..a family formed by four or five couples. Just one family...And afterwards they just didn't want to know and there were lots of problems.
> (Sra MP, Villa Azul, May 1993)

The arrival of new waves of migrants had led to a profound change in the internal organisations of the *villa*, as the fledgling *Junta Vecinal* gave way to a new structure of local authority based around the personal followings of a number of 'strong men' (*caciques*)[14] and the rivalry of large extended families. As various *caciques* sought to establish themselves and the political situation in the country as a whole became more chaotic, the *villa* suffered increasing violence and internal strife. This culminated with the murder and 'disappearances' of several important community figures.

Had the state authorities so desired they could have intervened to prevent the emergence of *caciquismo* in Villa Azul. They were, however, reluctant to do so. There are indications that members of the *Junta Vecinal* had been sympathetic to, if not directly involved in, left-wing Peronist factions, including the '*Montonero*' guerrillas.[15] The increasingly right-wing national government was prepared to turn a blind eye to *caciques*, some of whom, it was claimed, were nominally aligned to a rival, right-wing Peronist faction. According to one resident:

> Other people weren't in agreement with him [the president of the *Junta*] for political reasons...[he had] political links with the *Peronists*, a certain faction of *Peronists*...and had problems with this other group who were also *Peronists*..but the conservative, right-wing faction of *Peronism.*
>
> (Sr JR, Villa Azul, June 1993)

This was a similar strategy to the encouragement of the *Junta Vecinal* at the expense of the *Sociedad de Fomento* in Villa Jardín in the mid-1950s.

The bitter experience of the *Proceso* period was frequently referred to by present-day residents and community leaders, suggesting that it had an important effect on subsequent attitudes towards local activity. Unlike Villa Jardín, there is no indication that churches took on a more important role in Villa Azul during the period of military rule, nor were they exempt from the general repression. Indeed, a radical Catholic priest was kidnapped and killed in neighbouring Villa Itatí.

Redemocratisation led to a slow re-emergence of local activities, especially local Peronist and communist groups, who had an office in the *villa*. These facilitated the upgrading of basic infrastructure, such as the electricity supply. However, initiatives did not go beyond local party offices and, to a very limited extent, social assistance from a nearby evangelical church. The distribution of food parcels under the *Programa de Alimentación Nacional* from 1984 relied on trusted local individuals rather than local organisations. The *villa* remained in the grip of its traditional families and *caciques*, who learned to broker with outside actors, particularly the provincial and municipal governments.[16] Low levels of participation may also have reflected fears about the return to repressive policies. Although a 1985 government survey refers to the formation of a '*comisión vecinal*' (neighbourhood committee) the previous year, it goes on to identify:

> A continued lack of representation among the various organisations which operate in the community, displayed in the general ignorance of the activities which they pursue... (*Provincia de Buenos Aires*, 1985)

In 1987 local initiatives in Villa Azul entered a new phase of evolution, with the creation of a *Sociedad de Fomento* (the *Sociedad*) along with the receipt of a large grant from the Province of Buenos Aires and UNICEF for the construction of a nursery school and health clinic and the improvement of the sewerage system. At the same time the *Grupo de la Tercera Edad* (Group for the Elderly) was established (examined in detail below). This marked a broadening in local concerns away from simply upgrading the physical infrastructure to the social problems of vulnerable groups such as young children and the elderly. The nursery school building became an important community centre and was used by the *Grupo* for its weekly meetings. Despite these changes, local *caciques* were able to maintain their positions of control by obtaining posts on the committee of the *Sociedad* and preserving links with the outside authorities, including the police and municipalities. This may have been largely achieved by intimidation: gunfights between rival groups were not an infrequent occurrence during this period.[17]

1989 proved to be another important watershed for local activities in Villa Azul. This reflected a combination of circumstances, including economic crisis, the change of national and provincial government, the death of the most influential *cacique* and the imprisonment of several others. The economic hardship resulting from hyperinflation prompted residents and Quilmes municipality to organise a soup kitchen, which provided daily meals for over 300 children and around 10 elderly people. The *Peronist* victories saw new policies and encouraged greater local participation among its followers. These political discontinuities also reduced the external influence held by the *caciques*, whose status in the eyes of the authorities moved from power brokers to opponents and criminals. Recognising the change in circumstances a number of the most powerful *caciques* chose to leave the *villa*. By the 1990s a new group of local activists, many of them linked to left-wing Peronism had been able to challenge the position of traditional leaders. Following allegations of corruption, two *caciques* were excluded from the *Sociedad*. This new group also dominated the two housing co-operatives which had been established in each municipality, as part of a national plan to sell off land to the *villeros*.[18] Despite its purported commitment to open, democratic, non-partisan participation, the new movement revolved around a handful of key figures.[19]

Although Villa Azul had had a shorter and less rich history of local organisation than Villa Jardín, there were number of similarities between their experiences. Both had suffered internal conflicts between traditional Peronist and less politically modern factions. Government agencies had at times sought to encourage these rivalries and, during the *Proceso*, to clamp down on local organisations in general. Democratisation and the worsening poverty of the 1980s had seen a shift towards less fractious and more welfare-oriented modes of organisation, including the first instances of initiatives specifically concerned with elderly residents. Villa Azul's experiences illustrate the close relationship between internal organisation and supralocal political change. This was apparent in general developments, such as the struggles between Peronist factions, the emergence of the *caciques* and, from 1989, the re-establishment of traditional Peronists. Whilst most residents welcomed the disappearance of the *caciques*, there were signs that this had led to a weakening of structures of local authority, as gunfights were replaced by drug abuse and delinquency:

> What's terrible now are those yobs who're all on amphetamines...This didn't used to happen...it's just been the past year, never before.
>
> (Sra MP, Villa Azul, May 1993)

Other elderly residents complained of a sudden increase in muggings and burglaries. These developments were of particular concern to vulnerable groups such as the elderly and, if they were to escalate, would have a serious effect on their economic and general welfare. They showed that the *villa* was at a critical juncture as new organisations sought to obtain through welfare the level of legitimacy the *caciques* had won through intimidation.

Villa Zavaleta: the setting

Villa Zavaleta is located just inside the Federal Capital, five kilometres down the Riachuelo River from Villa Jardín. It is an ugly place, wedged between two dual carriageways, a large waste collection plant and an area of warehouses and workshops (see Map 4.4). Zavaleta was founded in 1969 as one of three temporary camps (*núcleos de habitación transitorio* or NHTs), for people displaced from *villas* eradicated elsewhere in the Federal Capital. The *Comisión Municipal de la Vivienda* (CMV) was charged with the general administration of the camp. As such, Villa Zavaleta was the direct outcome of a government initiative, rather than the result of ad hoc, illegal land occupations. As will be seen, this distinction had an important effect on the subsequent development of the *villa*.

The outline proposals of the NHT programme stressed the temporary, spartan nature of the new settlements:

> The project has attempted to take every consideration into account, including a minimum level of comfort, the camps' transitional and

> precarious nature and the use of materials which may be of most value when the homes are taken down again.
>
> (Argentine Republic, *Ministerio de Bienestar Social*, 1968:11)

And:

> It is hoped that the strict regime and hard conditions will stimulate and sharpen the desire for something better.
>
> (Argentine Republic, *Ministerio de Bienestar Social*, 1968:24)

The original camp consisted of 30 rows (known as *tiras*) containing a total of 560 identical back-to-back units. These were built of brick, with corrugated iron roofs and consisted of three small rooms with an inside bathroom. Some basic services, such as running water and electricity, were provided,

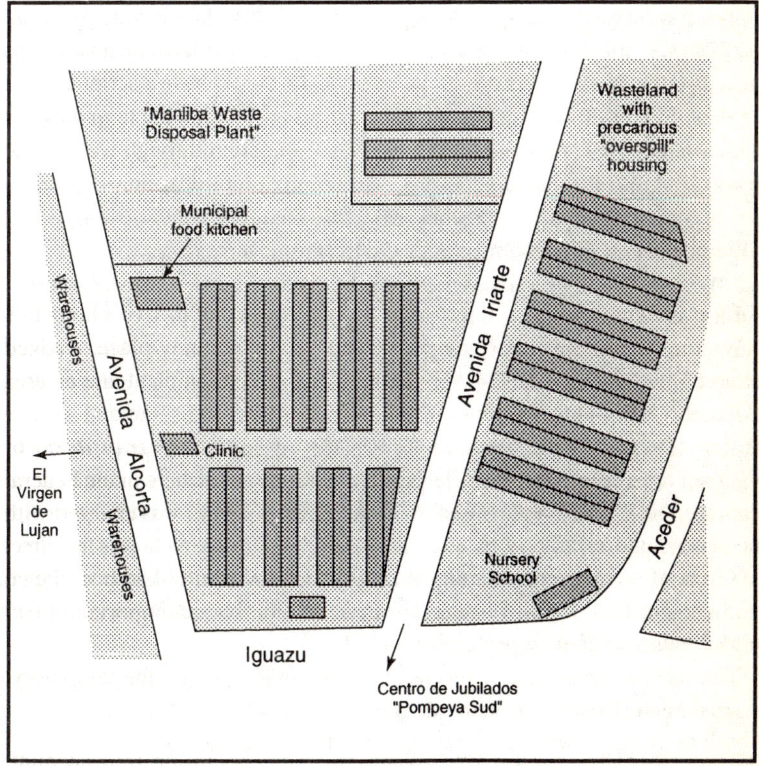

Map 4.4 Villa Zavaleta

but the camp lacked an effective sewerage system and surfaced roads. Reflecting its supposedly transitional nature, no provision was made for shops or communal buildings.[20] Thus, on balance, it is hard to say whether the camp's general facilities represented an improvement on the conditions in the *villas* which had been eradicated.

The construction of NHTs in the late 1960s and early 1970s coincided with a programme to provide low-interest loans for cheap accommodation.[21] This may partly explain why, at least during its early years, the majority of Villa Zavaleta's inhabitants only remained for short periods before moving to improved accommodation. These were replaced by subsequent waves of displaced *villeros*. Housing loans were only to be made available to people included in social insurance programmes, which may have caused the gradual accumulation of unprotected groups in the *villa*. The rapid turnover of population probably reduced residents' incentives to maintain its facilities, causing the physical infrastructure of the camp to decay: electric meters were replaced by illegal connections and some units no longer received running water. Gradually, Villa Zavaleta began to take on the appearance of any other *villa miseria*.

By early 1993, the camp still had the appearance of a temporary settlement, despite being over 20 years old. The passageways between the *tiras* remained unsurfaced and the surrounding wasteland had not been developed. There was less street life than in the other two *villas*. Gangs of youths, some openly taking drugs or inhaling solvents, would intimidate passers-by. The only commonplace sign of improvements to the original houses was the addition of reinforced doors and window bars.

Interviews with residents suggest that the turnover of population in the camp began to slow during the 1980s, as opportunities for escape were reduced.[22] This led to a problem of overcrowding and from 1990 small clusters of makeshift accommodation began to spring up in areas of surrounding wasteland (see Map 4.4). These largely consisted of overspill population from the camp and contained very few elderly. Consequently, they were not included in the survey.

The original plans for the camp made strict provisions for the maintenance of law and order. Indeed, the tenancy contracts which residents were obliged to sign went as far as to prohibit:

> noisy disturbance of any kind, especially in the hours of sleeping, which will be fixed according to the judgement of the Director.
>
> (Argentine Republic, *Ministerio de Bienestar Social,* 1968:78)

This reflected the broader authoritarian tendencies of the military government of that time. The outline proposals also stressed the need to:

> Instil security and confidence in oneself, motivate and direct the energy which every citizen should apply in obtaining a better level of living for those who aspire to improve themselves.
>
> (Argentine Republic, *Ministerio de Bienestar Social,* 1968:28)

These utopian ideals could not provide a sharper contrast with the grim realities of life in the camp. One local resident described her horror upon arrival to find the *villa* in the grip of violence and crime. She mentioned her attempts to obtain a night watchman from the CMV and added:

> Villa Zavaleta was appalling. There were so many bad people who were always robbing and assaulting everyone else. It was a very ugly situation...I had the luck [ironically] to be placed alongside some particularly unpleasant people who nobody could get rid of...They terrorised us.
>
> (Sra MB, Villa Zavaleta, June 1993)

Over the years, these problems of crime and delinquency became considerably worse. Commonplace illegal activities included the supply and use of various drugs, looting warehouses in the adjacent neighbourhood and holding up cars which passed along the two main avenues.

Unlike Villa Azul, the camp had no structure of local authority and few norms or values which residents could abide by. This made the guarantee of 'safe passage' to an outsider virtually impossible, whatever their role or status may be, and partly accounted for a number of other features. First, as will be seen, there was a low level of local organisation in Villa Zavaleta. Secondly, there was a complete absence of state involvement in the camp. Interviewees maintained that the CMV had had few dealings with the *villa* in recent years and that visits made by a social assistant had been discontinued two years previously. Third, the risks inherent in working in the neighbourhood had discouraged academic study. The researcher was unable to find any research specifically relating to the *villa.* This element of danger partly restricted the scope of the investigation. The researcher was only able to enter the camp when accompanied by the local Catholic priest, reducing the number of individual interviews which it was possible to conduct.

The daily lives of the elderly in Villa Zavaleta were greatly affected by these problems of security, with many afraid to leave their homes and interviewees generally put the fear of robbery and violence before economic and housing problems. According to one elderly woman:

> They [the elderly] are terrified because they think something will happen to them, people without any defence, like has happened before...There's a couple who've been broken into three times and had everything inside taken. They're two little old people who just can't defend themselves...and when the lady is left on her own in the house and they see she's there alone they [local youths] take advantage, they're so brazen. This a very serious problem for the elderly here.
>
> (Sra MB, Villa Zavaleta, June 1993)

By further reducing the mobility of elderly people, this fear served as an additional obstacle to completing the paperwork for social security benefits.

The reasons why Villa Zavaleta experienced such a social breakdown, whilst the other *villas* studied remained relatively safe and law-abiding are not entirely clear. From the outset, the neighbourhood contained a concentration of 'bad types' many of whom, it was claimed, came from the eradication of the notorious slum of Bajo Flores:

> Lots of bad people were brought here or came from other places to live here. It was really very bad, very bad...Here there are more bad types [than other *villas*]...because they came from so many places, like when those people were thrown out of Flores *villa*, Bajo Flores, and they all came here...that *villa* was – how should I put it? That *villa* was real badlife...The CMV had chosen the people, done a census and seen what they were like, so they shouldn't have let them come here.
>
> (Sra MB, Villa Zavaleta, June 1993)

A number of studies observe that government agencies applied some form of negative discrimination when selecting families for the NHTs:

> The relocations took no account of preserving existing communities: rather they sought to break groups up, particularly local leaders. And those placed in the NHTs were people considered to be inferior: single mothers, alcoholics, the most socially marginalised.
>
> (Davalos et al, 1987:23–4)

It has also been claimed that a process of selection for those to be given more permanent accommodation existed, and that this took into account the payment of rent and other factors. If this were the case, it could have bequeathed a residual population of 'social undesirables'.

The reduced level of state involvement in Villa Zavaleta may have been both a cause and an outcome of the rise in delinquency there. One resident argued that the *villa* was better-run during military governments when the authorities made more of an effort to maintain basic facilities and clamp down on crime. During the 1980s, government involvement in the neighbourhood became virtually non-existent. According to one community leader:

> The CMV has had five projects to begin reconstructing the *villa*. These include a [community] centre. On their plan there's a free space where they could build a community centre. But there isn't the political will to do anything other than talk about it. The plans can say what they want but...I suppose the [CMV] assistants will end up retiring without anything being built. (Sra CB, Villa Zavaleta, May 1993).

This both impeded the development of local initiatives and heightened the sense of exclusion and anomie felt by residents, including the elderly.

Table 4.10: INDEC data for Villa Zavaleta's census district, 1980

	Lacking basic needs
Total households	686
% of total households in district	18.5
Total population	2 903
Total over 64 years	362

Source: INDEC, 1984:46, 54 (district V.1).

Since it was located in the Federal Capital, not the Province of Buenos Aires, the camp was not included in the 1980 survey of *villas miserias*. INDEC data from the 1980 national census are available, but provide a less direct picture of conditions in the camp than they do for Villa Jardín. The census district which is used includes various other wealthier neighbourhoods. Thus, the overall figure of 18.5 per cent of households lacking in basic needs (see Table 4.10), is not representative of conditions in the camp alone. It is also feasible that the accuracy of the census data may have been affected by the reluctance of officials to run the risk of entering the *villa*. However, it is interesting that the total number of households with unsatisfied basic needs was 685, since this almost perfectly matches the number of housing units originally in the camp. This suggests both that Villa Zavaleta accounts for the vast majority of population lacking basic needs and that the total population of the camp consists of families living in sub-standard housing.

If these assumptions are valid, several more specific conclusions about the camp can be drawn. It can be concluded that in 1980 the *villa* had a total population of 2903 (the total number with unsatisfied basic needs). Of these 364, or 12.5 per cent, were aged over 64 (Table 4.10). This is a slightly lower proportion than that for the district as a whole, but far higher than in the other *villas* studied. This reflects the greater concentration of elderly in the Federal Capital than in the Province of Buenos Aires.

There are no surveys specifically relating to Villa Zavaleta or its elderly population. On one hand, they possessed more opportunities to reduce their marginal status: they formed a relatively high proportion of the total population and were located within the Federal Capital, whose insurance coverage and assistance expenditure were far higher than in the Province of Buenos Aires. On the other hand, the high levels of disorder and delinquency may have left many elderly as virtual prisoners in their own homes. One social worker estimated that, in 1992, at least 15 per cent of over 60 year-olds in the neighbourhood lacked any kind of benefit and that a significant proportion of these were seriously disabled.

Grassroots organisations in Villa Zavaleta

The original NHT proposals made much reference to the importance of local organisations. These were to include: 'literacy classes, medical check-ups, groups in each *tira*, *sociedades de fomento* and recreation for the elderly' (Argentine Republic, *Ministerio de Bienestar Social*, 1968:64–8). Yet, despite its early foundation and location within the Federal Capital, by 1993 Villa Zavaleta had a lower degree of local organisation than any of the other neighbourhoods studied.

Clearly, conditions in the *villa* were hardly propitious for local associations. As a government-run camp, initiative was stifled in the early years. One study of NHTs describes the relation between the authorities and residents as top-down 'imposition-control' (Yujnovsky, 1984:165–6). The rapid population turnover in the early years may also have discouraged local initiatives, although this had not been the case in the other two *villas* surveyed.[23] However, the greatest barrier to progressive organisation was without doubt the high level of crime and violence in Villa Zavaleta.[24]

The first known case of local organisation in Villa Zavaleta was the *Consejo Deliberante* set up in 1976. The *Consejo* provided a limited range of services for the *villa*'s needy (including some elderly residents), such as the distribution of free medicines. Sadly the *Consejo* ceased to function after just a few months. The reasons for this are not clear. It is claimed that, whilst it received no support from state organs, at least the *Consejo* did not suffer repression during the *Proceso*. Most probably, the *Consejo* fell victim to the generally unfavourable conditions for organisation within the *villa*.

Reference is made to other attempts at local initiatives, but these proved to be equally short-lived. The *villa* received some aid from the PAN programme, but this was said to have been handled corruptly. In 1989 a small number of local residents set up a new *Comisión Vecinal* (NCV) which survived, at least in name, until the time of this investigation. The NCV obtained funds from the local council[25] for a feeding centre (which a small number of elderly regularly attended) and a health clinic. It also distributed monthly parcels as part of a municipal food aid programme.[26] Of the 100 or so beneficiaries of this programme in Villa Zavaleta, it was claimed that the majority were elderly *villeros*. In addition, the NCV president helped local residents, including several elderly, obtain identity papers as a first step to gaining a range of contributory and non-contributory benefits.[27] Indeed, the president would appear to have been the key figure within the organisation and was credited with most of its successes. With his illness and death, the NCV's committee split, with some members remaining in control of the feeding centre and others running the health clinic. By 1993 considerable animosity existed between the two sides, with claims that the feeding centre refused to cater for some sections of the *villa*. Most of the NCV's activities had been discontinued by this time, although plans were being aired to hold fresh elections.

Grassroots political organisations were never able to establish a permanent presence in Villa Zavaleta. It was generally claimed that these organisations failed to carry out their promises and were, more often than not, managed corruptly. In 1992 an attempt to set up a *unidad básica* (Peronist office) in the *villa* was abandoned when its premises were burnt down by local vandals. Likewise, Church organisations never played a large role in the *villa*. As in Villa Azul, this was largely because no churches were located within the settlement. The NCV never established contacts with Caritas nor other religious bodies in the surrounding neighbourhoods. In the early 1990s, the arrival of a new priest prompted one local Catholic church to begin to take a greater interest in the *villa*, leading to the formation of several new local initiatives. These are examined below.

The past failings of local initiatives served to further reduce residents' willingness to participate in new ventures. According to one community leader:

> The elderly don't participate very much...I used to see them with their arms folded. They don't have much hope...They don't get involved. They lack the confidence to. (Sra CB, Villa Zavaleta, May 1993)

This contrasted with the active, participative attitude apparent in at least a proportion of elderly in Villa Azul and Villa Jardín and with the political mobilisation of *jubilados* elsewhere in the Capital. Local residents also differed from those of the other two *villas* studied in that they did not distinguish between credible and non-credible initiatives. The failure of all earlier attempts to organise encouraged residents to view subsequent initiatives with suspicion and scepticism. This posed another serious obstacle for progressive organisation in the *villa*.

The history of organisation in Villa Zavaleta was also characterised by the inability of residents to work together against common problems. Active members of the community often preferred to work individually than in concert, indicating the general lack of solidarity and trust in the *villa*. Conflicts within and between organisations only served to worsen the 'social chaos' of Villa Zavaleta.[28]

GRASSROOTS ORGANISATIONS CONCERNED WITH ELDERLY WELFARE

A number of general observations can be made about the organisation of elderly residents in the three *villas* studied. Most importantly, in no case had an attempt been made to establish a formal pensioners' day centre or *Centro de Jubilados*, along the lines advocated by PAMI. As discussed in Chapter 3, several hundred of these centres had been set up in Greater Buenos Aires by the early 1990s. There are a number of possible explanations for why these never took root in the *villas*. First, this may have been because there were too few aged in each neighbourhood to justify such an initiative. As has been seen, the proportion of elderly residents in the *villas* was markedly less than in the city as a whole. Alternatively, it is possible that the *villeros* displayed less capacity to organise themselves than did residents of other neighbourhoods. However, whilst this may have been the case in Villa Zavaleta, the large number of grassroots organisations in the other *villas* would seem to suggest otherwise. Other explanations are more closely related to the nature of PAMI itself. To begin with, it should be remembered that PAMI was almost exclusively concerned with the welfare of pensioners or *jubilados*. If large numbers of elderly *villeros* were without retirement benefits, they were automatically excluded from the bulk of activities organised by the *Centros de Jubilados*, thus reducing their operational feasibility. Another possibility is that PAMI was primarily concerned with middle-class elderly and therefore discouraged, or at least made no special efforts to foster, the involvement of *villeros* in its programmes. This would appear to have been discounted by the involvement of current and former PAMI officials in the formation of NGOs such as CEPEV. Nevertheless, it also begs the question why similar programmes could not have been developed through PAMI itself. Moreover, there were clear signs that, at the local level, existing *Centros de Jubilados* did not wish to include local *villas* in their remits. This point was made especially forcefully by the two centres located on the fringes of Villa Zavaleta.

Despite the absence of PAMI, the *villas* studied contained a variety of grassroots organisations which displayed some degree of interest in elderly welfare. These ranged from organisations catering exclusively for the elderly to those addressing much more general concerns. They included initiatives developed through the Catholic Church, other religious orders, political clubs and community development groups. Despite the differences between the neighbourhoods studied, it was possible to find examples of each type of initiative in each site. As such, it would seem that the absence of *Centros de Jubilados* did not reflect the small numbers of elderly *villeros* nor their inability to organise.

These grassroots organisations are now examined in the light of the general conditions in each *villa*. Rather than look at each location in turn, this section establishes a typology of organisations, beginning with those primarily concerned with the elderly and moving on to those with only minor interests. The analysis is based on general (sometimes participant) observations, as well as interviews both with individuals who were active in the organisations and with other elderly residents. Where possible, use was also made of documentary evidence, such as minutes books and NGO reports.

Organisations primarily concerned with elderly welfare

El Centro 'Los Jóvenes del Noventa'[29] *(the Centro), Villa Jardín*

The *Centro* had been operating in Villa Jardín for three years, providing legal advice, serving as a pressure group and also a social forum for all elderly, whether *jubilados* or not. In this respect, it differed from the model for *Centros de Jubilados* developed by PAMI and reflected the *Centro*'s philosophy of promoting solidarity among the elderly, whatever their economic circumstances. Indeed, since it lacked the requisite number of *jubilados* among its membership (a minimum of 100), it was ineligible for most of the assistance automatically granted to conventional *Centros de Jubilados.*

Whilst it was entirely independent of any other organisation, the *Centro* owed its creation to initiatives taken by a Buenos Aires-based NGO: *El Centro de Promoción y Estudios de la Vejez* (CEPEV). As explained in Chapter 3, CEPEV sought to extend its successful experiences in the slum district of

La Boca to another poor urban neighbourhood outside the Federal Capital. It conducted pilot studies in Villa Jardín, developed contacts among elderly residents and arranged a number of social events and group discussions. As a result of these initiatives, the *Centro* was founded. Although it still maintained very close links with CEPEV and often received technical assistance, decisions were made and activities executed by the *Centro*'s membership. It had a democratically elected president and steering committee, which comprised both elderly with pensions and those without. By the end of 1992 the *Centro* had 265 members, the great majority of whom (187) were women.

The *Centro* held two meetings a week: one for all members and one for its steering committee. These combined social activities with the provision of advice about how to obtain contributory and non-contributory benefits. Largely because of the personal contacts of some CEPEV workers with government organisations, the *Centro* was immediately successful in obtaining the assistance pension offered by the *Dirección Nacional de la Ancianidad* (DNA). Whilst not all applications were successful, by November 1991 it had secured DNA benefits for 84 members; out of a total of roughly 5000 granted in Argentina as a whole. Indeed, CEPEV became concerned that the *Centro* might just be seen as a means of obtaining these benefits. In December 1992 the DNA ceased to pay assistance pensions and there were no indications that these would be resumed.

The cessation of the DNA benefits caused a degree of disillusionment among members and might have threatened the continued success of the *Centro*, had it not been able to diversify its activities. According to one elderly man:

> The only real thing we got out of the *Centro* was that monthly benefit...But now they've even cut that, so there's nothing left at all...It's a nice enough place. You can go there to have a bit of fun, have a chat and things like that, but in financial terms, to tell you the truth, there's nothing going on at all and nothing is going to happen in the future.
>
> (Sra JM, Villa Jardín, February 1993)

The *Centro* had a small pool of funds, which came from a number of sources, including membership dues (one peso a month), raffles, jumble sales and dances. Rather than provide direct economic assistance, these funds were used to pay for social activities, including barbecues, monthly dances and theatrical productions staged for local schools. It also ran daily classes in the Catholic church. The weekly general meetings were treated both as a source of information and as a social occasion. In addition, the *Centro* organised tours and day trips, offered to members at greatly reduced prices thanks to subsidies from PAMI and the municipality.

The *Pro-Bienestar* programme, administered by PAMI and initiated in late 1992, provided a new source of finance for the *Centro*. This initiative aimed to set up feeding centres for those elderly on the minimum pension. The *Centro* objected to establishing such a centre in Villa Jardín, arguing that it would be both inefficient and degrading to pensioners and that it would exclude poor elderly without *jubilaciones*. It succeeded in replacing this proposal with food parcels to the value of 60 pesos a month. It also agreed with PAMI to put forward a joint proposal to the local council to fund the provision of identical food parcels to non-*jubilados*. By July 1993, the *Centro* had obtained 35 food parcels from PAMI but had not yet had any success with its approach to the local council.

By early 1993 the *Centro* was also pursuing claims for assistance pensions with the municipal office of the *Administración Nacional de Seguridad Social* (ANSES). Eligibility criteria for these benefits were more complex and the *Centro* organised visits by representatives of ANSES to claimants' homes. Members of the *Centro* pursuing ANSES benefits claims found the process far from easy. One elderly woman complained that:

> It's a very arduous job. To get hold of their attention is, in the first place, an exceptional achievement. It isn't something that I can rely on automatically on other occasions...Our experience with local council social assistance is really bad...People [in Villa Jardín] point out that those responsible for social services in the council have a very unpleasant manner...If you do manage to get an interview with a social assistant it's so complicated – all the paperwork you have to get because you have to prove what the exact situation of the whole family is. The family are obliged by the '*Ley Argentina*' to provide for the elderly. This [interpretation of the family] is very broad: not just the children, but siblings, older grandchildren and so on. (Silvia Simone, CEPEV, May 1993)

These bureaucratic obstacles were well illustrated in the case of one member, described as 'a blind lady, poor as a rat, abandoned in a little house' (Silvia Simone, CEPEV, May 1993), who had the misfortune to possess the singularly common name of María Martínez. This woman was obliged to make a legal declaration (by fingerprint since she was illiterate) that none of the several hundred other 'María Martínezes' listed in the provincial register of property owners were related to her. This delayed her claim by several months. Despite such problems, the *Centro* had secured ANSES pensions for three members by July 1993.

Through contacts with a national deputy, CEPEV had been promised a number of 'honorary' political pensions for members of the *Centro*. It was hoped that these would be granted at a rate of ten per month. If this were done, it would more than replace the role played by the DNA benefits when the *Centro* first began. CEPEV accepted that this arrangement was 'a political favour, which will be hard to repeat [elsewhere]...Even if the destination is justified, in its origin this is just as illegitimate as any other political favour' (Silvia Simone, CEPEV, May 1993), but felt that 'legitimate' channels provided no valid alternatives.

Despite these numerous successes, the *Centro* still did not have its own premises by 1993. Weekly meetings were held in the buildings of the local *Sociedad de Fomento* and parties were usually thrown at the Catholic church community centre, the '*Ateneo*' (see Map 4.2). This partly reflected the absence of unused spaces in Villa Jardín and very high land values due to its proximity to the Federal Capital. At the same time, sharing pointed to a degree of co-operation with other local groups and might in fact have been a more efficient use of the limited resources in the *villa*. Nevertheless, members stressed the importance of obtaining funds from PAMI or the local council for a building which would ensure their organisation's continued survival and to enable it to develop new services such as a health clinic, which were seen as:

> concrete elements, through which and around which people can construct some type of organisation which deals with other needs such as literacy, artistic expression or recreation...which are also very important.
>
> (Silvia Simone, CEPEV, May 1993)

The *Centro* had a considerable amount of contact with a wide range of outside actors; indeed, its main *raison d'être* was to channel the benefits and services offered by such actors, be they NGOs, PAMI, the DNA or the local council, to their members. At the same time the *Centro* was cautious about compromising its independence and apolitical status by ceding control to other organisations. It shunned contacts with some local associations which it regarded as controlled by political forces. It had some links with organisations linked to the Catholic and Protestant churches as well as the local *Sociedad de Fomento*, but these were more often the result of overlapping personnel than formal ties. Even the role of CEPEV was restricted to the provision of technical advice and this was gradually being reduced.

The *Centro* had achieved considerable success in the first three years of its existence, both in terms of improving the economic condition of local elderly and in reducing the social isolation often resulting from old age. The establishment of an organisation both *for* and *by* the elderly in Villa Jardín had no equivalent among younger generations living there. This may have partly reflected the greater necessity of co-operation during the early, difficult years of settlement which inculcated a strong sense of solidarity among the older generations. It may also have resulted from the greater amount of free time available to those elderly who were retired from the labourforce and free from commitments to other family members.

By developing new social programmes the *Centro* had been able to maintain the high level of interest generated by its early success with the DNA. In many respects, the *Centro* could be considered an ideal model for local initiatives by elderly *villeros*, against which others can be compared. Its success reflected a large number of factors, of which the most important were the progressive spirit of the *villeros* and the expertise and professional contacts of CEPEV. These factors are best demonstrated by comparing the experience of the *Centro* with elderly associations in other *villas*.

After three years of operation, the *Centro* appeared to have established itself as a permanent presence in Villa Jardín. Nevertheless, those involved felt that it was still too early to make this claim:

> All groups have their own life-cycles, don't they...I feel that, after two year's work, we [the *Centro*] are still at a stage of expansion, but I wouldn't like to say whether this will be permanent. I hope that the *Centro* is able to consolidate itself. (Silvia Simone, CEPEV, May 1993).

Until the *Centro* had secured its own premises and had proved itself to be independent of outside actors, CEPEV included, its long-term prospects would remain uncertain.

El Grupo de la Tercera Edad 'Unión y Esperanza'[30] *(the Grupo), Villa Azul*

This organisation was founded in Villa Azul in 1987, experienced a period of rapid growth and intense activity up to 1989 and then went into steep decline. After a two-year hiatus, some old committee members made efforts to renew the organisation, but met with little initial success. As such, the *Grupo* provides an interesting case-study of a local initiative for the elderly which fell apart and, possibly, of the nature of organisational lifecycles.

As with Villa Jardín's *Centro*, outside actors played an important role in the foundation of the *Grupo*. Three social workers from the provincial Ministry of Social Action, all of them women, began to advise elderly on hygiene and preventative healthcare. They organised informal discussions, held in a *villero*'s house, and day trips for the elderly. Subsequently they suggested starting a group and provided advice on how this could be done.

These social workers continued to support the *Grupo* for the first year of its existence, but then broke off contact.[31] This may have been due to changes in job responsibilities, a wish to give the *Grupo* more autonomy or a change in power within the provincial government (from the Radicals to the Peronist Party).[32] None of the surviving members of the *Grupo*'s committee can remember the full names of any of these social workers, nor precisely which section of the provincial government they represented, indicating that local participation was extremely limited.

The *Grupo* developed quickly in the months following its establishment and by the end of 1988 had attracted over 60 members. A committee had been elected and meetings were held roughly every month. Several committee members already had experience of local action and established contacts with both local councils, enabling the *Grupo* to obtain formal recognition from both provincial and municipal tiers of local government.[33] Whilst the gender balance of the total membership roughly matched that of elderly in the *villa* as a whole,[34] women filled twelve of the thirteen positions in the original committee. This indicates that, as with Villa Jardín's *Centro*, women participated to a much greater extent than men. Reasons for this are explored in detail below.

The official statute of the *Grupo* set out a series of objectives. However, these were couched in such general terms as to give little idea of the activities its members would be expected to undertake.[35] The range of services offered by the *Grupo*, as mentioned both in the minute books and by ex-committee members, was impressive. It included:

1. Direct assistance: funds raised from parties, raffles and donations were in part used to establish an emergency kitty. They covered the costs of funerals, accommodation and food for those members deemed to be in extreme need by the committee;
2. Legal advice: the *Grupo* helped around 50 members put their identity papers in order. The possession of such papers was a prerequisite for access to almost all forms of state assistance. The *Grupo* also assisted around 100 members, almost all of them elderly, to obtain non-contributory pensions from the provincial government;
3. Social forum: the *Grupo* organised a number of social events as well as conducting classes in literacy, knitting and embroidery. Whilst the statute stipulated that it was not to engage in religious activities, the *Grupo* at times provided catechism for its members;
4. Strength through numbers: whilst the statute also forbade the *Grupo* from conducting overtly political activities, it was able to send frequent

delegations to local government to ask for financial aid, food parcels and more holidays for its members. These were sometimes provided.

This range of activities was far broader than those conducted by the elderly group in Villa Jardín. However, there are indications that many of them were very limited in their effects. Only one of the elderly interviewed made any reference to literacy classes. Cases of direct economic aid to needy individuals were usually one-off events. No mention is made in the minutes about negotiations for assistance pensions nor identity documents for members. The impression given is that these services were only partially realised, that they were mainly performed by social workers and that the committee had little direct input.

Following 1988, the *Grupo* went into decline. This is reflected in the number of formal meetings recorded in the minutes books.

Table 4.11: Annual number of meetings held by the Grupo de la Tercera Edad 'Unión y Esperanza', *Villa Azul*

1988: 15	1989: 6	1990: 5	1991: 1	1992: 1

Source: *El Grupo de la Tercera Edad,* 18 January 1988 to 16 November 1992.

More frequently, the minutes refer to the failure of committee members to attend. There was also a general reduction in participation[36] and by 1991 the *Grupo* had effectively ceased to function.

When asked why the *Grupo* failed, interviewees provided a variety of explanations. Often, reference was made to the death and illness of key members, including the president, vice-president, treasurer and secretary. These, combined with the withdrawal of support by the social workers from La Plata (the capital of Buenos Aires Province), led to considerable disruption. Remaining activists in Villa Azul lacked experience and links with the authorities. In 1990 an attempt was made to re-establish the committee with new elections, but these were never held.

Following 1988, the *Grupo* was unable to obtain further assistance benefits for its members. It would appear that its early success stemmed from specific political conditions which subsequently changed. The granting of pensions by the provincial government may have been prompted by elections for national deputies in 1988.[37] One recipient referred to a large presentation ceremony in neighbouring Villa Itatí, in which 24 elderly people were awarded pensions, having been chosen by some form of lottery. A large number of senior politicians, including the provincial governor, were present as well as an impressive press entourage. Another mentioned a similar ceremony held in a local school. These circumstances changed once the election campaign had ended. The subsequent switch in provincial office-holders from Radicals to Peronists may also have disrupted the links which had been established by the *Grupo* and may also have heralded a new attitude towards social assistance. Indeed, the loss of contact with the social workers may have simply reflected the Province's lack of interest in providing further assistance benefits. Whatever the reasons, the failure to obtain fresh benefits was a major setback for the *Grupo*, as these had been the principal attraction for members. This indicates that, as was the case with Villa Jardín's *Centro*, the primary function of the organisation (at least in the eyes of its rank and file membership) was to obtain and distribute resources from state agencies.

Throughout its history, the *Grupo* was never able to obtain its own premises, despite the efforts of the committee who recognised both the concrete utility and symbolic value of this. Their failure partly reflected poor communications between the *Grupo* and other organisations in Villa Azul. The president was invited to be a committee member of the *Sociedad de Fomento* (which owned a building with several spacious rooms) but only attended twice. She claimed that this was partly because she did not want to become too involved with the *caciques* then running the *Sociedad*. In 1989 the two organisations came into conflict over the allocation of funds for new office by Quilmes council. According to members of the *Grupo*, these funds were allocated to the organisations jointly but they could not agree whether the building should be divided into one room each or a single large unit. The final result was that the *Grupo* was denied the use of the premises. One ex-committee member regarded the subsequent rupture of relations with the *Sociedad de Fomento* as the principal cause for the collapse of the *Grupo*.

The *Grupo* maintained better relations with the UNICEF-funded nursery school, which was where it most frequently met. It also had a number of contacts with church organisations. At one point a local priest offered the use of a chapel on Calle Azul for two years. This promise was subsequently broken, however, and relations with the Catholic Church were consequently soured.[38] This may have resulted from the hostility towards *villeros* apparent in the surrounding district and even voiced by some Caritas volunteers (see below). As in Villa Jardín, guaranteed access to a suitable meeting room was considered extremely important by local organisations and the failure to achieve this certainly contributed to the *Grupo*'s demise.

The *Grupo*'s relations with government agencies were both erratic and problematic. Meeting the bureaucratic requirements to maintain formal recognition took up a significant share of the committee's limited resources. Indeed, the problems posed by bureaucratic red tape were sometimes as serious for local organisations as for individual benefit claimants. In addition, promises made by the local councils were, more often than not, broken. The minutes show that Quilmes promised a regular monthly payment to the *Grupo* in September 1988 and monthly food parcels in April 1990. However, there is no mention of these being received after the first month in each case. This suggests these offers were simply intended as devices to serve the local government's short-term political ends. Relations with Avellaneda council were less developed, although this may have been less due to municipal disinterest than a failure of the *Grupo* to develop contacts.[39] The failure of committee members to establish firmer relations with, and follow up the promises made by the councils is another indication of their high dependence on the original social workers, who were themselves representatives of local government.

Finally, the *Grupo* missed opportunities to establish contacts with organisations in surrounding neighbourhoods. The minutes book observes that by early 1988 the *Grupo*'s activities were being talked about in Villa Itatí and beyond. Some attempts were made to hold joint meetings with a group of elderly people from Villa Itatí, but the proposal foundered because many members of both groups found the walk across the motorway too arduous. Contacts with such organisations might have increased the *Grupo*'s bargaining powers *vis-à-vis* the authorities and might also have helped it through the difficulties it subsequently faced. The organisation in Itatí was still holding regular meetings and organising outings in March 1993.

The failure of the *Grupo* did not result from the achievement of its original objectives nor the disappearance of its main raison d'être. Instead, the *Grupo*'s demise resulted from a combination of problems, including the loss of personnel, the failure to acquire proper premises and poor contacts with actors inside and outside the neighbourhood. Villa Jardín's *Centro* had been much more successful in meeting at least two of these challenges. In 1993, partly prompted by the greater interest being taken in Villa Azul's elderly by the *Sociedad de Fomento*, some of the *Grupo*'s old committee members organised new assemblies, reopened communication with Quilmes council and elected a new committee. However, by July 1993 they had yet to translate their words and plans into concrete activities of benefit to elderly residents.

El Centro de la Tercera Edad 'La Virgen de Luján'[40] *(CVL), Villa Zavaleta*

This was one of several initiatives which resulted from the renewed participation in Villa Zavaleta by a local Catholic church 'La Virgen de Luján' (see Map 4.4). The CVL shared its premises with a local Caritas branch and many of its volunteers were active in both organisations. Most interestingly, it was the first recorded instance of outside actors taking a proactive role in local organisation in Villa Zavaleta. These were the local priest and a part-time PAMI official who also provided catechism in the same church.[41] Unfortunately, as will become clear, these outside actors showed no more capacity for working together than the *villeros* themselves.

The CVL was established in 1992 following the arrival of a new priest who took a particular interest in Villa Zavaleta's social problems and, especially, the high concentration of elderly living there. It was also prompted by the implementation of PAMI's *Pro-Bienestar* programme, which sought to encourage the organisation of elderly and the establishment of feeding centres for pensioners. Meetings were organised with elderly active in the local church, none of whom lived in the *villa* itself and all of whom had contributory pension benefits. It was hoped that these would provide an 'example' to *villeros* and form the core of the new organisation. A door-to-door survey of elderly was then conducted inside Villa Zavaleta, noting ages, addresses and benefits held.[42] Such a survey was possible without provoking a violent confrontation due to the volunteers' links with the Catholic Church, the only institution which appeared to hold any authority in the *villa*.

By late 1992 fortnightly meetings with *villeros* were being held in a church building and the principal objectives of the new organisation had been agreed upon. Recognising the lack of community spirit in Villa Zavaleta, a principal goal was to teach residents how to work together and to set a precedent for other local initiatives. The new group was to be structured according to PAMI's guidelines for a *Centro de Jubilados* and was to provide a channel for the food aid being offered by the *Pro-Bienestar* programme. However, in contradiction to the PAMI guidelines, the group was to have a strong religious role, seeing to the spiritual as well as the material needs of the elderly. Every meeting was preceded by a short religious service in the adjacent church. According to the social worker:

> I think it's important that the elderly have a space for reflection about the transcendental side of life...we changed the [PAMI's] normative model in this respect. So far, the *Centros de Jubilados* which deal with social issues only really meet to dance, play cards and go on trips. And the reputations of these *Centros* have really fallen.
>
> (Sra CB, Villa Zavaleta, May 1993)

The CVL's meetings combined catechising with the dissemination of information about PAMI programmes and other assistance benefits. By early 1993 the PAMI worker had helped three local elderly obtain non-contributory invalidity pensions. Largely through the efforts of the local priest, the group obtained a grant from the newly-formed *Secretaría de la Tercera*

Edad (STE) for healthcare and housing improvements for over-60-year-olds without a pension. The full sum paid to the CVL was never disclosed but some members alleged that 300 pesos of it had gone towards the purchase of a new statuette for the church.[43] Other than a vaccination programme jointly funded by the STE and PAMI, no health or housing programmes were undertaken for elderly lacking insurance cover.

The initial meetings attracted upwards of 40 elderly from the *villa* and membership quickly rose to above 70. However, by mid-1993 attendances had slumped to less than ten and it appeared that the CVL could be dismissed as just another initiative in Villa Zavaleta that failed to take off.

As in the case of Villa Azul, it is instructive to examine why an organisation of the elderly which showed some initial promise then fell apart. The principal reason given by those involved was the conflict between the PAMI worker and the local priest. The former saw the priest's role as purely spiritual, whilst the latter sought to play a major, if not the dominant, part in all CVL activities. It was claimed that this often went to the extent of excluding the elderly *villeros* themselves from the decision-making process. This conflicted with the PAMI worker's objective to encourage participation among the membership. Tensions between the two outside actors worsened over the months, until the PAMI worker withdrew her support and was prevented from participating. Members, many of whom considered the PAMI worker to have been the initiator and key figure in the CVL, were left bewildered and disillusioned. According to the vice-president:

> It all began when Cecilia [the PAMI worker] began to go door to door to talk with people...But she hasn't come by or been at a meeting for the past two months. I more or less agreed with what she used to say. But now she doesn't come to meetings, well... [shrugs shoulders and tails off].
>
> (Sra MB, Villa Zavaleta, June 1993)

Whilst the rift between the two initiators of the CVL indubitably had a very negative effect on the group's fortunes, there are indications that this may have been a final blow to an organisation which had already lost its way. Attendances at meetings had already gone into steep decline[44] and, other than helping a small number of members with paperwork, the CVL had yet to put its plans into practice. This may have reflected the attitudes taken by the two outside actors and their lack of specialised knowledge about the complex system of official programmes and assistance benefits. Both were opposed to forming a group which gave priority to organising outings and parties, feeling that this would be incongruous with their religious objectives. As has been seen, such social activities were often a major attraction for elderly in other *villas*. The church service and a tendency to pepper discussions with religious references may also have discouraged some elderly from attending. Thus, although the behaviour of key individuals led to the final collapse of the CVL, many of its difficulties had arisen from institutional weaknesses.

Despite working for PAMI, the social worker's views often ran counter to those of more senior officials responsible for the *Pro-Bienestar* programme. She insisted that the feeding centre would provide for all over-60-year-olds in Villa Zavaleta, not just those with contributory pensions. This misunderstanding may have been because she was employed in PAMI's Women's Section rather than a department dealing specifically with food aid. Neither the PAMI worker nor the priest were aware of several types of assistance benefits potentially available to members nor did they have personal contacts with influential officials.[45]

It would appear that many initial participants simply lost patience with the CVL. After nearly a year of operation none of its members had yet benefited from PAMI food aid. Plans for a feeding centre were replaced by attempts to obtain individual food parcels. The process of obtaining these parcels, requiring the completion of a simple index card by members, was less complex than that for many other benefits. However, in July 1993, after several months of the operation, only a handful of the cards had been completed and none had been handed over to PAMI. Few volunteers were prepared to make further efforts or sacrifice their time for such activities. Similarly, the process of obtaining full recognition from the Buenos Aires council proved to be very protracted. As a result, the CVL was able to offer very few material benefits to its members. According to its vice-president:

> people here are always telling me, 'Nothing has happened yet. I'm not going to go anymore.' You see, the people here are like that. If they don't see an immediate benefit, they begin to drift away.
>
> (Sra MB, Villa Zavaleta, June 1993)

By mid-1993 there were few signs that the CVL would be able to overcome these difficulties.

Some of the reasons why the CVL was unable to succeed were similar to those which thwarted the *Grupo* in Villa Azul. In neither case did elderly *villeros* play a large role in day-to-day decision-making. In the case of the *Grupo*, local interest ebbed when its early successes were not followed up. Likewise, the CVL's inability to obtain quick, tangible economic benefits for participants led to a rapid fall in support. Had this not occurred, the subsequent tensions between its initiators might not have arisen.

Local Caritas branches[46]

Branches of Caritas, the charitable wing of the Catholic Church, ran programmes in all three of the *villas* studied. However, despite belonging to the same overarching organisation and sharing the same religious views, the activities of each branch differed widely. As will become clear, this reflected the personalities and attitudes of key participants as much as it did the varying problems and opportunities found in each neighbourhood.

A key difference between Villa Jardín and the two other locations was that the local Caritas branch was located inside the *villa* itself, not in an adjoining site. Indeed, the church and other Catholic buildings provided an important focus for community life in the neighbourhood. Villa Jardín's Catholic parish church was first consecrated in 1953 but the parish did not assume an important welfare role until the early 1970s. This development was largely attributed to the arrival of Padre Luís Stokler, a German priest, who was able to obtain substantial funds from his home country for local projects. These included the construction of a new church, a large community centre (the '*Ateneo*') and a football ground, all of which were located in the heart of the Villa Jardín (see Map 4.2). Villa Jardín's local Caritas branch was formally established in 1978 although the church was already involved in a variety of assistance projects. During his ten years in the *villa*, Padre Luís became an almost mythical figure and his photograph was often prominently displayed in *villeros'* homes. According to one elderly resident:

> You used to be able to go and tell him: 'Look here, Padre, this person's died, or one thing or another' and he'd come straight away, straight away. No car, none of that. Rain or shine, you used to be able to go and he'd lend a hand. He was a very important man and did very good things here.
>
> (Sra JM, Villa Jardín, February 1993)

Villa Azul's nearest Catholic church was located just three blocks away, in an area of modern middle-class housing in Avellaneda district. It was permitted by the local ecclesiastical authorities to include those parts of Villa Azul located in Quilmes district within its activities. However, interviews with *villeros* indicate that, whilst assistance from the church had occurred over a long period, this was both limited and sporadic. Unlike, Villa Jardín, the local branch of Caritas was only established in 1990. The original plans for Villa Zavaleta had made no provision for community buildings such as churches. In this case, the nearest Caritas branch was located a three-minute walk away, on the other side of a busy dual carriageway. Again, activities specifically targeting *villeros* had been extremely few and far between before the 1990s.

The principal activity of all three Caritas branches was to distribute food to households facing acute financial difficulties. In Villa Jardín, the distribution of monthly parcels had grown slowly, beginning with a single household in 1976 and had reached five by 1978. Following the formal inauguration of the branch, parcels became increasingly important and were being distributed to around 180 homes by 1992. It was claimed that these sought to provide short-term relief to households in extreme need, regardless of their religious persuasion.[47] Households were identified by 17 part-time voluntary workers, mainly women, each of whom was responsible for monitoring the economic conditions of families living in a cluster of blocks. The monthly parcels usually contained basic food items such as pasta and rice along with soap and, in some cases, medicine.

There were no formal eligibility criteria for Caritas help in Villa Jardín. This was left to the judgement of individual volunteers, who put in a claim to the director of the local centre. Thus, the director only exerted a negative control, vetoing cases she deemed inappropriate, rather than a positive, proactive one, identifying claims ignored by less conscientious volunteers. In an informal conversation, the director admitted that this may also have been because some volunteers made more of an effort to keep up to date with local requirements than others.[48] Volunteers were expected to combine their Caritas duties with a degree of catechism, which might have discouraged less than devout Catholics from seeking their assistance.

Food parcels were partly financed by a small contribution of between 50 centavos and 2 pesos from beneficiaries (compared to a market value of around 60 pesos for the products they contained).[49] The local Caritas also received monthly donations of food and money from church collections. In addition, surrounding, relatively wealthy parishes permitted volunteers from Villa Jardín to collect second-hand clothes in their own districts. The best quality clothes were sold, raising up to 900 pesos a month. The rest were distributed free among needy families.

Whilst these food parcels and used clothing were not specifically targeted at the elderly, volunteer workers claimed that this group received a disproportionately large share. However, they were unable to show the investigator their records or give precise figures, providing some grounds for concern both with regard to their efficiency and their openness.[50] In theory, the food parcels were intended to target households going through short periods of extreme need, as opposed to those experiencing more permanent difficulties. This might have excluded poor elderly who had little chance of improving their position. In cases where elderly were in great economic need but received no support from nearby family members, Caritas sometimes arranged for one of the two local padres to visit and talk over the situation with relatives.

In 1993 a number of modifications were made to the food parcel programme, resulting in a halving of the number of beneficiaries. At the same time, the number of items in the food parcels was increased. It was hoped that this would enable the targeting of aid towards households with no potential breadwinners, such as single mothers with large families and elderly living alone. Rather than reflecting altered economic conditions within Villa Jardín, this new approach was the consequence of changes in personnel. The preceding year had seen the arrival of a new parish priest and the retirement of Caritas' long-serving director. Insufficient time had elapsed between these changes and the completion of the investigation for their impact to be fully assessed. However, a number of elderly interviewed in Villa Jardín complained that they had lost out under the new system:

> Yes, I used to get them [food parcels]. And now they've cut me off...last month they cut me off. So now I have to go to see José Martínez [the new padre] so that he can give me a new form. And for this they want twenty pesos! What if I don't have it? If I had twenty pesos I'd go out and buy the stuff myself. (Sra JM, Villa Jardín, February 1993)

Conversely, none of the elderly residents interviewed claimed to have obtained new Caritas benefits through the targeting strategy. Given that the majority of households in Villa Jardín had basic needs unsatisfied, this targeting could have caused the exclusion of many needy cases, including needy elderly. It was also an implicit recognition that the local branch could not aspire to fill all the gaps in state welfare protection. Indeed by the early 1990s most local Caritas initiatives specifically for the elderly had been discontinued.[51] No references were made to volunteers directly pursuing benefits at state agencies or obtaining places in rest homes. This both reflected the formation of the '*Jóvenes de Noventa*' centre and the change in personnel.

By 1993 the Villa Azul Caritas was also distributing free food parcels to needy families on a weekly basis. These parcels contained a similar range goods to those provided in Villa Jardín. However, of a total of 34 beneficiaries aged over 55 years, only nine came from the Villa Azul itself. The majority lived in the surrounding middle-class district and already received minimum pension benefits. Most of these cases had begun to receive help after Caritas carried out a door-to-door survey in 1990. Despite containing far higher concentrations of poverty than other parts of the parish, Villa Azul had not been included in this survey. As in Villa Jardín, the local Caritas collected used clothing, although the bulk of this was resold with only leftover items being distributed free.

In Villa Azul Caritas received funding from a wide variety of sources. These included the sale of clothes, church collections, fund-raising by local schools and donations of food and medicines. The director stressed that funds sometimes dried up and so the provision of food parcels was not always reliable. This was put forward by the director as a reason for being unable to develop programmes specifically targeting *villeros.*

Rather than provide food parcels free of charge, the Villa Zavaleta branch had opted to provide them at a discount of 20–30 per cent compared to the usual price. This economy was largely achieved by buying the food in bulk at a local warehouse. Volunteers argued that it was possible to help a larger number of families by providing smaller discounts than in Villa Azul and Villa Jardín. The local Caritas kept index cards for the 2000 or so families who had received aid. However, it had made no effort to establish a network of volunteers inside the *villa*, as had been done in Villa Jardín. This would have been difficult due to the lack of solidarity and security in the *villa* but, for the same reason, would have been very beneficial. Villa Zavaleta's Caritas also collected used clothing, all of which was distributed free.

Although Caritas as a whole was particularly concerned with the unemployment of household heads, the Villa Jardín and Villa Azul branches also provided services specifically for the welfare of local elderly. According to the ex-director in Villa Jardín:

> Caritas began [to pursue claims for] assistance pensions when I became involved in 1978. It was me who started them, but there was nobody [in the authorities] to provide this type of assistance. 'Come back tomorrow!' So I'd come back tomorrow. 'Return the day after!' So I'd return the next day. 'Come back at such a time!' So I'd come back then. They couldn't get rid of me until I'd got what I wanted...There weren't many pensions at first, but then they were all I could manage. We also used to send people to the council and others to the Social Welfare office in the Federal Capital...Afterwards we began to help people who were living alone find places in rest homes. (Sra EH, Villa Jardín, February 1993)

Whilst the numbers involved were small, these measures represented an unprecedented series of initiatives for the local elderly, involving both direct assistance and bureaucratic advice.[52] Villa Jardín's Caritas had recognised the failure of official welfare agencies to provide elderly with adequate information and advice about obtaining appropriate benefits and had therefore decided to take on the responsibility itself. It had also become aware of the formidable bureaucratic obstacles which lay in the path of those seeking assistance. According to the ex-director:

> People don't insist. They're afraid of authority [she enacts a dialogue]:
>
> 'Good morning.' They enter the office. 'I'm from such-and-such a place and need such-and-such a thing.'
> 'Come back tomorrow.'
> 'Alright, then. Bye.'
>
> I don't handle it that way. I go straight up to them and tell them:
>
> 'I'm Estefanía from such-and-such a parish and such-and-such a group and I've come to ask for this, this, this and that: altogether so I don't have to make separate visits.'
> 'But the person you require isn't here', they tell me.
> 'Isn't anyone taking their place?', I ask.
> 'Yes, I am.'
> 'In which case, can't you help me with these things?'
> 'Yes, but its not supposed to be my job.'
> 'Come on, you're only twenty. I'm three or four times as old as you. You're not going to send me away again.'
> 'I could get you a reply', she ponders, 'but the boss isn't here.'
> 'Where's the boss?'
> 'In a meeting.'
> 'That's alright. I brought my rosario. I'll sit down and pray that the meeting ends soon.'
>
> And I stay put. They know I'm not going to go and so they have to do something. (Sra EH, Villa Jardín, February 1993)

The ex-director's story graphically demonstrates the difficulties of obtaining aid from state assistance agencies. It also shows that the administrative problems of social security systems went beyond budgetary inefficiency. The incompetence and lack of motivation of personnel in many state agencies had engendered a culture of Kafkaesque stonewalling, which usually proved insurmountable for individuals less confident or well-informed than the Caritas director. This issue is explored further in Chapter 5.

By 1993, Villa Jardín's Caritas had become much less involved with assisting elderly with benefit claims. Instead, information about appropriate cases was passed on to the '*Jóvenes del Noventa*' Centre. Nevertheless,

Caritas workers were planning to develop a programme of legal advice for elderly and other groups. This was to be given by a local lawyer who would provide his services free of charge.

None of the Caritas branches located in the other two *villas* had taken significant steps to assist local elderly with their benefit claims. In early 1993 Villa Azul's Caritas also began to provide a limited amount of free legal counselling through a local lawyer. By April one elderly man, from the neighbouring area not the *villa*, was using this facility to apply for a contributory invalidity pension. At this time, none of the elderly interviewed in Villa Azul were aware that Caritas offered this service, again indicating a lack of contact. In Villa Zavaleta Caritas provided no services specifically targeting elderly welfare concerns. This would have been considered an unnecessary duplication of activities with the '*Virgen de Luján*' Centre, which was located on the same premises.

Contacts between the different Caritas branches and other grassroots organisations as well as the *villeros* themselves were highly variable. In Villa Jardín, Caritas had a number of links with the '*Centro de los Jóvenes del Noventa*'. For example, it provided a hall for the *Centro*'s monthly birthday parties. The retired Caritas director was an active member of the *Centro*'s committee and provided a vital bridge between the two organisations. Several of the Caritas volunteers discussed the *Centro*'s activities with the elderly in their respective areas of responsibility. Villa Jardín's Caritas had no links with other local initiatives, although it was considering the possibility of operating with a local Protestant organisation in a housing renovation project (see below). It maintained a distance from organisations such as the *Junta Vecinal*, the *Sociedad de Fomento* and local Peronist offices (*unidades básicas*), which, according to Padre Jorge (who succeeded Padre Luís as head of the parish church), 'never get things done' and were too closely tied to party politics.[53] By contrast, Villa Jardín's Caritas had good links with higher levels in the Caritas hierarchy, through monthly meetings with the bishopric of Lanús.

In Villa Azul links between Caritas and other local organisations had been virtually non-existent before 1993. The director claimed that this was because most organisations operating in the *villa* made false promises and were corrupt. The dominant position of local *caciques* in *villero* politics up to the late 1980s was no doubt a serious barrier to greater church participation. However, these links were improved during the period of the investigation and several joint meetings were held with the *Grupo* and the local *Sociedad de Fomento*. Plans were made to co-ordinate future projects, including a poverty census and workshops for youths and elderly. Several members of the *Grupo* registered to receive food parcels and to take advantage of free legal advice.

Local organisations inside Villa Zavaleta had developed some links with Caritas, which had provided funds for an extension to the defunct *Comisión Vecinal*'s feeding centre. In general, however, the lack of effective local initiatives in Villa Zavaleta reduced the scope for collaboration. As in the *Virgen de Luján*, the local priest played a large part in Caritas' day-to-day management. Indeed, it was often difficult to distinguish initiatives taken by Caritas from the *Virgen de Luján* or the individual actions of the priest.

In Villa Jardín Caritas provided few opportunities for the participation of elderly *villeros* and did not aspire to do so. Its director was appointed by the chief parish priest and most policy decisions were made between the two of them. None of the voluntary workers at the time of the survey were themselves elderly, although they were *villeros*. Thus, the local Caritas constituted an initiative *for* (at least in part) the elderly rather than an initiative *by* the elderly.

In Villa Azul scope for *villero* participation in the running of the local Caritas was even more limited. As mentioned above, the bulk of Caritas activities in Villa Azul were directed at needy families living in the middle-class district rather than in the *villa* itself. The failure to develop a network of voluntary assistants within the *villa* may partly have been because the local branch was established at a time when the middle classes were suffering from a sharper fall in living standards than poorer sectors.[54] However, there are also indications that the attitudes of individual Caritas workers precluded initiatives in Villa Azul. Coming from surrounding middle-class districts, many of Caritas workers considered the proximity of shanty towns as a 'threat' to the neighbourhood and were in favour of eradication. During an untaped interview in April 1993 the director gave a very negative view of the *villa* and its inhabitants, who were portrayed as lazy, untrustworthy scroungers.[55]

In Villa Zavaleta there was slightly more involvement of *villeros* in the day-to-day running of Caritas. This reflected the strong interest taken in the shanty town. Nevertheless, the great majority of Caritas volunteers were from outside the *villa*; often from the same families as those elderly who were to provide 'examples' in the *Virgen de Luján* group. Moreover, the local priest monopolised decision-making and appeared to consider *villeros* incapable of playing a major role in any initiative.

Although there were some similarities in terms of the programmes offered by the Caritas branches in each *villa*, their attitudes towards and their impact on the economic welfare of elderly *villeros* were often at variance. In Villa Jardín membership of Caritas consisted entirely of local residents, who did not feel that they required external support in decision-making or organisation. Nevertheless, since elderly *villeros* did not participate in the branch, they may have been vulnerable to increasingly rigorous targeting which appeared to prioritise other groups. That Caritas played a very different role in Villa Azul appeared to be largely due to its location inside a middle-class neighbourhood many of whose residents felt hostile towards the *villeros*. Whilst this hostility was not apparent in the case of Villa Zavaleta, *villeros* were often viewed in a rather patronising and negative light. Here, there would appear to have been a sharper conflict between welfare provision and religious concerns than in the other *villas*. The contrasting priorities of these different Caritas branches indicate that the organisation as a whole did not play a consistent part in providing economic support for elderly *villeros* across the city. Indeed, individual parish priests often had more influence over local initiatives than did national guidelines. As such, Caritas could not be considered, in any sense, a homogenous safety net for those poor elderly who were without sufficient means from other sources.

Other religious grassroots organisations

'El Centro Urbano Nueva Parroquia' (CUNP), Villa Jardín

This organisation co-ordinated the activities of several Protestant churches in the neighbourhood.[56] It did not, however, simply constitute a Protestant version of the local Caritas. CUNP first became active as part of a general upsurge of outside interest in Villa Jardín during the 1960s, when its activities combined a degree of evangelising with improvements to the local infrastructure. During the *Proceso* period relations with the military government were not as good as those enjoyed by the Catholic Church. Accordingly, CUNP did not enjoy the freedoms granted to Caritas: several members were arrested and its activities discontinued.[57]

CUNP was re-established in the 1980s, in response both to redemocratisation and a sudden upsurge of evangelical Protestantism across the country.[58] Rather than distribute food parcels, CUNP sought to provide local employment opportunities through training programmes and small workshops. These included a fresh pasta factory and a number of sewing groups. By their nature, such activities were more directed at the needs of local youths and women than those of aged *villeros*. Only two CUNP programmes were of clear benefit to the elderly. One, the provision of free legal advice from a local lawyer, overlapped with similar programmes run by several other organisations. The other, the creation of a feeding centre inside Villa Jardín, had been attempted unsuccessfully on several previous occasions. These centres provided for both children and elderly and it was claimed that between 10 and 15 of the latter would come to eat on a regular basis. They were run by elderly *villeros*, who would be given a small wage. One of CUNP's directors explained that the latest initiative had failed due to a lack of financial support from the local council. However, local residents mentioned that people working there had been assaulted by local youths, who may have been angered by CUNP's heavy-handed evangelising amongst those who attended. This reflected an inevitable tension between CUNP's religious and social functions, which it was admitted often led to disagreement within its co-ordinating committee.

CUNP had a variety of links with other organisations both inside and outside Villa Jardín. Indeed, although it owned premises inside (the *Centro Comunitario*, see Map 4.2), its main offices were located just outside Villa Jardín. Unlike the local Caritas, CUNP received part of its funding from a national body: *La Federación Argentina de Iglesias Evangélicas*.[59] Unfortunately, the exact nature of its relationship with this organisation was not made clear by those CUNP members interviewed.

CUNP collaborated with Caritas and other local organisations in the distribution of emergency food aid during the hyperinflationary crisis of 1989. When this programme was discontinued in 1991 ties with Caritas became much weaker. CUNP members claimed that this was largely due to the arrival of Padre Jorge, the new Catholic priest, but refused to say why this was the case. The most probable cause of the rift was tension arising from CUNP's predilection to combine assistance with evangelising. Whatever the reason, it indicates the importance of good personal relations between respective members for maintaining collaboration between local organisations. There were also indications that collaboration with the other groups had created a number of problems. The assistant director of CUNP complained that the local *Junta Vecinal* development organisation had been suffering much internal conflict and had been too compromised by personalism to operate effectively.

These bad experiences partly explained why CUNP was wary of establishing links with other local associations. Thus, although CUNP provided CEPEV support and advice for establishing the *Centro*, these close ties weakened over time. When the *Centro* first succeeded in obtaining DNA pensions it invited CUNP to send along any eligible elderly. This was done but CUNP refused a subsequent offer to send a representative along with the *Centro*'s delegations to various social security agencies. Since then, there had been no contact between them. The breakdown in collaboration may have partly resulted from a gradual increase in ties between the *Centro* and Caritas.

CUNP's general impact on the economic welfare of the elderly in Villa Jardín was very small. This partly reflected its particular concerns and priorities. However, the failure of the feeding centre and the duplication of legal advice might have been avoided if links with Caritas and the *Centro* had been kept up. These, in turn, might have been facilitated if CUNP had been able to separate its evangelising mission from its other activities. Unfortunately, there were no indications of this being done.

Villa Azul's evangelical church

The general lack of interest and even hostility of the local Catholic church to the residents of Villa Azul appeared to provide evangelical Protestants an opportunity to attract new converts. There was, however, little indication that they had been able to do so. A single evangelical organisation still maintained premises in the *villa*, on Calle Azul, but none of the local residents interviewed had seen any signs of activity in recent times. One interviewee who received economic assistance from them in the early 1980s mentioned that these programmes had since been discontinued. Another received occasional help through a contact at a church in the neighbouring district of Bernal. Neither was able to throw any light on why the evangelists had stopped coming to Villa Azul. According to the vice-president of the local *Sociedad de Fomento*:

> There have always been evangelicals around here but, as far as I can see, they were never really accepted...I don't just mean large-scale support...Yes, they have a few followers, but they're not at all important for most people.
> (Sr JR, Villa Azul, June 1993)

This suggested that the evangelists may have lost heart due to the failure to realise large-scale religious conversions.

Local development organisations

As has been seen, in all the *villas* studied there were attempts, some more successful than others, to develop grassroots associations seeking to promote general neighbourhood improvements. Such initiatives are part of a strong tradition of community organisation in Greater Buenos Aires, which goes back to the start of the century.[60] In order to obtain legal recognition from local government, these organisations were, theoretically, barred from political activities. Surveys of local development organisations in the city as a whole, observe that they declined in importance after a brief resurgence during the years of democratic transition. This trend was less apparent in the *villas*. Here, community organisation took longer to recover from the repression of the *Proceso*. When they did re-emerge, organisations began to place more emphasis on social problems than they had hitherto done.

Although this tended to prioritise groups such as children, adolescents and women, the elderly also received some consideration.

La Junta Vecinal (the Junta), Villa Jardín

The *Junta* was re-established in 1988 and carried forward its predecessor's tradition of improving the local infrastructure, such as drainage and power supply. Whether it also carried forward the tradition of representing the interests of *intrusos* within the *villa* is less apparent. Although *Junta* members made no reference to this matter, they admitted that it only worked within a handful of blocks surrounding their meeting room (see Map 4.2). This comprised one of the poorest parts of Villa Jardín, the vast majority of whose residents were probably *intrusos*.

From 1992 the *Junta* began to diversify its activities, providing various forms of social assistance for women, children and, to a lesser extent, elderly. As elsewhere, the *Junta* provided free legal advice for elderly attempting to claim contributory and assistance pensions. By May 1993 30 elderly had used this service, although only one had so far been successful in obtaining a benefit.[61] This is yet another indication of both the formidable bureaucratic obstacles facing benefit claimants and the relative success of the *Centro*. Indeed, members of the *Junta*'s committee were unaware of the full range of non-contributory pensions potentially available to members nor did they have privileged personal contacts with the staff of state welfare organs, as had been the case with CEPEV.[62]

The *Junta* sometimes provided direct economic assistance to poor elderly. In 1992, it received an undisclosed number of food parcels from the provincial government in La Plata, which were to be distributed among those it considered most needy. However, this service was no longer occurring by early 1993. The *Junta* also obtained food aid from the local council, but this was ear-marked for mothers of young children. Occasionally the *Junta* distributed food donated by political parties, some of which may have gone to elderly. None of the elderly individuals interviewed in Villa Jardín made any reference to these programmes, indicating that their scope must have been extremely limited.

The *Junta* had plans to develop new activities during 1993, some of which might have been of benefit to the elderly. It was hoping to co-operate with the council in the distribution of a new set of food parcels targeting the most needy families. This would appear to be a separate scheme to that proposed to the local council by the *Centro*, since it was not to be exclusively for the elderly.

In the past, the *Junta* had largely relied upon the co-operation of the local residents for the financing of its activities: for example, families in a block pooling the cost of a road improvement. In addition, registered members of the *Junta*, of which there are around 300, were required to pay a due of two pesos a month. However, as is indicated by the above activities, the *Junta* was beginning to develop stronger relations with local government. Its formal registration by Lanús Council in 1992 coincided with the delivery of the first food parcels and the *Junta* continued to have meetings with the municipal Secretary of Social Assistance about once a month.[63] Although the *Junta* maintained that these links did not compromise its non-political status, several elderly respondents disagreed, equating the activities of the *Junta* with grassroots political groups and complaining of false promises and political manipulation. According to one elderly woman:

> some of them get things done when there's a political [campaign]. They start to mobilise everyone, helping this person, helping someone opposite. And then they just forget about it all...Because its just for politics, for politics more than anything else. (Sr JM, Villa Jardín, March 1993)

The *Junta* also received a small amount of funding from a national NGO, *La Fundación de Vivienda y la Comunidad,*[64] which channelled aid from the Italian, French and German governments. The *Junta* wanted to develop closer links with other organisations working in surrounding areas but had no contacts with the *Centro*, due to the latter's reservations about its competence and political status. Other than recognising their mutually agreed spheres of influences or 'territories', it had few links with other *Juntas Vecinales* in the surrounding neighbourhoods.

As with the CUNP, the impact of the *Junta* on the welfare of local elderly was limited by its own priorities. Moreover, both organisations encountered similar problems of credibility within Villa Jardín, resulting from tensions between the desire for social improvements and to win over new converts to their respective causes. In the case of CUNP, their promotion of evangelism conflicted with the Catholic beliefs of the majority of *villeros*. Hence mixing religion with assistance caused more problems than it did for Caritas. By contrast, the alleged Peronist leanings of the *Junta* coincided with the political ascriptions of most residents. Its lack of credibility was partly due to false promises and an absence of professionalism in the past, as well as a widespread disenchantment towards clientelistic modes of organisation in the *villa*.

El Sociedad de Fomento, Villa Azul

As explained above, the *Sociedad* received its initial stimulus from the construction of a nursery school in 1987 and later, in 1989, from emergency government policies designed to reduce the impact of hyperinflation. According to the ex-president:

> [the hyperinflation] was the key moment because...Maglana became the president [of the *Sociedad*], the vice-president was Nino (who isn't in the *Sociedad* any more but is still actively working for social issues) and this other guy called Martín who used to be an active member of the Communist Party back then and after they stopped he began to work with us in the *Sociedad de Fomento*. He was the president of the last committee but, well, for personal problems he couldn't carry out his duties and he had to resign a few months ago. (Sr JR, Villa Azul, June 1993)

Thus, by 1992 the *Sociedad* had passed from the hands of local *caciques* such as Nino and Maglana, and from non-Peronists to a tightly-knit group of Peronist activists who were also dominant in the two housing co-operatives.

For most of its history, the *Sociedad* had primarily been concerned with the physical fabric of Villa Azul and conducted no activities specifically targeting the elderly. Its only contact with the *Grupo de Tercera Edad* resulted from the conflict over premises in 1989. By 1993, however, the *Sociedad* was taking increased interest in the elderly. This change may have been prompted by several considerations, including the demise of the *Grupo*, the acquisition of substantial funds and political opportunism.

In 1991 the *Sociedad* obtained a substantial grant via the provincial '*Plan de Justicia Social*',[65] which was used to construct a sports centre and community buildings alongside the nursery school (see Map 4.3). These were nearing completion in July 1993 and it was planned that they would be used to provide a daily feeding centre for the Villa Azul's elderly. According to the vice-president, the committee were confident that they would receive funding from the PAMI *Pro-Bienestar* programme. They were also confident that all elderly residents aged over 60 included in their 1992 census would be entitled to use the feeding centre. This clearly contradicted the line taken by PAMI that the programme would only benefit those with contributory pensions.

It is clear that the *Sociedad* had been very successful in obtaining funding and executing projects. As such it had become the focus for local participation in Villa Azul. It is also apparent that much of its success stemmed from personal contacts which originated in the party political activities of some committee members. During the internal Peronist elections of May 1993 several were openly campaigning for a local councillor who had previously been Secretary for Social Assistance in Quilmes council and was presently working for the '*Plan de Justicia Social*'. It was also disclosed that the councillor's sister worked for PAMI in Quilmes council and had been their original contact with the *Pro-Bienestar* programme. The vice-president of the *Sociedad* was himself working in Quilmes, as part of the *Dirección de Cooperativas*, set up by the *Plan Arraigo*. In this respect the attitude of the *Sociedad* was a marked contrast to that of organisations in Villa Jardín. According to the vice-president:

> There are people in the Comission, the *Sociedad de Fomento*, the Co-operative, who are politically active...Our success with the sports centre was partly because we had realised that what we need more than anything is an organisation in the neighbourhood. But if this organisation doesn't have political contacts, then, unfortunately it won't be successful: it has to be done the other way. (Sr JR, Villa Azul, June 1993)

The *Sociedad*'s attitude to the reactivation of the *Grupo* was at best ambivalent. The vice-president argued that the *Grupo*'s committee members were too old to be able to take on major responsibilities and hinted that they might be about to lose formal recognition from Quilmes council. He felt that, since the *Sociedad* had itself obtained funding for the feeding centre, they would be unable to delegate the full responsibility for its management to another organisation. He argued that either the *Sociedad* should have a strong supervisory role in the affairs of the *Grupo* or that they should take it over completely.

The attitude of the *Sociedad*'s new leadership towards the 'old guard' of the *Grupo* was in part a continuation of the struggle against individualistic modes of organisation which had previously been dominant. It could also be interpreted more cynically, as an attempt by one group of activists to extend their political influence within Villa Azul at the expense of another. Interestingly, one of the *caciques* who had lost his post in the *Sociedad* began to take a much more active, behind-the-scenes role in the renewal of the *Grupo*. These potential conflicts were resolved, at least superficially, by the election of a *Sociedad* member on to the *Grupo*'s committee in May 1993. Yet the *Sociedad* did little to encourage the participation of elderly. Indeed, its attitude towards the *Grupo* suggested it believed that the elderly were not capable of running an organisation.

The *Sociedad* had obtained several tangible benefits for Villa Azul, although none had been of direct nor exclusive benefit to the elderly. Its success had stemmed from a very different approach to that taken by organisations such as Villa Jardín's *Centro*. Alignment with dominant elements in local government had clearly paid short-term dividends and won the *Sociedad* the backing of most *villeros*. However, this must also have left it vulnerable to the sort of external political changes which had previously undermined the *Grupo*. The crucial difference between the two was that the *Sociedad*'s committee had considerable organisational and political experience and therefore were not dependent on the decisions and expertise of outside actors. This left it in a much stronger position. The large sports hall, which dominated one end of Villa Azul, was concrete proof that the *Sociedad* was able to obtain material benefits for residents and had had a galvanising impact on local support. This contrasted with the *Grupo*'s failure to even acquire its own office.

Grassroots political organisations

Unidades básicas and other grassroots political associations

Of the three neighbourhoods, Villa Jardín had a particularly strong tradition of political activity going back to the days of the first Peronist government. Whilst political organisations were ruthlessly put down during the last period of military rule, they quickly recovered following redemocratisation. By early 1993 the *villa* boasted at least three local Peronist offices (*unidades básicas*) and one belonging to the Radical party. Several more groups appeared during the Peronist internal election campaign of May 1993. Many of these distributed food on an ad hoc basis.

As with Villa Jardín's *Junta*, overtly political associations did not enjoy a high degree of credibility as unbiased purveyors of social assistance amongst those elderly interviewed. Frequent accusations were made of corruption and incompetence. According to one elderly woman:

> Well, when its election time, they come looking for you. They come looking for you to join up so they'll give you bread, so they'll give you groceries. They do the rounds for this short time. Then they don't give you anything anymore, nothing at all. Just during the elections and all that stuff and then they don't give you anything.
>
> (Sra AG, Villa Jardín, March 1993)

Another *villero* observed:

> They're always making lots of promises but never come up with the goods...Its the politicians who are responsible for sucking the blood of people living here, because politicians never work...They're pure lies, friend, pure lies. (Sr OM, Villa Jardín, February 1993)

These negative attitudes towards local political militancy partly explain the strong fear of overt party political compromise held by most other groups in Villa Jardín. They also suggest that the roles of *unidades básicas* and similar organisations in promoting welfare within the *villa* would remain slight.

LOCAL INITIATIVES FOR THE ELDERLY: CONCLUDING COMMENTS

This section compares the experiences of the three neighbourhoods studied and seeks to draw some general conclusions. It begins by examining factors which may have contributed to the success or failure of local initiatives in reducing the marginal status and improving the economic position of elderly *villeros*. It then considers how much successful initiatives were able to achieve.

Comparisons between neighbourhoods

Despite all being shanty towns located in the same city, the experiences of the three case-study locations were extremely varied. By 1993, Villa Jardín contained a large range of initiatives which addressed the needs of elderly residents, either directly or indirectly. This was helped by a rich tradition of local organisation and participation and a general shift in priorities away from improving the physical infrastructure towards socio-economic problems. As such, the *villa* conformed most closely to the 'slum of hope' characterisation put forward in studies of shanty towns elsewhere in Latin America (Lloyd, 1979:39). Nevertheless, the contribution made by the *Centro* far outweighed those of all the remaining groups put together. It is not easy to establish whether the latters' tendency to prioritise other issues was due to the emergence of the *Centro* or reflected the continued marginality of the elderly within the community. Thus, were the *Centro* to run into difficulties the general profile of the elderly within Villa Jardín might be substantially reduced.

By contrast, Villa Azul had failed to establish an organisation comparable to Villa Jardín's *Centro* and its local initiatives provided far less economic support for the elderly. This could largely be attributed to the decision of CEPEV to become involved in one area and not the other and the different priorities of the local Catholic priests. By contrast, local government had taken more interest in the plight of Villa Azul's elderly than it had in Villa Jardín, sending social workers and providing assistance benefits. A change in local government undermined the *Grupo*, cutting off an important source of outside assistance for the elderly. By 1993 these needs were being rearticulated by an organisation which had better links with the new power structure. In both of these initiatives, participation by elderly *villeros* was much lower than it had been in the *Centro* and there was little indication that it had reduced their marginal status either within or outside the *villa*.

Potentially, local initiatives could have been of more benefit to local elderly living in Villa Zavaleta than in the other *villas* studied. Their most important contribution would have been to reduce the sense of fear and isolation experienced by many of the elderly there. The relatively high number of elderly, the majority of whom it was claimed possessed contributory pensions, would have increased the bargaining power of organisations *vis-à-vis* official agencies such as PAMI. Sadly there were few signs that any of this could be achieved until a degree of order was established in the *villa*.

Requisites for success

Outside actors

For the purposes of analysis it is useful to distinguish between those actors that form an integral part of local initiatives and others that are less directly involved. These are referred to as 'integral' and 'non-integral' actors.

None of the three *villas* contained examples of elderly residents organising themselves spontaneously without outside help. This was largely a consequence of the problems of double marginality referred to at the beginning of the chapter. In every case, outside actors (be they social workers, the Church or political parties) were integral both in initiating activities and, more often than not, in their day-to-day management. When this external support was interrupted many initiatives foundered. Similarly, the inability or reluctance of outside actors to work in a *villa* was a major obstacle to the organisation of elderly there. This partly accounted for the fact that Villa Zavaleta contained no successful initiatives, despite having by far the highest number of elderly.

Whilst outside actors were ubiquitous, their roles varied considerably. This partly reflected the type of actor involved (religious, political, state or NGO) and their reasons for becoming involved in the *villa*. On the one hand, CEPEV sought to make groups fully independent of outside help after a few years, so that its resources might be directed elsewhere. On the other, religious or political actors had an interest in maintaining permanent links with local initiatives (to put bums on pews or crosses on voting slips).

The presence of outside actors provided local initiatives with a series of opportunities and constraints. They provided *villeros* with basic organisational skills, information about available state or non-state resources and, in many cases, direct access to resources through personal or institutional contacts.

Personal contacts were particularly important. The case-studies indicate that access to resources was frequently a question of 'who you know, rather than what you know'. Examples of this included the Villa Azul *Sociedad de Fomento*'s political patron's links with PAMI staff and CEPEV's contacts with the *Dirección Nacional de la Ancianidad*.

Permanent dependence on such actors tended, however, to stifle initiative and participation within the groups making them more vulnerable to changes in external support. It could also lead to conflicts between social and other objectives. The failure of CUNP's feeding centres and the *Virgen de Luján* partly reflected the dangers of mixing religion with assistance. Political links were often perceived negatively by *villeros* and generally proved to be unreliable. It should be stressed that divisions between state and party politics were often confused in Argentina.[66] Ruling factions generally filled government posts with their own party faithful. CEPEV identified:

> The predominance of a centralised, 'strongman' pattern in the exercise of power and distribution of resources on the part of local government.
> (CEPEV, 1990:14)[67]

Thus, close association with a specific state agency might bring with it the same drawbacks as links with a political party. If elections led to a change in the political party of office-holders, *villa* organisations' links with local government might be badly damaged.

All the local initiatives studied also maintained non-integral relations with outside actors. These included a wider range of institutions, with local government particularly important. Again, such contacts offered local groups both advantages and disadvantages. Local groups usually took the initiative in developing such ties, often motivated by a desire to obtain resources held by the outside actor. At times, substantial barriers had to be overcome in order to develop formal links. Again, such contacts could open doors to previously inaccessible resources. Likewise, they could also increase external dependence or foster political or religious compromise. However, since these relations were by definition less intensive, both the risks and opportunities they conferred were usually less significant.

Incentives

Local initiatives for the elderly were unable to maintain high levels of participation nor justify monthly dues unless they could provide concrete benefits for their members. The experiences of the neighbourhoods studied suggest that these must include a tangible economic gain for a large proportion of members. This might be food aid or facilitating access to cash benefits. Whilst parties, vaccinations and day trips increased the solidarity and confidence of local elderly, they were not enough on their own to ensure participation.

One problem which confronted by most groups was that it was sometimes impossible to obtain benefits without having already achieved a high level of participation, yet local elderly were unwilling to join until they saw clear evidence of economic aid.[68] Often it was not possible to break out of this unfortunate cycle. According to the Villa Azul *Grupo*'s ex-president:

> The people here are rather non-committal. I don't know if they're afraid or what...It's hard for me to talk with them, convince them and even, to be frank, lie to them in order to motivate them.
>
> (Sra MP, Villa Azul, May 1993)

Secure premises

Access to suitable premises was another key requisite for the success of local initiatives. This reflected both the concrete utility and the symbolic value of the building. Premises could have been offered to or shared with other organisations, increasing co-operation between them. Space may also have been rented out, providing organisations an additional source of income. Ideally, the building should have been centrally located: the lack of community buildings inside Villa Zavaleta severely restricted its development. The failure to secure a regular meeting room contributed to the demise of Villa Azul's *Grupo* and limited the activities of Villa Jardín's *Centro*.

Broad participation

All of the organisations studied were dominated by a small number, sometimes just one, of key participants. In some cases these were outside actors, in others they also included local residents. Whilst this was probably inevitable, maximising the number of active members from the locality was important for the long-run success of initiatives. The *Virgen de Luján* and Villa Azul's *Grupo* both provide examples of organisations which foundered because key members became inactive. Clearly, the risk of death or illness was higher if initiatives were run by a small number of elderly people.

In most of the initiatives studied notions of democratic participation were somewhat limited. Again in both the *Virgen de Luján* and the *Grupo's* elections for committee members, only one person was nominated per post. Few votes were taken on day-to-day decisions, and, when this was done, they generally consisted of an informal show of hands. This lack of democracy can only have served as a disincentive to participation and to concentrate decision-making in fewer hands.

Generally speaking, women participated in local initiatives for the elderly to a much greater degree than did men. Other than parish priests, local Caritas volunteers were virtually all female. Women dominated both the general membership of the *Centro* and the committee of the *Grupo*. This gender imbalance was more pronounced than that for the total population of elderly *villeros* and requires explanation. Levels of female participation may have reflected the importance of elderly women in the national human rights movements of the late 1970s and early 1980s (Leis, 1989). The military regime was unable to suppress these activities with force, since it feared public reaction to the sight of elderly women being manhandled by police and soldiers. This experience increased the confidence and capacity of elderly women to organise themselves. However, its importance should not be overestimated, since there are no indications that *villeros* were involved in these activities. Moreover, none of the elderly women interviewed in the three villas made any reference to the human rights movement.

Various neighbourhood studies draw attention to the importance of women in maintaining contacts with friends and neighbours through informal networks (Lomnitz and Pérez-Lizaur, 1979:166; Ramos, 1981:55–6; Jelín, 1991:183). This may partly have been because, while for men the workplace represented the principal focus of social life and organisation (hence the predominantly male ethos of much of the trades union movement[69]), for women these functions were more usually located in and around the home. Consequently, elderly men who were no longer working were less able to maintain social contacts than were women in the same situation.

Data for Argentina as a whole indicate that elderly women were less likely to be in employment than were men (Table 3.17). Whilst this does not take activities such as unpaid housework into account, it could have meant that elderly women had more free time to devote to local activities. It should not be assumed, however, that national patterns of economic participation were replicated in the *villas*. The disproportionate number of elderly women in local associations may also have reflected greater levels of material need or more formidable obstacles to state assistance.[70] These issues are returned to in Chapter 5, which provides detailed comparisons of the economic conditions between the sexes.

The impact of local initiatives

The local initiatives described in this chapter sought to reduce elderly *villeros'* marginal status, both in terms of access to resources and by fostering a higher social profile. In other words, they aimed to compensate for some of the gaps and dualism inherent in the macro-structures described in Chapter 3.

The impact of local initiatives varied substantially among the neighbourhoods studied. Nevertheless, some general comments can be made. The provision of direct economic aid and advice by local organisations were usually the principal functions of such organisations. Their capacity to do so was limited by a number of factors, including a lack of information about benefits and their unfamiliarity with complex bureaucratic procedures. Whilst a number of local organisations sometimes resorted to pressuring government agencies for additional resources, this was usually on an ad hoc basis rather than as a systematic strategy. Thus, they could not be considered to be pressure groups in the same sense as other pensioner protest organisations.[71] Rather than this, many local organisations actively strove to formalise and develop relations with government agencies along clientelistic or apolitical lines.

The reluctance of elderly *villero* organisations to protest against or confront the state could be interpreted in a number of ways. In one sense, it could be considered a rational strategy, averting the risk of alienating agencies which might be able to provide short-term material relief. It is unlikely that overtly political organisations would have been afforded formal recognition by local government, thus excluding them from initiatives such as the PAMI *Pro-Bienestar* programme. This might also be interpreted as a conscious strategy of top-down social control. However, the political passivity of such organisations may also have been a reflection of the double marginality of their membership. Many elderly may simply not have been able to afford the bus fare to take them to demonstrations in the city centre or may have been too frail or unwell to make the journey. There were also psychological barriers to participation in such activities. As has been shown, the repression and violence of the *Proceso* years had been particularly intense in the *villas*. This would have discouraged future political activity and increased fears of official violence. According to one elderly woman:

> If you go to Plaza de Mayo or Plaza del Congreso [scene of demonstrations] you just go and shout and what do you get out of it? You just leave all battered and bruised. That's why we won't go to Plaza de Mayo. What does it solve?...They punch you, kick you, all sorts – I've seen what they do on the television. This is what the [mockingly] *jubilados*, the *jubilados* from the Capital get up to. (Sra Eugenia B, Villa Azul, June 1993)

Moreover, elderly *villeros* generally did not equate their plight with that of *jubilados* living elsewhere in the city. According to one resident of Villa Azul:

> What do those *jubilados* from the [Federal] Capital do for people in the Province [of Buenos Aires]?...Because maybe they'll give them things if they ask for this, then for that. But the Province just gets worse...The people living badly are in the Province...The situation in the Province is very different. (Sr JS, Villa Azul, June 1993)[72]

Local organisations were more successful in providing the elderly with a social forum, including parties, classes, outings and other activities. Although these were not of a political nature they may have served to increase the confidence and collective identification of members and thus lay the foundations for future mobilisation. There were, however, few signs that this had occurred as yet in the *villas* studied.

Thus, whilst local initiatives often met with some success, they were never able to resolve all the shortcomings of the broader institutional structure of economic support for the elderly. Assuming that all the requisite factors mentioned in the previous section were in place, it is instructive to examine what 'external' effects reduced the role of local initiatives.

First, it was apparent that the elderly were generally given little attention by their fellow *villeros*. Partly because of this, many local initiatives emphasised the needs of other groups – young children, single mothers or unemployed men – rather than the aged. This bias was also reflected in local government social assistance programmes, so that often resources simply were unavailable for local organisations dealing with elderly. The marginal status of the elderly within the *villas* was compounded by the negative attitudes of outsiders towards *villeros* in general (as voiced by the Villa Azul Caritas or the *Centros de Jubilados* around Villa Zavaleta). This discouraged some neighbouring organisations from getting involved in the *villas* and deprived elderly *villeros* of the opportunity of mixing with and learning from residents of other neighbourhoods.

Local organisations seldom had good information about the range of benefits available to their members. As was seen, there was much confusion about who would be the eventual beneficiaries of PAMI's *Pro-Bienestar* programme. No organisation other than Villa Jardín's *Centro* was even aware of the existence of the *Dirección Nacional de la Ancianidad*. This mainly reflected the failing of the agencies concerned to publicise their services, which, as was shown in Chapter 3, was largely due to budget constraints and the way funds were allocated.

Since the rising number of elderly in shanty towns, many of whom lacked insurance cover, had been a relatively recent phenomenon, many external agencies had yet to adapt to the changing circumstances. This was well illustrated in PAMI's advocation of model *Centros de Jubilados*, which were geared to the needs of those who already had contributory pensions. These were clearly inappropriate to the needs of the three neighbourhoods studied here.[73] In some cases outside actors proved to be inconsistent. In the case of Caritas, assistance programmes varied very much by parish, often reflecting the preferences and concerns of the local priest. Outside aid from political agencies was extremely erratic and this was sometimes also the case for benefits provided by the state.

Local organisations in each of the three neighbourhoods often exhibited a lack of co-ordination and collaboration. This sometimes resulted in overlapping service provision, as was clearly the case in Villa Jardín, where, by mid-1993, it might have been possible to receive food parcels from a number of sources: Caritas, CUNP, the *Centro* or the *Junta Vecinal*. Similarly, legal advice might have been obtained from either CUNP, the *Centro* or the *Junta*. This lack of co-ordination may even lead to rivalry when organisations are competing for the same resources from an outside agency. In Villa Jardín, both the *Centro* and the *Junta* made requests for food aid from Lanús Council. In Villa Azul, the *Grupo* and *Sociedad de Fomento* fought over council funding for a meeting hall.[74]

Common services, common links with external agencies and, most importantly, a common aim to alleviate the poverty of elderly are all very strong reasons for organisations to develop close mutual ties. Several factors may explain why this often failed to occur. These included:

(i) The fear of compromising religious or political status. This was apparent in Villa Jardín's *Centro's* attitude to the *Junta*. Similarly, Church organisations were often bound by hierarchical guidelines about collaboration with other agencies.[75] The local Caritas in Villa Azul had very little knowledge of initiatives inside the *villa*, and vice versa.

(ii) A lack of information. Ignorance of other organisations may lead to suspicions and false claims that they 'never get things done'.

(iii) Personal motives. As was seen in Villa Zavaleta, failure to co-operate may result from personal conflicts between key members of organisations. These individuals may shy away from links with other groups because they fear their own positions of authority could be usurped. This fear was apparent in the attitudes of the *Grupo*'s old committee to the *Sociedad de Fomento* in Villa Azul.

A key theme throughout this chapter has been the 'double marginality' faced by elderly shanty town residents: the marginality of the slum and the marginality of old age. Local initiatives have sought to reduce this marginality but, in the case of Villa Zavaleta at least, were often unable to overcome the barriers it imposed. State agencies sometimes compounded this marginality through their own prejudices or their inability to adapt to changing circumstances. Whilst the experiences of the three *villas* were very mixed, all of them displayed less propensity for local organisation than more affluent neighbourhoods. Community-specific income maintenance was shown to be patchy and biased against the most vulnerable groups of elderly. This compounded the fragmentary and skewed pattern of coverage afforded by agencies outside the *villas*. At the same time, the exceptional success of Villa Jardín's *Centro* shows what can be achieved through enlightened outside actors and should be considered a model to be applied in other poor urban neighbourhoods.

5 The Case-studies: Individual Strategies

INTRODUCTION

This chapter focuses on the economic experiences of individual elderly *villeros*, which complement the macro and community-level perspectives given in the two preceding chapters. Its findings are largely based on two sources of data, a household questionnaire survey and a number of longer, semi-structured interviews. The chapter begins with an explanation of the methodology. The data are then presented and analysed. This analysis includes comparisons between the different neighbourhoods studied and according to a range of other criteria such as gender and previous employment. It looks at different sources of income in isolation, before examining them as a whole. A central concern is to demonstrate the complexity of potential income maintenance strategies pursued by elderly *villeros*. These strategies are located in a broader context of economic marginality and barriers to state protection. As such, they reflect the multiple constraints facing poor urban elderly rather more than the opportunities open to them.

SURVEY METHODOLOGY

The questionnaire survey was conducted in the three *villas* between November 1992 and June 1993. It did not aim to provide a representative sample of all elderly *villeros* living in Greater Buenos Aires and its findings should be not be interpreted as such. The number of returns for two neighbourhoods (Villa Jardín and Villa Azul) was large enough to be representative for all elderly living there. As such, they can be treated as two specific case-studies, continuing the analysis of the preceding chapter. Unfortunately, the number of questionnaires completed in Villa Zavaleta was much smaller due to the high risk of assault. In this case, the returns cannot be assumed to be representative for elderly in the *villa* as a whole. Because of this, data from Villa Zavaleta are only used when grouped with findings from the other two neighbourhoods.

The questionnaire survey includes 129 separate households, each with at least one member aged over 55, giving a total of 181 'elderly' *villeros*. Whilst the survey sets out to provide a representative sample of the economic conditions of the elderly living in each *villa*, it does not make use of orthodox sampling techniques. Given the lack of a complete, single source of information on the addresses of households containing elderly, it was impossible to construct sampling frames embracing whole *villas* or even sections of them. Instead of selecting a random sample, the survey identified a number of streets whose housing and infrastructure appeared representative of the *villa* and interviewed all the available elderly living on them. Whilst this method does not yield data as robust as a properly conducted random sample, its reliability is high since the size of the sample relative to the total universe is large.

The questionnaire is broken down into several sections.[1] These concern: (i) living conditions, household composition and quality of accommodation; (ii) individual data for elderly members, including labour histories, access to state benefits, economic relations with family and neighbours and other income sources; (iii) the interviewee's appraisal of his or her own condition; and (iv) a recapitulation and summary of the income sources of the elderly individual.

Difficulties encountered in conducting the survey included obtaining the addresses of households with elderly, gaining access to them and ensuring the reliability of responses. The problem of addresses was resolved in several ways: first, by using membership registers of local organisations dealing with the elderly; secondly, by relying on the personal knowledge of local community leaders and thirdly, by asking interviewees for contacts with other elderly living nearby. This provided a good mix of members of various local organisations as well as people with no links to any group. Working with organisations which were generally well-respected in the *villas*, also ensured safety and helped gain entrance into households and obtain the trust of their members.[2]

The problem of reliability was less easily resolved. In cases where the respondent was clearly confused, his or her answers contradictory or where the information given clearly contrasted with the evidence of the interviewer's own eyes (such as the man eating beef steak and reading that day's newspaper, whilst claiming to be living on an extremely low income), the lack of reliability was recorded in the questionnaire. Of the 129 households surveyed, 11 were identified as apparently unreliable. Rather than excluding the data provided from these cases and thus imply that all this information is false and that all the remainder is correct, no such distinction is made. Instead, the proportion of apparently reliable results is used as a rough indicator of the degree of reliability of the survey as a whole.

Information about the value of household income is probably the least reliable of the data sets obtained from the questionnaires and interviews and for this reason is not used as a major element in the elaboration of the research. Elderly residents were not always aware of the income of all household members. Figures given for earnings for similar occupations, such as domestic service, often varied to such a degree that they could not be assumed to be reliable. Also, some income sources, such as occasional gifts of food from neighbours, were difficult to quantify. Because of these limitations, the analysis of income values is restricted to identifying those sources which provide a substantial income and those which are less significant.

The questionnaire survey was followed up by 11 more detailed semi-structured interviews. The households interviewed were selected to represent the various types of income maintenance strategy encountered in the questionnaires: pensions, odd jobs, reliance on family support and so forth. These interviews were recorded and serve, in part, to illustrate the findings of the household survey. However, they also provide a source of richer, qualitative insights, which complement the narrower focus of the questionnaire.

It should be stressed that neither the questionnaire nor the interviews seek to provide an objective, 'correct' view of the income maintenance opportunities afforded elderly *villeros*. Rather, they give a subjective version of reality, which may at times be at odds with that held by better-informed actors and may even contradict itself. This is useful in two respects. First, the perceptions of elderly *villeros* of surrounding phenomena condition the way they respond to them. Secondly, disparities between the views held by such individuals and larger agencies reflect the incomplete diffusion of information both from above to below and vice versa. It is, however, important to avoid confusing the views held by respondents with those of the author. Attention is drawn to cases where there are clear discrepancies between the two and reasons are put forward to account for the particular views of the respondent.

SURVEY RESULTS

General characteristics and origins

Table 5.1 shows the age and sex structure of the sample survey. The gender distribution is more biased towards women than is the case in Argentina as whole.[3] This may have simply reflected a greater likelihood that women were available to answer questionnaires (although information about men in the same households would have been automatically provided). Another possibility is that differentials between male and female adult life expectancy were greater in the *villas* than elsewhere, perhaps due to violence, harsh working conditions and the more widespread occurrence of alcohol abuse among men. Since the sample is not fully representative, these conclusions cannot be extended to poor elderly in Buenos Aires as a whole. Nevertheless, they raise the question to what extent old age and urban poverty is a predominantly female issue.

Table 5.1: Age and sex structure of sample households, 1992/3

	55–59	60–64	65–69	70–74	75–79	80+	Total
Azul men	1	6	9	6	0	3	25
Azul women	1	7	11	5	4	2	30
Jardín men	6	6	12	10	1	5	40
Jardín women	5	14	22	8	3	3	55
Zava men	1	4	4	2	1	1	13
Zava women	6	3	1	2	3	3	18
All men	8	16	25	18	2	9	78
All women	12	24	34	15	10	8	103
Total	20	40	59	33	12	17	181

Source: Questionnaire, Buenos Aires, 1992–3 (Villa Azul, Villa Jardín and Villa Zavaleta).

The age distribution also differs in a number of ways from the national pattern. The higher number of elderly in the 65–9 age group, compared to those in younger cohorts is not easily explained. It may have occurred because larger numbers of younger age groups were in full-time employment and therefore unavailable for interview. Also, younger age groups may not have considered themselves to be elderly and therefore may not have joined local organisations. Since the age of an individual can affect his or her potential entitlement to numerous state benefits, it follows that the lower proportion of elderly in younger age sets should be reflected in above-average levels of access to state benefits.

Table 5.2: Place of birth

	Greater Buenos Aires	Other part of Argentina	Overseas
Azul	2 (3.7%)	46 (83.6%)	7 (12.7%)
Jardín	6 (6.3%)	81 (85.3%)	8 (8.4%)
Zavaleta	6 (19.4%)	23 (74.2%)	2 (6.5%)
Total	14 (7.7%)	150 (82.9%)	17 (9.4%)

Source: Questionnaire, Buenos Aires, 1992–3.

Table 5.2 shows elderly *villeros'* places of birth. In both Villa Jardín and Villa Azul the majority came from Argentine provinces lying beyond Greater Buenos Aires. Most of these were provinces in the far north-east and north-west of the country, rather than the surrounding Pampas region or relatively nearby cities such as Rosario or Córdoba. General surveys of internal migration between 1947 and 1980 found that these less distant locations accounted for the highest proportion of those coming to Greater Buenos Aires (Torrado, 1992:85–9). There was, therefore, a heavy regional bias among those migrants who settled in the two *villas*. This was not surprising, since the relative poverty of northern Argentina meant that this group would have been unable to afford housing elsewhere in the city.

As such, the data in Table 5.2 support the general view that *villas* served, at least initially, as reception centres for opportunistic migration from impoverished rural districts. This is reflected in the experiences of Sra EC of Villa Jardín:

> When I was fourteen or so...in Posadas in [the north-eastern province of] Misiones, it's part of Argentina you know...first, I worked in the Misiones regional hospital in my village...cleaning...and then I started work in the maternity ward...I was nineteen when I came here [the *villa*] from Misiones...to get my midwifery qualification.
>
> (Sra EC, Villa Jardín, February 1993)

However, it would be dangerous to assume that movement to the *villas* always resulted from economic opportunism. The relatively recent origins of such settlements suggest that the small number of *villeros* who were native to the city had mainly originated from less precarious neighbourhoods. For this group, arrival in the *villa* was more likely to have resulted from economic destitution rather than opportunism (that is, 'push' rather than 'pull' factors). This was clearly illustrated by the circumstances of Sra HF, a resident of Villa Azul:

> We left [La Boca in the Federal Capital] because my daddy had come to live in Bernal [in Quilmes municipality]. There we lived in a very big house...Daddy kept animals and we were very comfortable. Then, you know how it is, one person got ill and then the next one did. Doctors and other blokes, loan sharks, had us over a barrel. They just came and took their money. What with all the expenses and one thing and another, they took away our house. When daddy died, we had to move somewhere else in Bernal with mummy...We rented a place until mummy died...Then my brother came and said 'What are you going to do? Mummy's dead and

> you're living here all on your own. Come and with me to live in Córdoba...' Then I got ill...because the air is so strong out there...So I came back to Bernal... a good friend of my mummy's lent me a plot of land...but the lady had to sell it. So we grabbed our things and came to live in the *villa*.
>
> (Sra HF, Villa Azul, June 1993)

Sra HF's demise partly reflected a failure of the social security system to compensate for the cost of nursing and the loss of the household's main breadwinner, her father. At the time of his death, in the early 1930s, public healthcare and insurance were still at an early stage of development. Her difficulties were compounded by the failure of other family members to provide for a vulnerable relative – her vague comment about the 'strong air' of Córdoba may have been a means of avoiding reference to a family dispute. Similar references were made at other points in her interview. Whilst the experience of Sra HF was by no means typical, it shows that the course by which elderly individuals came to live in the *villas* was sometimes very complex and cannot always be reduced to a single set of circumstances.

Only 17 elderly were born overseas and all but four of these were from Paraguay. Interestingly, only four foreigners received any type of state insurance or assistance benefit. Comparisons of factors such as past employment and date of arrival show no significant difference to Argentine nationals. Whilst Argentine citizenship is not a requirement for obtaining most state benefits, possession of documents proving the right of residence is.[4] Since, however, almost 90 per cent of elderly *villeros* were native Argentines, this problem should not have had a substantial influence on general patterns of access to benefits.

Table 5.3: Date of arrival (Villa Azul and Villa Jardín)

	Azul	Jardín	Total*
Before 1950	0	28 (29.8%)	28 (18.8%)
1951–60	11 (20.0%)	34 (36.2%)	45 (30.2%)
1961–70	20 (36.4%)	18 (19.1%)	38 (25.5%)
1971–80	11 (20.0%)	6 (6.4%)	27 (18.1%)
1981–90	9 (16.4%)	1 (1.1%)	10 (6.7%)
Since 1990	4 (7.3%)	2 (2.1%)	6 (4.0%)
Do not remember	0	5 (5.3%)	5 (3.4%)

*This excludes Villa Zavaleta, many of whose residents were simply relocated from *villas* elsewhere in the city.

Source: Questionnaire, Buenos Aires, 1992–3.

Table 5.3 shows the date at which the elderly came to live in the respective *villas*. The higher proportion of elderly coming to Villa Jardín before 1970 reflects that settlement's relatively early foundation and the use of all available land by this time. The date elderly arrived in the *villas* is significant in a number of respects. First, those elderly who arrived in Villa Jardín and Villa Azul after 1990 displayed various differences from the sample as a whole. In all but one case their children owned the house in which they lived and in every case family support was their principal source of income. This indicates that they came to the *villas* because they had no other source of economic support and were unable to maintain a separate household. Secondly, the proportion of elderly in Villa Jardín whose principal employment had been in the formal sector was roughly twice as high for those who arrived before 1960 than for those who came subsequently.[5] Similarly, the proportion of those lacking a benefit was twice as high for post-1960 arrivals as for those who arrived before 1960.[6] These relationships reflect the broader shifts of employment and the dynamics of *villa* growth outlined in Chapter 2. By using 1970 as a cut-off point in Villa Azul no significant differences occur. This is probably because levels of formal sector employment were generally much lower there.

Principal lifetime employment

Table 5.4 refers to the principal occupations held by respondents during their working lives. As was shown in Chapter 2, Argentina's economic performance after the Second World War was highly erratic, with marked cycles of growth and decline. Moreover, from the 1960s there was a steady increase in the relative importance of the urban informal sector. This increased the probability that elderly *villeros* had changed their occupations at least once, if not frequently, during their working lives. The necessity to keep the questionnaire short and simple prevented the collection of precise information about individual labour histories. Thus, rather than provide full accounts of each respondent's past experiences, the analysis is restricted to those occupations which respondents perceived as their principal job.

Patterns of male employment in the two *villas* were fairly similar, although a slightly higher share of those in Villa Jardín (53 per cent) were engaged in factory work or other formal activities than was the case for Villa Azul (44 per cent). This may have been because Villa Jardín was founded earlier and was located closer to erstwhile concentrations of heavy industry along the Riachuelo River. However, the small number of men surveyed prevents more concrete conclusions. In both *villas*, principal male employment was split roughly evenly into urban formal and urban informal activities, whilst only a very small number had been rural workers. This is in line with the finding that the vast majority of respondents had lived in the *villas* for more than 20 years.

Table 5.4 Principal employment during lifetime[7]

Villa	Sex	Factory work	Other formal sector work	Construction	Domestic service	Other urban informal sector work[8]	Rural work	Housework
Azul	M	7	4	10	0	1	3	0
	F	1	0	0	21	2	2	4
Jard	M	13	8	7	0	10	2	0
	F	8	2	0	27	3	0	15
Total*	M	23	15	23	0	12	5	0
	F	10	4	0	54	7	3	25

* Includes Villa Zavaleta.

Source: Questionnaire, Buenos Aires, 1992–3.

Male employment was much more diverse than that of females, who were almost entirely engaged in domestic service or housework. However, even within female employment there were clear differences between the two *villas*. In Villa Jardín a larger proportion were engaged in housework and a small but significant group found employment in factories. The increased likelihood of unpaid housework in Villa Jardín may have been related to higher overall levels of male formal employment there, which, if better remunerated, would have reduced the need for female waged labour. At least half of women who had been engaged in housework had husbands who participated in the formal sector.[9] Greater opportunities for formal employment around Villa Jardín would also explain the success of some women in obtaining factory work.

Domestic service accounted for at least 52 per cent of female employment in all *villas*, rising to 70 per cent in Villa Azul. This compared to 6–8 per cent for the national workforce (both sexes) between 1950 and 1992 (PREALC, 1992, 1993). The extended interviews indicated that this concentration was due to a lack of alternatives rather than any genuine preference. Sra JM put it bluntly:

> I didn't have any education. I didn't have anything. So was I going to walk along swinging my handbag in the air, go with men, become a whore? It was the only alternative. (Sra JM, Villa Jardín, February 1993)

Within domestic service there were differing degrees of formality, reflected in whether the worker was paid on an hourly or monthly basis. The latter was more stable and sometimes afforded the employee more rights. One interviewee noted that her daughter-in-law, who was paid by the hour, did not receive the annual bonus, whereas she herself used to.[10] Another contrasted the unstable, casual nature of her hourly work with the security of her monthly paid job as a hotel cleaner. Very few of those interviewed had lived in the houses where they had been employed. More typically, domestic service was a part-time occupation and was often combined with other jobs as well as housework. According to Sra EC:

> I used to work in lots of different houses in the Capital. Sometimes it was by the hour, sometimes by the month. Sometimes I worked in the morning by the hour and in the afternoon by the month...Do you know why? Because I had children and so that I could get more money, well, you understand? (Sra EC, Villa Jardín, February 1993)

Thus, although factors such as date of arrival in Greater Buenos Aires and location exerted some influence over principal lifetime employment, gender divisions had the strongest effect. Individual testimonies indicate that the higher proportion of men in the formal sector mainly reflected a lack of opportunities for women, rather than their desire to pursue informal employment.

Contributions and benefits

Table 5.5 shows respondents' social security contributions, along with their sex and principal employment. It is probable that the figures for those who made some or all the required contributions are slightly exaggerated, since not all respondents produced documentation to verify their claims. A number of reasons were given for this, some of which were more credible than others. In one case, an elderly *villero* stubbornly claimed to have made contributions to the self-employed workers' fund for longer than it had been in existence. Several maintained that they had lost their papers in fires or floods. The physical conditions of *villas* (wooden structures, accumulations of litter, lack of drainage) may have increased the likelihood of such events. Others claimed to have left their paperwork behind before migrating to Buenos Aires. Since it was impossible to assess which of these accounts were accurate, it may well have been that levels of social insurance evasion were higher than those indicated.

For the three main national funds, a minimum of 15 years' contributions was required to be eligible for a pension. There were pronounced differences between the sexes, with 53 per cent of men having made all the required contributions and only 15 per cent of women. The respective figures for no contributions were 24 and 72 per cent. It was, however, difficult to establish whether the underlying cause for these differences was gender or occupation. In exclusively female activities, such as domestic service and housework, levels of contribution were extremely low. Nevertheless, when women worked elsewhere, they were as likely to make contributions as were men. These relationships between occupation and contributions roughly coincide with information obtained for Argentina as a whole (Frediani, 1989:80).

Table 5.5: Principal lifetime employment and social security contributions

	Type of work	Sufficient to qualify	Insufficient	None
Women	Domestic	5	8	41
	House	0	1	24
	Urban informal sector	0	1	6
	Factory	8	2	0
	Other formal sector	2	2	0
	Rural	0	0	3
	Total	15 (15%)	14 (14%)	74 (72%)
Men	Construction	11	5	7
	Urban informal sector	1	4	7
	Factory	18	4	1
	Other formal sector	11	3	1
	Rural	0	2	3
	Total	41 (53%)	18 (23%)	19 (24%)
Total		56 (31%)	32 (18%)	93 (51%)

Source: Questionnaire, Buenos Aires, 1992–3.

Interviewees who made no contributions put forward a number of explanations. In some cases it was pointed out that formal social security protection did not exist for the activities they were engaged in until relatively late in their working lives. More frequently, however, a lack of spare cash was the main reason. Sra JM observed:

> I was worried about the future but I needed a hundred of those little pesos, the type that don't exist any more. I needed them to be able to get a *jubilación*, to make the contributions, to be able to go to a *jubilación* fund. Well, us women are always worried about keeping up the house.
>
> (Sra JM, Villa Jardín, February 1993)

In such cases exclusion from social insurance would appear to have been a matter of constraint rather than choice. Sra JM's testimony suggests that policies which lead to a fall in real wage levels or redistribute income away from poorer groups will have an adverse effect on social insurance coverage. However, her husband, who also failed to make insurance contributions, put forward another set of reasons:

> I always used to work in a firm called 'Picasso' in Luna Park. And then the firm finished because the boss was already pretty old. So I began to work for myself, doing *changas* [odd jobs], always *changas*, nothing else...I made about three months' contributions, when I was working for one company...[I ask if he was ever worried about the future]. No, to tell you the truth I wasn't. Because once I left them I always worked in black...I had all my work papers but because you earned more working in black, well. Imagine it. At that time we earned 150, 120. That was talking money!...So it paid me to work like that. And I did. I've been working like that ever since. (Sr OM, Villa Jardín, February 1993)

Here, exclusion from social insurance involved elements of both choice and constraint. A lack of occupational stability, with frequent shifts from self-employment to working in semi-formal firms, discouraged continued contributions. In the case of Sr OM, this might have required transferring from the general employees' (or, before 1967, construction workers') fund to the self-employed one and back again. At the same time, Sr OM showed a clear preference for 'working in black'. This reflected a number of considerations, which should not be dismissed as irresponsibility or an unwillingness to defer consumption. Ageing was a fairly recent phenomenon in the *villas* and, as such, making provision for later life may not have been perceived to be economically rational. It is possible that *villeros* were aware, at least to some degree, of the vagaries of insurance benefit values and the high levels of administrative wastage in such programmes. These, coupled with bureaucratic obstacles, may have meant that the perceived opportunity cost of pursuing contributions was higher than the future benefits. Working in relatively informal activities afforded some *villeros* an opportunity to opt out of insurance programmes which was denied to formal sector workers.

Comparing the testimonies of Sra JM and her husband would seem to support the conventional wisdom that female breadwinners tend to devote a greater proportion of their income to general household expenses than do men.[11] One outcome of this would be that women have less disposable income to pay for social security contributions. More specifically, the very low levels of coverage for women working in domestic service sometimes occurred because they did not expect their employers to pay their own share of contributions. According to one elderly woman:

> I could have paid...But you know that when you work by the hour the *patrones* [domestic employers] don't have anything to do with the domestic service fund, they don't pay them, they don't discount you or anything. So why would a person want to pay if she isn't going to keep her half of the deal? That's what happens. (Sra AG, Villa Jardín, March 1993)

Other interviewees, both male and female, who expressed an opinion generally blamed themselves for not making contributions, admitting that they could have found the money if they had really wanted to. Sra EC observed:

> *EC*: You had to make your contributions, you know. I worked as a cleaner and I had to pay into the cleaners' fund...but I never did.
> [*Interviewer*: Because you didn't have enough money to?]
> *EC*: No. I just didn't want to.
> [*Interviewer*: Didn't you think about the future?]
> *EC*: No, I never thought. That's the way it was...I had money before...enough to bring up my children and even buy a little house. (Sra EC, Villa Jardín, February 1993)

However, in blaming themselves, it is possible that some respondents were taking an idealised view of their earlier circumstances which played down the hardships they had had to face at that time. This confusion was apparent in one interviewee who stated:

> Yes, of course I was irresponsible not to pay them [contributions] – I had to pay them. But I couldn't find the money.
> (Sra AG, Villa Jardín, March 1993)

Taken together, these testimonies indicate that the reasons why a relatively high proportion of elderly *villeros* did not make contributions were complex and cannot simply be reduced to choice and constraint. Attention must be paid to the opportunity costs as perceived by the elderly *villeros* during their prime working years. What was the rationale of making contributions if, in the meantime, the individual would not have enough income to subsist, the individual was unlikely to reach old age or the benefits received did not match the resources (both financial and paperwork) paid in? Whilst it would be unrealistic to assume that respondents' past decisions had been entirely based on a considered appraisal of opportunity costs, the interviews indicate a general awareness of these issues.

Table 5.5 also shows that 22 per cent of respondents had made some contributions but that these were insufficient to make them eligible for an insurance benefit. The only occupation where this did not occur was factory work. It should be noted that such individuals were unable to withdraw their partial payments and thus directly financed pensions which were denied to them. The average amount of contributions made by respondents in this category was seven years.

The payment of some, but not all, insurance contributions cannot be explained in terms of past perceptions of opportunity costs. In some cases, respondents had planned to make the required number of payments but had lost their jobs. An extreme case was that of Sra AG, who claimed (probably exaggerating) that she had lost her job only lacking one month's contributions:

> I went to the fund...and they told me that I'd have to pay a thousand and something. And I couldn't...I didn't have enough money. I didn't have enough to make up the [outstanding] contributions...it was a lot of money to have to pay. (Sra AG, Villa Jardín, February 1993)

Although no interviewees made reference to it, it is possible that some *villeros* were forced to discontinue contributions from the mid-1970s as formal employment contracted, real wage levels fell and income distribution worsened.

Tables 5.6 and 5.7 show the number of respondents who received the various types of state benefit. The proportion over the minimum retirement age (65 for men, 60 for women) who received no insurance benefits was 63 per cent: far higher than figures for Greater Buenos Aires or Argentina as a whole.[12] However, the proportion who received no benefits whatsoever accounted for only 45 per cent of the total. This was because assistance benefits were almost as widespread as social insurance pensions (49 and 51 respondents respectively). Available data show that assistance coverage for the city as a whole was much lower than this, indicating that the low level of insurance coverage in *villas* was partly off-set by a degree of targeting of assistance benefits.[13] As is shown in Table 5.7, average assistance benefits (113 pesos per month) were worth substantially less than insurance ones (185 pesos). Even so, the importance of assistance pensions in the *villas* studied was beyond dispute. To date, the general literature on social security in developing regions has neglected the importance of such non-contributory pensions for the poor.

Table 5.6: Type of social security benefits held

	Total	Men	Women	Azul	Jardín
None	82 (45%)	37 (47%)	45 (44%)	29 (53)	39 (41)
Spouse D	7	6	1	0	7
Spouse A	2	2	0	0	0
Spouse I	12	1	11	3	6
Employee	31	23	8	7	21
Public	3	3	0	1	1
Self Emp.	3	1	2	1	1
Widow(er)	14	0	14	1	7
Total ins	51 (28%)	27 (35%)	24 (23%)	10 (18%)	30 (32%)
Old age	21	6	15	15	4
Invalid	8	3	5	1	2
DNA	20	5	15	0	20
Total ast	49 (27%)	14 (18%)	35 (34%)	16 (29%)	26 (27%)

Key: None = Receive no benefit, but spouse may do so.
Spouse D = Spouse with DNA.
Spouse A = Spouse with assistance benefit.
Spouse I = Spouse with insurance benefit.
Employee = Private employees' insurance benefit.
Public = Public employees' insurance benefit.
Self emp. = Self-employed insurance benefit.
Widow(er) = Widow(er) insurance benefit.
Total ins = Total insurance benefits.
Old age = Assistance benefit for elderly.
Invalid = Invalidity assistance benefit.
DNA = *Dirección Nacional de la Ancianidad* subsidy.
Total ast = Total assistance benefits and subsidies.

Source: Questionnaire, Buenos Aires, 1992–3.

Table 5.7: Average benefit values (1993 pesos)

	Average	Maximum	Minimum
Employee	185	310	140
Public*	320	500	210
Self emp.*	243	450	140
Widow(er)	170	245	140
Assist.	113	140	110
Invalid.	122	153	102
DNA	100	100	100
Men	143	500	100
Women	113	450	100
Total	125	500	100

*The low numbers of respondents with these benefits reduce the reliability of these figures.

Source: Questionnaire, Buenos Aires, 1992–3.

As with principal employment, there were sharp divisions between men and women in the distribution of state benefits. Men (35 per cent) were more likely to receive an insurance benefit than were women (23 per cent). This largely reflected the greater likelihood that men had made contributions during their working lives. Conversely, a much higher proportion of women (34 per cent) received assistance benefits than did men (18 per cent). This meant that a slightly higher overall proportion of women received some form of benefit, although, as Table 5.7 shows, the average value of their benefits was less than those received by men. Also, women were more likely to have a spouse with an insurance pension. However, whether this was of benefit to them depended on the degree of pooling of income. Pooling between couples could not be taken for granted: according to Sra JM:

> If I'm without I wouldn't even ask him [points to husband] for help. I know that he has money but I wouldn't ask him for any. I wouldn't ask for money even to buy bread, even to buy an aspirin.
>
> (Sra JM, Villa Jardín, February 1993)

Comparisons between *villas* also reveal some important differences. At 53 per cent, the proportion of residents of Villa Azul without any benefit was clearly higher than in Villa Jardín (41 per cent). This difference was largely accounted for by access to insurance pensions, which, in turn, reflected the levels of formal employment in the two *villas*. In Villa Jardín 32 per cent received insurance benefits, compared to only 18 per cent in Villa Azul. Levels of access to assistance were very similar in the two locations, but there were important differences in the type of benefit. Whilst DNA grants accounted for the vast majority of assistance benefits in Villa Jardín, nobody in Villa Azul received or had even heard of them. Conversely, Villa Jardín contained a far smaller proportion of elderly in receipt of better paid and more reliable assistance pensions. Thus, in Villa Jardín economic divisions between *jubilados* and other elderly respondents were more pronounced than in Villa Azul. These variations largely resulted from the particular contacts and information at the disposal of local organisations and testified to the impact of such activities.

As Table 5.7 shows, in every case average benefit values were only a small fraction of 1250 pesos, the amount which the state statistics agency estimated was needed to provide for the basic requirements of a 'typical' household in 1992.[14] All of those who expressed an opinion in the extended interviews claimed that the benefits fell a long way short of meeting their basic needs. According to one elderly man in Villa Azul:

> It's impossible, impossible. Try to imagine it. How can we survive for a month on a million, one hundred [110] pesos? How much does bread cost us? How much does a kilo of sugar cost us?...Now bread's gone up [in price] to 8 pesos to buy half a kilo.[15]

The same man estimated that his assistance pension was roughly a third of the money he required to eat and dress himself properly. According to Sra Eugenia B, whose husband had an insurance pension:

> Because this money that the government gives you doesn't even last for 15 days...Why should I have to wait in line three or four hours for a pathetic amount of money?...Because I can't just live like that, just bread and water...Some people tell us 'Well you're alright because he's got his *jubilación*.' [she laughs] They don't know what it's really like...the pathetic amount of money the government gives us.
>
> (Sra Eugenia B, Villa Azul, June 1993)

Whilst a large number of residents of Villa Jardín had been in receipt of the DNA grant, most complained that the benefit had been paid irregularly and so could not be budgeted for. None had received payment for several months at the time of the interviews and few expected the benefit to be resumed. Most recognised that, unlike pensions, payment of grants was not obligatory:

> Now they're not going to pay us any more...They owe us lots. Well no, no they don't owe us because it isn't really our money.
>
> (Sr OM, Villa Jardín, February 1993)

If the discontinuation of the DNA grant is taken into account, access to state benefits for women in Villa Jardín was far more limited than in Villa Azul. Indeed, insurance pensions become almost the only available source of state support in Villa Jardín. This underlines the importance of securing guaranteed payment for both insurance and assistance benefits.

The means-tested PAMI supplement for *jubilaciones* was introduced during the period of interviewing. Consequently, it was not possible to ascertain its overall distribution, although later interviews with *jubilados* in Villa Azul showed that a large proportion had not obtained the supplement. Occasionally, *villeros* would refer to other forms of state support, including food aid. However, no elderly villeros directly benefited from this type of assistance during the interview period.

Given the contributions requirement, it is logical that variations in access to insurance pensions were largely conditioned by previous employment. By contrast, the distribution of assistance was most strongly governed first by location and then by gender. The locational effect is easily explained by the irregular diffusion of information about different benefits and the haphazard nature of contacts between local organisations and the authorities. Reasons why uninsured women should be more likely to receive assistance than their male counterparts are less obvious. There was no evidence of conscious targeting by support agencies. As was mentioned in Chapter 4, a disproportionately large number of women actively participated in local organisations in the three neighbourhoods studied. This may have in part reflected a greater degree of female involvement in informal networks. As a result, women would have been better-informed about available support.

Present employment

Table 5.8 shows that roughly a quarter of respondents were still employed at the time of interviewing. Whilst levels of economic activity for 60–64-year-olds were not much higher than those recorded for Argentina as a whole (27.55 per cent in 1990 – see Table 3.17), employment of over-64-year-old *villeros* was much higher than the national average (7.2 per cent). This indicates that elderly *villeros* were more likely to remain in employment than were their counterparts in other neighbourhoods.

Table 5.8: Present employment

Type of work	Under 65 years	65 years and over	Total
Urban informal sector	10	11	21
Domestic service	6	2	8
Construction	2	6	8
Informal laundry	2	3	5
Factory	1	1	2
Other formal sector	1	1	2
Total	23 (37%)	25 (21%)	48 (26%)

Source: Questionnaire, Buenos Aires, 1992–3.

A national survey of elderly attitudes cited in Chapter 3 found far more expressed a desire to continue working than were able to do so. As such, the disproportionately large number of *villeros* who continued employment into old age could have resulted from privileged access to work. However, it may have also have been because elderly *villeros*, as a result of their greater necessity, performed tasks which other groups would have shunned. Also, casual forms of employment, such as clothes washing and odd jobs, which accounted for a high share of *villero* employment, may not have been registered in larger, official surveys. Consequently, disparities between the *villas* and other areas may have been smaller than the data indicate.

The survey results show that a large proportion of elderly *villeros* would have liked to have obtained employment had they had been capable of working. The incidence of severe health problems and frailty explain why levels of economic activity were far lower among over-65-year-olds than for younger respondents. Several respondents had been forced to abandon work because of accident or illness. Of those without either employment or a benefit, 31 (46 per cent) claimed to have serious health problems. According to Sr JJ:

> I don't work because I can't, thanks to the business with this knee of mine which I can't rely on...Really, I need to go about the place, doing things since the money I have isn't enough. But I haven't been able to...for a year now. (Sr JJ, Villa Azul, June 1993)

Employment opportunities were also limited by rising levels of unemployment in Greater Buenos Aires at this time. By 1993 this had reached 11.1 per cent, the highest level ever recorded. Some interviewees pointed out that even younger household members often had difficulty finding work.

The data for present employment show far smaller proportions working in the formal sector than was the case for principal lifetime occupation. This is in keeping with findings for elderly in Argentina as a whole and was the result of two processes. First, it reflected the withdrawal of formal sector workers from the labour force. Of the 50 respondents principally engaged in formal activities, only 12 were still working at the time of the interview. Employment patterns also reflected the transferral of formal labour into the informal sector. Seven of the 22 working in *changas* had originally been formal sector workers.

As explained in Chapter 3, increased informality was part of a more general downgrading of employment between the respondents' main periods of economic activity and their old age. The great majority (73 per cent) were working on a casual, part-time basis, which reflected the limited availability of employment rather than their desire to work fewer hours. According to Sr OM:

> *OM*: I do *changas* when there are any, but right now they're screwed...You see, when there are any *changas* I'll go and do them. Every two or three months, every month, maybe every week there'll be some *changas* that I can do and so I get on with them.

[Wife interrupts: Come on. You haven't done any work for the past five months.]

OM: You know, the other day there was this *changa* and they told me to come back the next day for the money. [Emphatically] 200000 australes! [20 pesos]. But then they didn't have any money. Well, what do you expect me to do, what do you expect me to say?

(Sr OM, Villa Jardín, February 1993)

A similar process of downgrading occurred for women who had been working in domestic service. The physical rigours of this work meant that only a small minority (22 per cent) of these continued in employment. Of these only one, a 60-year-old, was engaged on a full-time basis. Several moved into informal laundry work, an occupation which none had pursued during their prime working years. The low income and, possibly, the social stigma attached to this activity may explain why no younger residents covered in the survey worked as washerwomen. One interviewee with a crippled arm washed clothes, whilst her retarded son would wring them for her. She was aware of the resulting stigma:

I do it sometimes, sometimes Mondays and Tuesdays. When the weather's fine like today for example, then I can wash. Today I could wash. The clothes would dry and tomorrow I could iron everything...They pay by the dozen [items], 60 or 70 [6 or 7 pesos] for the dozen...I only do it because I need to...I mean, I could wash twice a week, every week...I don't have any problems about it. When my neighbours come 'Can you do this for me?' 'Yes, I need the money.' And I have to do it because I need the money.

(Sra EC, Villa Jardín, February 1993)

Another female interviewee, Sra VT, found an alternative form of employment to domestic service and clothes washing: assembling small metal components for a local factory. She was able to do this at home but had to work very long hours to obtain an adequate income:

The lady who lives behind me used to do it. I used to work with her because she's on their books. Well, these things are called 'collectors'. They say that they're used to make bobbins. That's what they say. I take them from the factory...When I finish them off I take them back and if they have any more they give me those, I do them again, bring them back and that's the way it is...[interviewer asks if she is paid well] No. I get paid for the

> month...sometimes I may get seven hundred and something [70 pesos] and sometimes six hundred and something. Its never enough for me, never.
>
> (Sra VT, Villa Azul, June 1993)

Unlike her neighbour, Sra VT was not on the factory's 'books' and therefore had no formal or legal status with her employer. The fact that she went to the factory in person indicates that the company actively colluded with her illegal employment as a means of reducing labour costs.

It is unclear to what extent this downgrading of labour was related to lifecycle transitions and how much it resulted from the general contraction of formal employment in the city since the 1960s. Many *villeros* who had worked in factories, the docks or the railways were made redundant by closures. One interviewee explained how her deceased husband had lost his job as a stevedore during a bitter dock strike:

> And then in this port there was some bother, I don't know what, and he didn't go there any more. I've no idea what happened. They closed down and then people started to go back to work. But he didn't go back there any more. He started up with his *changas*. Just *changas* and he never made any more [social insurance] contributions.[16]

Conversely, despite the rapid decline in middle-class standards of living during the 1980s, domestic service was still the predominant form of female *villero* employment and elderly participation here was only limited by frailty.

Thus, the possibility of obtaining income through continued employment was restricted by the elderly's ability to compete with younger age groups in an environment of high unemployment. Those who found work were usually occupied on a highly informal, part-time basis. Few distinctions could be drawn between insured and uninsured elderly, men and women or locations: all appeared equally willing to work.

Economic relations with household and family members

Tables 5.9, 5.10 and 5.11 provide information about respondents' relations with other household members. Defining household units in *villas* was complicated by a tendency for several family members to occupy adjacent buildings on the same, jointly owned plot of land. In cases where cooking and bathing facilities were also shared, the survey elected to define households as a single unit. Where this did not occur, they were treated as individual units.

Table 5.9 shows that the great majority of respondents of all ages (72 per cent) lived with relatives other than a spouse. Conversely, only 11 per cent lived completely alone. Of those respondents living with other relatives, over half were in households of three to five members, rather than large extended units. These figures are roughly compatible with findings for Argentina as a whole (Table 3.11). The survey found few significant differences between elderly aged over or under 70 years, although the proportion of the younger group still living with their partners was slightly higher, reflecting the greater likelihood that he or she was still living.

Table 5.9: Size of household

Age	Alone	Partner	3–5	6+	2*
70+	6	7	18	19	11
Under 70	14	23	47	24	12
Total	20	30	65	43	23

* Not including partner.
Source: Questionnaire, Buenos Aires, 1992–3.

Table 5.10: Degree of economic dependence on household members other than partner

Age	Complete	Substantial	Slight	None
70+	3	7	14	37
Under 70	5	19	25	71
Total	8	26	39	108

Source: Questionnaire, Buenos Aires, 1992–3.

Table 5.11: Nature of economic ties within the household

Age	Win	Lose	Neutral	None
70+	7	15	20	19
Under 70	23	17	35	45
Total	30	32	55	64

Key: Win = Clear net economic gain for respondent.
Lose = Clear net economic loss for respondent.
Neutral = No clear net gain or loss for respondent.
Source: Questionnaire, Buenos Aires, 1992–3.

The degree of economic dependence on household members, as shown in Table 5.10, is not a quantitative measurement and, in part, reflects an element of subjective judgement by the investigator. This is based on both the frequency, type and value of support obtained from the household, as well as other sources of income at the disposal of the respondent. An absence of dependence on household members did not necessarily reflect an absence of economic relations, but rather that the respondent did not benefit directly from them.

Table 5.10 shows that 19 per cent of elderly *villeros* were either completely or substantially dependent upon the economic support of other household members. However, levels of such assistance may have been greater than the results indicate. First, it is probable that some respondents were embarrassed to admit their true levels of dependence on other household members. According to one *villero*:

> I don't go to my children for anything because it makes me ashamed to ask them. (Sra JM, Villa Jardín, February 1993)

Also, respondents may have been unaware of a number of important indirect benefits of living with other family members. For example, scale economies such as bulk buying and the sharing of costs could have substantially reduced individual expenses without any internal transfer of income.

Another important reason why the elderly did not feel dependent on other household members was the reciprocal nature of assistance provided. As argued in Chapter 3, it is misleading to reduce relations between the elderly and other household members to a unidirectional flow of income to the former from the latter. Table 5.11 identifies those cases where the flow of income was clearly in favour of the respondent and those where it clearly went the other way. It shows that roughly a quarter of respondents who had economic relations made a net gain, with a similar proportion making a loss. This suggests that other household members were just as likely to be economically dependent on the elderly as vice versa.

Nevertheless, the claim by the majority of respondents to be independent of household assistance, although probably exaggerated, cannot be dismissed and requires further explanation. The pattern of relations with other household members reflected a number of factors, including their relative economic positions and the priorities of individual members. In 20 of the 32 cases where the elderly made a net loss, they were the only source of household income. Of these, 13 were living with grandchildren, 8 with ill relatives and 7 with unemployed family members. One interviewee suggested that other household members would have supported her had they been able to:

> They can't help at all because they're just as poor as I am. They have to work to be able to eat too...I never think about going and troubling people,

do I? What can I do?...When they started working then as soon as they got paid they would go and buy what we needed and that was that. But now they haven't got any work.

(Sra Elsa B, Villa Jardín, March 1993)

This indicates that the rapid increase in urban unemployment had reduced the capacity of family members to provide for the elderly.

Individual willingness to provide support was reflected in the degree of income pooling between members. In the survey, 24 respondents lived in households where some members held back a share of their personal incomes from the common pool and in another seven cases there was no pooling whatsoever. However, in the vast majority of households members would pool all their individual incomes. The pensions and benefits received by elderly members took on particular importance when the incomes of other family members were less reliable and were sometimes ear-marked for basic items.

The willingness of other family members to offer support and the willingness of the elderly to accept it was compromised when this reduced the resources available for young children in the household. According to Sra JM:

'La Morena' [her daughter] helps out when she can, when I tell her to. And I can't really ask her either. I'm not going to ask her for her children's bread. They'rc her children. She has to look after her children like I looked after mine...The children – one's just started going to secondary school, he's in his second year, and the others are practising to play football. You have to buy them their shoes, you have to buy them their vitamins, you have to buy them the food they're eating, pay their bus fares.

(Sra JM, Villa Jardín, February 1993)

The overriding priority given to the needs of young children by both their parents and grandparents paralleled the main interests of local organisations in the *villas*. Both local community leaders and the elderly themselves tended to put children first.

Elderly respondents did not just contribute to the economic welfare of households through the pooling of income. Respondents were sometimes responsible for the care of grandchildren, freeing the child's mother for waged employment. A more frequent and potentially more significant contribution was the provision of accommodation. Whilst virtually all the homes surveyed had no legal entitlement to the land they occupied, this did not mean that these houses were without value. Several interviewees made references to informal property markets in the *villas* and to the gradual improvements they had made to their houses over time. According to Sra AM:

> We moved in paying 150 a month to an old lady who lives in that place there, opposite. Now they work as scavengers there...This boy came and told me 'The lady, my granny told me that you're to stay here. You're doing it all up'...And we were doing it up, because before it was all made of bits of wood, just bits of wood...its still not finished, but we're still working on it. When there was money we used to buy cement or something and get on with it. That's how it was. (Sra AM, Villa Jardín, March 1993)

Of those elderly surveyed, 140 (77 per cent) owned (either individually or with their partners) their own home. Of these, 90 were living with other adults. Few respondents attached any importance to this form of economic support and none referred to any form of rental arrangement. However, various surveys of household expenditure in the early 1990s found that accommodation accounted for a high and increasing share of costs.[17]

Table 5.12: Degree of economic dependence on other family members

Age	Complete	Substantial	Slight	None
70+	1	11	15	34
Under 70	2	28	35	55
Total	3	39	50	89

Source: Questionnaire, Buenos Aires, 1992–3.

Table 5.13: Nature of economic ties with other family members

Age	Win	Lose	Neutral	None
70+	24	1	4	32
Under 70	41	5	24	50
Total	65	6	28	82

Source: Questionnaire, Buenos Aires, 1992–3.

Tables 5.12 and 5.13 provide information about family members who did not form part of respondents' households. They indicate that more elderly obtained economic support from relatives living outside their domestic units (23 per cent) than from those within (19 per cent). This is reflected both in respondents' dependence on these ties and in the probability of their making a clear net gain from them.

Several explanations may account for this counter-intuitive finding. More economically successful children would have been more likely to be living away from their parents, since they would have been able to meet the cost of their own accommodation. Two interviews provide extreme examples of this. In both cases all the children but one, who was mentally retarded, had moved away from their elderly parents. Another explanation may be that elderly respondents generally had more children and close relatives living outside the home than in it. This increased the probability that some would be willing and able to help out. In many cases where support came from outside the home it was only provided from one of several children or close relatives. According to one interviewee:

> One [of my children] lives just opposite...He works as a street trader...He never sets foot in this house...Another [son] lives in Avellaneda...he's a builder and he sometimes calls in...I've another son who's a street trader, selling clothes. That one would never give me a penny either. And he lives on his own!...Another son lives near here in 'Las Saladas'...They can't give us anything because they've got seven kids to fend for. I could never ask them for anything. [Interviewer asks about her two daughters]. They're both very near...[one gives us] lots of things. Every month they give me what they can: 50, 100, 200 [pesos]. That's my girl, the youngest one...She's very good to me. [Interviewer asks if other daughter helps] No...she's got three children and they're all men and all working. But I'm not going to go begging to my children for anything. No way...Only the youngest daughter, only her. (Sra EC, Villa Jardín, February 1993)

Given that responsibility for providing economic support and general care for the elderly was not evenly distributed between household members, it is important to establish the degree to which women bore a disproportionate share of the burden. In fact, the responses of the elderly *villeros* do not present as clear-cut a picture as that usually found in studies of age care. Of those who obtained economic support from family members (from either within or beyond the home) 45 per cent claimed that both sexes assisted, 35 per cent stated that assistance came primarily from females and 20 per cent said it came from males. Thus, although women provided more support than men did, the difference was not glaring. The role of women was often limited because they tended to have fewer financial resources on which they could draw to offer assistance. Nevertheless, it is very probable that the role of women as general carers is understated by these figures since the questionnaire focused on economic issues and not the overall welfare of the elderly.

Whilst support from relatives beyond the household was more significant than that from those within, it should be noted that, for the majority of elderly (77 per cent), it was of slight or no importance. Economic ties were restricted in a number of ways. As seen in the previous testimony, the primacy given to the needs of young children was again important. Geographical distance was another potential constraint. One respondent mentioned that she would occasionally go to relatives who lived outside the city for help but that sometimes she did not have enough money to make the trip. However, proximity did not necessarily lead to economic ties. According to Sra AG:

> I've another daughter who's married and lives with her husband on the other side [of the street]...We're sometimes very friendly. Other times I'm ill and can't go over there. I can't walk very well...Sometimes they say to me 'Are you going to stay here to eat, mum?' 'No, I'm going', I tell them. They eat different types of food, strange food I don't like...Sometimes they come here. Very seldom...I can't help them out much either. We help each other in here [the house] and that's it. Inside here, but only here...Everyone has their own way of living, their own way of life. Everyone. Them in their house, me here...Everybody has their own house. They never come bothering me for anything and I don't go bothering them either. (Sra AG, Villa Jardín, March 1993)

Rather than distance, the important factor here was residential separation. Some studies have observed that informal reciprocal exchange contains a strong element of social symbolism, which has broad implications for the nature of the relationship between the two parties (Ramos, 1981:16–17). Accordingly, elderly individuals may have felt that to cross the threshold of another home to ask for assistance was a more considered, public gesture than to make ends meet within their own households.

Whilst respondents were more likely to profit from dealings with relatives living outside the household, economic support was not entirely one-way. Several respondents spent time caring for grandchildren whose parents lived outside the home. According to Sra Eulalia B:

> At one time I helped her [younger daughter] out a lot because...he [grandson] lost his place in the school, because he was at nursery school and he lost his place because she couldn't go and pay them the fee. They couldn't give the boy a place, they couldn't take him. So I looked after the boy...she [daughter] leaves her house at five in the morning and gets back at four in the afternoon...I looked after the baby between seven or eight in the morning until twelve...His father worked until twelve. When his father came back the boy would go over to him.
>
> (Sra EC, Villa Jardín, February 1993)

The survey found that 38 per cent of respondents were completely or substantially dependent upon family support, be it from within or beyond the household. This figure is considerably higher than those recorded by studies of Argentina as a whole (Table 3.16) but still only represents a minority of respondents. These economic relations were diverse and affected by a range of factors. As has been shown, the economic welfare of the elderly was partly dependent on that of other groups. Low and unreliable wages and a lack of state benefits for unemployment or invalidity reduced the amount of support relatives were able to provide. However, often relations were as much the result of individual volition as economic capability. Intra-family support was generally inequitable, with one child bearing a disproportionate share of the burden of caring for the elderly. Conversely, elderly respondents were sometimes left by richer relatives to fend for sick or unemployed children.

Economic relations with friends and neighbours

Numerous studies have stressed the importance of mutual trust for exchange and assistance between non-kin. As mentioned in earlier chapters, some of these maintain that a condition of common poverty and marginality promotes a stronger sense of solidarity within communities, enabling such assistance to occur with relative frequency.

Table 5.14: Degree of economic dependence on friends and neighbours

Age	Complete	Substantial	Slight	None
70+	0	3	11	47
Under 70	1	4	37	78
Total	1	7	48	125

Source: Questionnaire, Buenos Aires, 1992–3.

Table 5.15: Nature of economic ties with friends and neighbours

Age	Win	Lose	Neutral	None
70+	6	2	8	45
Under 70	12	5	31	72
Total	18	7	39	117

Source: Questionnaire, Buenos Aires, 1992–3.

There was little evidence to corroborate this view in the *villas* studied here. Tables 5.14 and 5.15 show that respondents received and reciprocated far less economic support with friends and neighbours than they did with family members. Among those who received no such support, many claimed only to have loose acquaintances and not to trust the local people. The most frequent view was that:

> Only acquaintances. 'Good morning, good afternoon.' No more than that.
> (Sra Elsa B, Villa Jardín, March 1993)

Some respondents went further, claiming to have been taken advantage of in the past. According to Sra EC:

> I don't like the people [here] because you [tend to] put a lot of trust in them and that's not a good idea...It happened to me lots of times...someone comes and makes themselves your friend, and that's when I lower my guard and then they rob me...I've never even asked anyone for a *yerba maté* [popular herbal infusion], never...and I've helped out lots of people here...I don't want to have anything to do with any of them because they paid me back badly. Because I, I gave them oil, pasta. I gave things to all my neighbours. And afterwards nobody thought about doing the same for me. So when I go out of here I don't even say 'Hello' to them.
> (Sra EC, Villa Jardín, February 1993)

In nearly every case where substantial support was received the respondent was in extreme economic straits, often with no other source of income at his or her disposal. According to Sr JJ some neighbours actively sought out those who might be in particular need:

> I have to go about a lot to be able to get by. Because there are neighbours round here who sometimes lend me a peso, a useless peso...Every time I pay a visit they give me something...There are some who come here and ask me 'Alright, do you need any money?' and I say 'Alright' ....and just like that they give me ten pesos, if I don't have any money for the next week, if I'm short. (Sr JJ, Villa Azul, June 1993)

This form of economic support was considered an option of last resort by takers and, sometimes, the givers. It provided a final safety-net for those respondents who might even have faced the threat of starvation if they had been abandoned by the community. As with family assistance, the burden of support was not spread evenly between all residents, but was provided by a small minority.

By contrast, the bulk of cases involving slight dependence consisted of reciprocal support, with each party careful not to put their own pride at stake. Sra JM's attitude was typical of many *villeros*:

> I tell you, my neighbours help me out lots of times. They give me plates of food, they bring me bread...You can't cook any type of food without oil, you know. If I want to eat lettuce, anything and I've not got a drop of oil, they ask me why I didn't ask. Look, if you don't have something, you don't want to show the other person that you don't. I don't like doing that. I have this pride...They have a plate of food and they bring it me without me asking first. I help them without asking them for anything in return and without them asking me first. I'm about to take a plate of food next door. I don't know if they need it and sometimes they needed it so much and they hadn't told me, they hadn't asked me.
>
> (Sra JM, Villa Jardín, February 1993)

As has been shown, there were two separate forms of economic interaction between neighbours. The first responded to dire need and involved no expectation of repayment. In these cases, the pride of the recipient was not an important issue. The second was usually a mutually beneficial arrangement, where participants took pains to defend their pride and stress that they were not financially dependent on the favours of another family. However, the great majority of respondents preferred to have no economic dealings of any shape or form with their neighbours.

Other sources of income

None of the elderly individuals covered by the survey claimed to derive any income from savings or rent. One couple in Villa Jardín had lived off the proceeds of selling their home but claimed that this money had since run out. The apparent absence of savings paralleled findings for Greater Buenos Aires and Argentina as a whole and was explained in Chapter 3. Likewise, little evidence was found of property renting in the *villas*, although one interviewee mentioned that she had previously rented her home from another elderly *villero*. In the few households which contained non-related individuals, these were generally treated no differently to relatives and were expected to pool earnings rather than pay rent.

Caritas provided economic assistance for 36 respondents. This generally consisted of monthly food parcels, although in some cases it was limited to the provision of basic medicines and used clothing. The proportion of respondents assisted by Caritas varied sharply amongst the *villas*, rising from

9 per cent in Villa Azul, to 15 per cent in Villa Jardín, to 54 per cent in Villa Zavaleta. It should be noted that the number surveyed in Villa Zavaleta was not large enough to be representative for the area as a whole and was probably exaggerated since most of the interviews were obtained through volunteers at the local church. The variations between Villa Jardín and Villa Azul reflected the different resources and priorities of the local Caritas branches.

As mentioned in the previous chapter, local Caritas branches generally sought to channel their aid to those households in the greatest economic need. Whilst none of the respondents were entirely without other forms of income, the majority appeared to be in more difficult economic circumstances than the average elderly *villero*. However, there were cases both of respondents suffering extreme poverty without Caritas help and those in relatively secure circumstances receiving it.

No other local organisations, religious or otherwise, were mentioned as sources of income in the survey, with the exception of one *villero* who made daily visits to a soup kitchen run by the neighbourhood council. In two of the extended interviews references were made to assistance from nearby evangelical churches. However, in neither of these cases did they provide a significant source of support at the time. Thus, other than Caritas, local organisations were largely insignificant as sources of direct economic assistance for elderly in the *villas*.

It is probable that a large number of elderly *villeros* received occasional economic support from past employers, particularly those who had engaged them in domestic service. This source of income was not included in the questionnaire, but its importance became apparent when frequent reference was made to it in the extended interviews. According to Sra EC:

> And when I go into the [Federal] Capital where I used to have my bosses; if I go to a boss's home they give me clothes, shoes, they give me all kinds of things...every year, once every year I go and visit them...they give me fruit, they give me meat to eat, they give me tuna fish, that's what they give me...I go when I feel like it and all of them give me some help...They were all very nice, very nice, because I was a very good woman to them...Sometimes they give me five hundred, a thousand, two thousand [50, 100 or 200 pesos]...I went visiting just a while back, before Christmas. I went to visit a lady, to spend a bit of time there, near to Chacarita...I went there early and stayed until the afternoon...she filled my bag...and told me 'Stay here and eat. You stay here and eat.'
>
> (Sra EC, Villa Jardín, February 1993)

This form of assistance was ad hoc, varying in intensity and content. In some cases it extended to providing elderly respondents' relatives with employment. However, not all those who had worked in domestic service received such support:

> I had a boss. I was with her for three years...now she doesn't [help] because I don't go there any more. Sometimes I meet them by accident, sometimes. I often bump into her husband...I saw him about two months ago...We only said hello. No more than that...Besides, I stopped working there because when the wage for domestic servants started to go up, they didn't want to give me a raise. (Sra Eugenia B, Villa Azul, June 1993)

Another interviewee pointed out that her employer had herself been a *jubilada* and had not been capable of providing any economic assistance. Similarly, it is likely that the worsening financial position of many middle-class families reduced their capacity and willingness to provide assistance to ex-employees. Consequently, this form of support did not compensate women who had worked in domestic service for the lack of social security protection they had received. Moreover, rather than being sought out, it was necessary for *villeros* to visit employers' homes and assistance was considered a special favour rather than an obligation. At its most cynical, it represented a paternalistic salve for the consciences of past employers, an extension of a mistress and servant relationship.

Only one example was found of informal support from past employers when the respondent had not been in domestic service. This was the case of an elderly *villero* whose dead husband had worked as an assistant in a solicitor's office:

> They're not obliged to give me anything. They give me stuff because, well I don't know, they're the people where my husband used to be. If they hadn't wanted to, they wouldn't have given me anything...The lawyer never paid our pension [contributions] or anything...when there are some clients who pay up...then they've got money and they give me some...sometimes two million [200 pesos] but when they give me two million I always owe more than two million. They haven't paid me now for about six months...I go looking for whatever money there is but there isn't anything. I've gone there so many times. (Sra Elsa B, Villa Jardín, March 1993)

Since no similar instances were reported by other respondents, it can only be assumed that this kind of arrangement was highly unusual.

Twelve respondents referred to use of an informal credit arrangement with local shopkeepers, known locally as a *libreta*. These involved bulk payments, usually made on a monthly basis, which enabled the customer to buy goods on account. This service was usually only offered to a select few customers deemed to be trustworthy and any failure to repay would lead to exclusion. It was unclear whether users were charged any kind of interest on the *libreta* and, therefore, whether it was essentially a mechanism which enabled respondents to budget more effectively or represented a drain on their resources. According to Sra Eugenia B:

> *EB*: We make use of it [*libreta*] at the grocer's. Well, it works because you have to put money in at the end of every month. You have to put money in and sometimes you pay, for example now I paid exactly a million [100 pesos]...
>
> [Husband interjects: We have to pay up. If we don't pay then we won't have anything to eat.]
>
> *EB*: If you don't pay up then there's no more credit. You've got to. [Interviewer asks if she pays interest]. Sure, because there are – sometimes there are no rises, no rises in food prices. They hear on a certain day a certain thing is going to go up...So when you go there to pay they really sting you. But there hasn't been a rise yet. With the money that we pay the grocer, she [grocer] goes and buys the food...to have it in for the month.[18]

A handful of respondents obtained income from a variety of other sources. Although a general lack of open ground prevented most *villeros* from raising livestock or keeping hens, one interviewee kept a small number of fowl. However, he did not consider these a potentially significant source of support. The same elderly couple were paid every month for minding a neighbour's child along with their own numerous grandchildren. Finally, three respondents were reduced to scavenging in rubbish tips (a practice known as *haciendo cirujas* and more commonly pursued by children) or begging in the streets of adjacent districts. This was a strategy of last resort pursued by those elderly *villeros* who had no alternative source of support. The stigma attached to this activity was reflected in Eugenia B's defiant pride:

> At one time, I told you, we were very poor. He [husband] searched for whatever he could get. He went looking for things to eat in the rubbish... Yes, we used to eat out of bins. I used to go out early in the evening with my son when he was smaller and I used to do the rounds of all the food shops. All of them. No – why should I be ashamed to say it?...I'm proud to say

that I ate from rubbish, that I ate out of bins. We ate and I fed my children out of the rubbish. (Sra Eugenia B, Villa Azul, June 1993).

In summary, the survey identified two significant sources of income other than benefits, continued employment or the support of family and friends: occasional handouts from past employers and Caritas food parcels. The former was almost entirely restricted to respondents who had previously worked in domestic service, whilst the latter targeted, albeit imperfectly, those elderly in direst need. However, for neither group did this support fully compensate for their position of relative disadvantage.

Summary of income sources

This section examines the relative importance of the income sources described above by analysing how they were combined by individual respondents. These income sources were distributed as follows:

Table 5.16: Commonly occurring income combinations

Sources	Number of respondents
Insurance benefit and household	15
Assistance benefit and household	15
Employment alone	15
Insurance benefit alone	12
Household alone	11
Assistance benefit alone	10
Spouse alone	7
Family alone	6
Insurance and family	6
Assistance and other	6
Employment and family	5
Spouse and family	4

Source: Questionnaire, Buenos Aires, 1992–3.

Table 5.17: Number of income sources

Number of sources	Number of respondents
One	65
Two	83
Three	31
Four	2

Source: Questionnaire, Buenos Aires, 1992–3.

As is apparent in Tables 5.16 and 5.17, the survey found a striking variety of income strategies: 55 different combinations for a sample of 181. For example, Table 5.17 shows that 64 per cent of respondents received more than one source. Some combinations were, however, much more prevalent than others. As displayed in Table 5.16, the six most frequent accounted for 78 (43 per cent of the sample) and the top 12 accounted for 112 (62 per cent). Conversely, all of the remaining combinations were pursued by only three respondents or less.

It is worthy of note that of the 100 respondents in receipt of benefits, 79 combined these with some other form of income. The proportion who did so was the same for both insurance and assistance pensions. Sometimes these combinations included sources of last resort: Caritas assisted 14 respondents who also received benefits, of which all but one were non-contributory. Five pensioners were forced to turn to neighbours for substantial amounts of economic support and one *jubilado* made regular scavenging trips. This supports the earlier finding that the values of all forms of benefit were insufficient to meet the basic requirements of elderly *villeros*.

A number of studies of the Argentine social security system draw attention to the problem of multiple benefits. In 1990 it was estimated that 7.7 per cent of beneficiaries of the national insurance system received two or more contributory pensions (Isuani and San Martino, 1993:21). Of those surveyed, only three respondents admitted to receiving multiple benefits and in two of these cases this involved an insurance and an assistance benefit. It is probable that a number of others chose not to disclose information about multiple pensions and so it is not possible to gauge the extent of this practice.

Current studies of social security in Latin America and elsewhere in the developing world make few, if any, direct references to the effect of factors other than principal lifetime occupation, thus implying that they are insignificant. Rather than accept this assumption at face value, it important to verify that factors such as gender, age and location were negligible. This can be done by making comparisons between sub-sets of the sample population.

Gender comparisons show significant differences in a number of areas. First, as indicated above, elderly women (15 per cent) were much less likely to have made social insurance contributions than were men (53 per cent). Gender differences for access to contributory benefits (35 per cent men, 23 per cent women) were clear but not as marked. This was largely caused by the relatively high number of women in receipt of widows' pensions, a result of their greater longevity. As has been shown, women were more likely to receive an assistance benefit or subsidy, but these paid less money and were less reliable. Finally, women (21 per cent) were slightly less likely to continue in employment than were men (29 per cent). Differences in current occupation paralleled those which had occurred during prime working years, with domestic service exclusively female and construction remaining a male reserve.

There were, however, some areas of income maintenance in which there were no discernible differences between the sexes. Overall levels of access to benefits were roughly equal for men and women (53 and 56 per cent, respectively). Similarly, levels of dependence on household and family members were almost identical. For both sexes similar proportions (40 and 37 per cent) were either completely or substantially dependent on these sources. Overall, differences in the types of benefits held and, to a lesser extent, continued employment meant that women were in a somewhat worse economic position than men. This was also reflected in the larger number of women (17 per cent) who were reliant on the support of their partner than was the case for men (10 per cent).

*Table 5.18: Gender comparisons for ex-informal sector workers**

Income source	Male informal	Female informal
Insurance benefit	7 (20%)	8 (13%)
Assistance benefit	9 (26%)	24 (39%)
Spouse support	2 (6%)	13 (21%)
Employment	15 (43%)	16 (26%)
Household support**	12 (34%)	19 (31%)
Family support**	10 (29%)	16 (26%)
Friends/neighbours support**	3 (9%)	5 (8%)
Other	8 (23%)	17 (28%)

*Includes construction and domestic service.
**Excludes cases of slight support
Source: Questionnaire, Buenos Aires, 1992–3.

To what extent were these gender differences essentially reflections of respondents' principal lifetime occupations? As was shown earlier, men (49 per cent) were much more likely to have worked in the formal sector than women (14 per cent). By comparing income patterns of men and women who worked exclusively in the informal sector, it is possible to isolate the gender effect. Table 5.18 shows that women who had worked in this sector were less likely to be in receipt of an insurance benefit than were their male counterparts. It is also worthy of note that virtually all such women were in receipt of widow's pensions and not benefits for which they personally had made contributions. By contrast, no male ex-informal sector worker received a widower's pension. Likewise, gender differences in access to assistance benefits, dependence on spouses and likelihood to continue in employment were as clear for informal sector workers as they were for the total sample.

Nevertheless, even gender differences between informal sector workers may have been influenced by the type of informal activity pursued. As has been shown, the majority of women in this sector were domestic servants, whereas men were most frequently engaged in construction. The proportion of the former who made sufficient contributions (9 per cent) was much lower than for the latter (48 per cent). There is no evidence to suggest that this reflected a greater predisposition among males to make contributions, and so the disparity must have resulted from a larger element of formality within construction, which obliged workers to contribute. Conversely, the greater likelihood of men to continue working in the informal sector may have reflected the nature of building work, which lent itself to occasional odd-jobbing *changas* much more readily than domestic service, which was usually based on a regular weekly schedule. Likewise, it is possible that gender differences for access to assistance benefits simply have resulted from higher levels of insurance coverage among men rather than greater female participation in local initiatives.

Thus, whilst it is evident that previous employment had a significant effect on income patterns, it is unclear whether this entirely discounted the influence of gender. Despite the problems of separating the effects of these two variables, it is clear that women who had worked in domestic service were in a particularly disadvantageous position, despite the support of past employers. This may partly account for their activism in local organisations.

Table 5.19: Comparisons of income sources between villas

Income source	Villa Jardín	Villa Azul
Insurance benefit	29 (32%)	11 (20%)
Assistance benefit	25 (27%)	16 (29%)
Spouse support	10 (11%)	9 (16%)
Employment	24 (26%)	13 (24%)
Household support	32 (35%)	21 (38%)
Family support	25 (27%)	14 (25%)
Friends/neighbours support	3 (3%)	6 (11%)
Other	11 (12%)	13 (24%)

Source: Questionnaire, Buenos Aires, 1992–3.

It is also useful to draw comparisons between the elderly living in Villa Jardín and Villa Azul. Here, again, it is important to take the effect of past employment into account since residents of Villa Jardín (32 per cent) were twice as likely to have worked in the formal sector as those of Villa Azul (16 per cent). This, in turn, led to a larger proportion with insurance benefits in the former (33 and 20 per cent, respectively). Table 5.19 shows that there were no other clear differences in elderly income sources between the two *villas*. However, as was mentioned earlier, the majority of assistance benefits in Villa Jardín were DNA pensions, whilst in Villa Azul the majority were provincial or municipal pensions. Thus, there were two identifiable differences between the *villas*: the likelihood of having worked in the formal sector and the type of assistance benefit received.

Table 5.20: 'Young' versus 'old' old

Income source	Aged under 70 years	Aged 70 and over
Insurance benefit	29 (24%)	21 (34%)
Assistance benefit	25 (21%)	24 (39%)
Spouse support	17 (14%)	6 (10%)
Employment	36 (30%)	6 (10%)
Household support	38 (32%)	24 (39%)
Family support	32 (27%)	16 (26%)
Friends/neighbours support	6 (5%)	4 (7%)
Other	22 (18%)	16 (26%)

Source: Questionnaire, Buenos Aires, 1992–3.

Table 5.20 compares sources of income for respondents aged under 70 and the rest. It shows a number of predictable disparities. Older respondents were more likely to be eligible for benefits and had participated in the labour market at a time when there were more opportunities for formal work: hence their greater coverage. Younger ones were more willing and able to continue in employment, which, in turn, reduced their eligibility for benefits. The larger proportion of younger respondents relying on income from a partner reflected the greater probability that both were still living. There were no clear differences for other potential sources of income.

Differences between the two *villas* and Argentina as a whole were much greater than differences between them or their constituent groups. As displayed in Table 5.21, these were evident for principal lifetime employment and all sources of income once elderly. Differences in access to insurance benefits roughly mirrored the relative importance of informal employment. This was only partly compensated for the targeting of assistance pensions and grants. Table 5.21 also shows that elderly *villeros* were more likely to remain in employment and receive support from other family members. It is understandable that these income sources took on more importance in the *villas*, given the reduced levels of access to state benefits.

As with gender, it is difficult to separate the effect of location from that of occupation. If high concentrations of informal employment in the *villas* occurred mainly because such workers were unable to live elsewhere, the underlying determinant remained occupation. However, it is also possible that residents had more difficulty in obtaining formal employment because of their status as *villeros*. For example, employers may have been reluctant to take on workers from neighbourhoods facing the threat of eradication. In this case, the critical factor would have been location.

Table 5.21: Comparisons between villas *and Argentina as a whole*

		Survey	Argentina (c. 1990)
Principal lifetime occupation[a]			
	Formal	29%	78.9 to 80.9%[c]
	Informal	23%	13.2 to 11.6%
	Domestic	30%	7.9 to 7.5%
	Housewife	14%	No data
Insurance[b]		28%	60.9%
Assistance[b]		27%	6.9%
Current employment[d]		20%	8.4%
Family support		38%[e]	10.3%[f]

Notes

[a] Not including rural labour or domestic service, based on PREALC's 1982 classification.

[b] Estimated coverage of population aged over 65 or more (author's estimate).

[c] 1950 and 1980 data.

[d] Population over 65 years old.

[e] Complete or substantial reliance.

[f] CELADE sample survey.

Sources: PREALC, 1982; ILO, 1986b; CELADE, 1989; Questionnaire, Buenos Aires, 1992–3; Isuani and San Martino, 1993.

It is, then, often difficult to separate the effects of factors such as gender, location and age from those of employment. Rather than discount their importance, however, it is useful to understand the ways in which they interact with each other.

ACTUAL VERSUS POTENTIAL ACCESS TO STATE BENEFITS

It has already been demonstrated that access to insurance benefits by gender and by neighbourhood roughly paralleled the relative importance of formal activities and pension contributions. However, Table 5.22 shows that this was not a perfect relationship, since 40 per cent of those who claimed to have made sufficient payments were not in receipt of a *jubilación*. Even taking into account that this figure may have been exaggerated by a number of false testimonies, it cannot be entirely discounted. Conversely, a small number of respondents who had made insufficient contributions had been able to obtain a benefit.

Table 5.22: Contributions and receipt of insurance benefit

	Sufficient	Some	None
None	23	28	93
Employee	28	3	0
Public	3	0	0
Self-employed	3	0	0

Source: Questionnaire, Buenos Aires, 1992–3.

Table 5.23: Criteria determining eligibility for assistance benefits

Criteria (cumulative)	Men	Women	Total
Without insurance or assistance benefit	37	44	81
Over 64 years old	21	22	43
Spouse without benefit	19	15	34
No potential household support*	11	10	21
Serious health problems	8	7	15

* Households where fewer members aged under 65 were receiving a regular monthly income than the total number of members.
Source: Questionnaire, Buenos Aires, 1992–3.

Eligibility criteria for means-tested assistance pensions were more complicated and partly depended on the subjective judgement of the assessor. Thus, it is less easy to compare patterns of potential eligibility and actual access to such benefits. Table 5.23 selects a number of criteria which were generally applied in means-testing: age, health, benefits held by spouses and household income. It shows that over half of those without any benefit were aged 65 or over. The number of respondents potentially eligible for assistance is gradually reduced as other criteria are taken into account. This leaves a total of 15 respondents who fulfilled all the criteria used here. It should be emphasised that these criteria are not necessarily the same as those which were used by means testing agencies for the various benefits. The fact that a large proportion of those who were receiving assistance did not fulfil all the criteria indicates that means-testing was inconsistent or less stringent than it might have been. Conversely, it is possible that other factors were taken into account. These may have included a general assessment of the claimants' living conditions, although it is probable that residence of a *villa* in itself would satisfy this criterion.

Taken together, Tables 5.22 and 5.23 show that, according to the information they volunteered, 37 respondents were clearly eligible for benefits which they did not receive. In addition, a much larger number were apparently no less eligible for state benefits than respondents already in receipt of them. It is therefore important to consider what factors helped create these disparities between potential and actual access.

Table 5.24: Respondents pursuing pension claims

	Men	Women	Total
Total	15	17	32
Under 6 months	5	7	12
Don't remember	1	2	3
Insurance	7	5	12
Assistance	8	11	19
PAMI supplement	0	1	1

Source: Questionnaire, Buenos Aires, 1992–3.

Disparities between potential and actual access to benefits were largely the result of a number of administrative failings. As mentioned in Chapter 3, Argentina compared favourably with other Latin American countries in terms of the proportion of its total social security budget devoted to administration. However, lower expenditure may not have reflected administrative efficiency: it is essential to take into account speed and effectiveness in delivering services.

Table 5.24 shows that 32 respondents were pursuing claims for state benefits. For those who had been doing so for over six months, the average period of pursuit was three and a half years. In seven cases, respondents claimed to have been pursuing claims for five or more years. Predictably, a larger number of respondents were making claims for assistance pensions than insurance ones. These results were in line with national data for insurance pension claims in early 1994, which revealed that 100000 were awaiting clarification, with an average delay of many months.[19]

The limited availability of information about the full range of benefits and how to obtain them partly accounted for the disparities between potential and actual access. A number of respondents were seriously misinformed about these procedures. Sra HF in Villa Azul recounted a conversation with her terminally ill mother and uncle:

> He said 'Look, Angelita', (Mother was called Angelita) and he said 'HF won't get the pension.' [Mother replied] 'Why won't they give it to her, why won't they let her have it. Yes, as far as I'm concerned I'm sure they'll pay her – an unmarried daughter [in fact, HF was also a single mother], she's 32, an adult, an only child. Of course she'll get the pension!' (I used to care for my mother and everything). My brother got up and said no, I wouldn't. (Sra HF, Villa Azul, June 1993)

A similar case was that of Sr JJ, who assumed that holding an assistance benefit would automatically disqualify him from pursuing a claim for a better-paid insurance benefit.

> *JJ*: I could have had been a *jubilado* not a *pensionado* [person in receipt of assistance benefit]...
>
> [*Interviewer*: And it would be worth your while to get a hundred pesos a month more?]
>
> *JJ*: Of course it would. Because if I was a *jubilado* they'd give me more than the thing I get now, wouldn't I...But I'll tell you this, I can't go and make a claim for it there [central offices in the Federal Capital], because the boys there are going to turn me down because I've already got the [assistance] pension. (Sr JJ, Villa Azul, June 1993)

Many respondents who lacked information about claims relied on local organisations rather than state agencies to obtain it for them. This was particularly important in Villa Jardín, whose *Centro Los Jóvenes del Noventa* was well-informed about bureaucratic procedures. According to Sra AM:

> [*Interviewer*: Are you making claims for any other pensions?]
>
> *AM*: No, no. I'd like to but – they gave me some addresses. But I don't know. What do I know? I don't know where to go to for it. I've got no idea what goes on. Norma [secretary of the *Centro*] told me that maybe I could do something to make a claim. At least something to be sure that they'll pay you every month. If you want a help: maybe just a little bit, but it's still a help.
>
> [*Interviewer*: And do you have information about this kind of pension?]
>
> *AM*: No. And I don't know where to go...It's a long time since I last saw her [Norma]. 'Maybe you can make a claim for a pension', she said 'that's better than this one [DNA subsidy]' she said. 'It's possible. There

are some people who've been getting it for the last ten years' she said...'So', she said 'It's worth your pursuing this, isn't it'.

(Sra AM, Villa Jardín, March 1993)

Sra AG provided a similar testimony:

[*Interviewer*: Are you pursuing any pension claims?]

AG: At this moment, only the one that they're doing over there [*Centro*]...This claim for the pension, for whatever pension it is that they're doing now...Silvia [founder of *Centro*] told me 'Why are you waiting?' She, Silvia, had told me that it wasn't right that my husband, who should have been a *jubilado* but hadn't been granted one, was still working. And then she sent me to make some photocopies...

[*Interviewer*: Who are paying out this pension?]

AG: I don't know. The state. What do I know?...

[*Interviewer*: What part of the state do you think is paying out this pension?]

AG: I don't know. They say that La Plata [seat of provincial government] is going to help, La Plata is going to pay. But I don't know when it'll pay.

(Sra AG, Villa Jardín, March 1993)

As was shown in the previous chapter, even local community leaders were sometimes ignorant of procedures. In some cases they relied upon the expertise of external professionals. In *villas* where local organisations were less developed or well-informed about pension requirements, elderly individuals had to seek advice from other sources, such as lawyers. In some cases these provided their services free of charge, but it was more frequently the practice to promise such lawyers a share of whatever benefits were eventually obtained. According to Sra VT:

VT: I'm always going and going to see this lawyer. I'm sick of her...

[*Interviewer*: And when did you start seeing a lawyer? Recently?]

VT: Just now...to see if I could get my *jubilación*. And they still won't give me it...When it comes I'll have to pay her.

(Sra VT, Villa Azul, June 1993)

As well as an economic cost, working with lawyers often involved a degree of risk. According to one elderly *villero*:

There are lawyers who specialise in this kind of thing [pension claims]...but it's always a risk because you never know if you're going to die while

> they're doing it. If you die the lawyer keeps all the *jubilación* for himself. And so there's no willingness to get it done fast.
>
> (Sra SH, Villa Jardín, February 1993)

Another gave a first-hand account of her treatment by an unscrupulous lawyer:

> You know he [husband] had a lawyer...Then he made a claim because he had fallen when he was working...both his legs were really bad...they sent him a lawyer, but this lawyer just disappeared. And he didn't give me back his identity papers...nor the papers for his *jubilación* or our marriage certificate...and this happened about four years ago. Well, my daughter-in-law went over to the pension office to find out what was happening. They told her we had to wait. We had to wait and that that lawyer wasn't to interfere any more. (Sra AM, Villa Jardín, March 1993)

Obtaining information was less difficult for those who had worked in large, formal sector firms, who often received free assistance from the company lawyers. Sra AG pointed out how straightforward the pension claim of her husband, a stevedore, had been:

> There in the port they did everything for him, they did it all...He didn't have to go around sorting it out...No, they gave him his *jubilación* right there in the port. They made all the contributions. All of them.
>
> (Sra AG, Villa Jardín, March 1993)

For the majority of those who had worked in the informal sector or had been self-employed the general lack of information about pension procedures made respondents dependent on the good will of local organisations or the services of untrustworthy lawyers. As has been shown, these third parties themselves often had incomplete information about all the available benefits. Clearly, then, the failure of state agencies to disseminate accurate information represented a serious obstacle to initiating and successfully concluding pension claims.

A second problem which confronted claimants was the complexity and bureaucracy of the procedure to obtain most benefits. According to Carmelo Mesa-Lago:

> the granting of [insurance] benefits [in Latin America] is usually conducted through judicial litigation in which the insured have to prove their rights

> through documentation, witnesses, and so forth. This makes the process more complicated, time consuming and expensive...
>
> (Mesa-Lago, 1991b:203).

Such problems could deny even relatively well-informed claimants the pensions for which they were potentially eligible. One elderly woman described the process of making a claim for an assistance pension:

> I had to make the claim, go to the tribunal...I had to come and go, you know. Sometimes they were there, sometimes there wasn't anybody...I had to go to Wilde [approximately 10 kilometres away] to Tribunal Number One...I made the claim for the pension. I did it for almost five years...Do you know how much I used to have to go from place to place?
>
> (Sra EC, Villa Jardín, February 1993)

During the period of interviewing a number of respondents were attempting to obtain the PAMI pension supplements which had just been introduced. Several had been thwarted by the number of visits they needed to make to different government offices. Sra Eugenia B described the process of obtaining the PAMI supplement for her invalid husband:

> I went to the [Federal] Capital to do all the paperwork. It was right opposite the parliament building. I went there to make the claim for him...I had to go there right away: that was where they sent me. And I did all the paperwork and then I had to bring the papers back here so that he could sign them and then I had to go back there again taking them the papers so that he'd also get this subsidy. After that he got the 50 peso subsidy. Also, this was here in PAMI, they sent me back there [to the Federal Capital] and it took me the whole day because I couldn't find the place. I walked around and around and I couldn't find it. At last, when I was tired out, I managed to find it. And I did all the papers there. I had to bring them here again for him to sign them and then go back.
>
> (Sra Eugenia B, Villa Azul, June 1993)

Sra AG gave a similar account:

> *AG*: I have to take [PAMI] the papers...They told me you had to go to the bank to ask for the supplement but...I went to collect the money and they told me it wasn't there yet...You have to take photocopies of your birth certificate, everything, his identity papers, his last wage slip...to PAMI...its on the corner of Chacabuco and Alsina streets in the [Federal] Capital...The

lady working there told me that I had to do this and that, make a sworn declaration, make photocopies of his last wage slip, show his identity papers.

[*Interviewer*: And where do they make the sworn statements?]

AG: They gave me a form there. I had to call the police [located a kilometre away from Villa Jardín]...to get it signed in front of them and pay the contributions which we still had to make.[20]

Often respondents were required to present large numbers of documents before they could make their pension claims. Documents included photocopies of their identity papers, receipts for past contributions, sworn statements about personal income and the wage slips of other relatives. Frequently, these papers were lost and obtaining replacements added to the bureaucratic obstacles of making a claim. Sra JM described how a neighbour would be able to obtain a new identity card:

She lost it recently, but I've already told her to go where everyone else goes. They'll give her a new card there. I've already told her. And she doesn't remember her [identity] number but it doesn't matter because they give it to you just the same...Yes, they do it just the same, because they'll go and look in the civil registry. (Sra JM, Villa Jardín, February 1993)

These problems were particularly serious for immigrants from neighbouring countries, many of whom had never obtained official identity papers in the first place. Similarly, a number of respondents who had made pension contributions to provincial funds in distant parts of the interior faced great difficulties in obtaining replacement copies. Also, those who wished to pursue claims for widow's pensions for partners who had not secured the *jubilación* before their deaths, had to overcome a number of severe obstacles. Even without these added complications, many elderly *villeros* found organising their paperwork a considerable challenge. Sra AG described the problems besetting her claim for an insurance benefit:

I had a problem with my boss and my boss didn't want to know me after that...What I had to do was ask him [employer] for all the papers to...present them to the Ministry of Social Action. I made the claim but my papers were wrong because one was signed for the year – I began to work there in 1977. I had worked two months. Then in 1979 I came back there again...and so I had worked there for enough time when I made the claim [in 1988]...This is the receipt I have from when I returned there...I've got lots of receipts. This is the only one here because I don't know where the

> other ones are because....all the things are jumbled up. I kept them all in a box and my son was moving some furniture. He picked it up and it broke and there was all the box where I'd put everything...There were lots of papers I'd gathered together and put there. I kept them for whatever might crop up. They told me to present all the papers that were there to a lawyer so that they could get me a pension.
>
> (Sra AG, Villa Jardín, March 1993)

This experience contrasted with the subsequent claim which Sra AG made for an assistance pension. Here, the *Centro Los Jóvenes Del Noventa* took on most of the responsibility for handling documentation.

> I have to provide two documents. I still need my boy's signature, and the signatures of my daughter and her husband and another daughter and her husband. That's all, just these papers. Then I hand over all of them to them [the *Centro*]. They're in the file which Norma [secretary of *Centro*] keeps.
>
> (Sra AG, Villa Jardín, March 1993)

The ability of respondents to obtain information, organise their papers and pursue claims varied considerably and was in part determined by factors such as education, motivation, health and financial resources. Of these, the respondent's health was often the critical factor. As displayed in Table 5.23, 15 respondents identified as potentially eligible for assistance benefits had serious health problems, including blindness and paralysis. In some cases other relatives were able to pursue the claim on their behalf. Even after the claim had been granted, elderly *villeros* had to find someone to collect the benefit for them every month. According to Sra Eugenia B:

> I'm going to have to waste three or four hours in a queue [which she did every month] because...he [husband] can't see any more. And I, because he can't stay standing for hours, I have to go. I go to collect it for him.
>
> (Sra Eugenia B, Villa Azul, June 1993)

She also pointed out the financial cost of making claims: bus fares, photocopying and other expenses may have been beyond the means of the poorest elderly.

> You have to have the money to go from place to place, coming and going. What if you don't have any? (Sra Eugenia B, Villa Azul, June 1993)

For Sr JJ, this had been an insurmountable obstacle:

> I made contributions everywhere, but I'm not going to go hunting for them because I don't have any money and you can't go in circles from place to place if you don't have any. That's why I'm not going to go looking for all that stuff. (Sr JJ, Villa Azul, June 1993)

The time, energy and money which *villeros* often needed to expend in order to obtain benefits, along with uncertainty about when, if ever, they would be successful, may have meant that the opportunity costs (either real or perceived) of pursuing claims outweighed the final gain. These costs were particularly high for those with poor education, the self-employed, the disabled and those lacking cash for bus fare and photocopies: the very groups most in need of assistance pensions.

A number of respondents were able to circumvent the numerous barriers to making claims by using personal contacts or resorting to clientelism. In the case of Sra EC, several years of unsuccessful attempts to obtain an assistance pension were brought to a sudden end due to the intervention of her son, who worked in the municipal mayor's office:

> I waited and waited. Then a lady came here from the municipality [Lanús], the chief. She came to my house and told me 'Sra Cristobál your contributions are all paid up.' And then my elder son and Quindimíl [municipal mayor] presented me with my papers. Quindimíl's from Lanús, have you heard of him?...he [son] came one night with a lady in a car, she was Quindimíl's secretary. We went off with my son and I was given the letter which gives me a pension. Yes, and Quindimíl presented it to me...He knows me very well because my son works with him. My son is a secretary for Quindimíl. (Sra EC, Villa Jardín, February 1993)

During informal conversations, another interviewee, Sra Eulogia B, made a series of references about cultivating links with the local Radical party association as a means to obtaining an assistance benefit. However, she was not prepared to discuss this in detail when the interview was being taped:

> [*Interviewer*: Also, you were speaking to people from the Radical party?]
> *EB*: Yes [laughs nervously].
> [*Interviewer*: What came of that?]
> *EB*: No, I didn't speak to them, I didn't go there...They sent me some letters but I didn't go and tell them anything.
> [*Interviewer*: What did the letter say?]
> *EB*: I didn't bring the letter here [she lived next door].
> [*Interviewer*: What did it say more or less?]

EB: That I come. That I help them with my vote, so that they, the Radicals, can keep up the good work.

[*Interviewer*: What are they going to offer you?]

EB: They didn't say anything. Work, just work. I didn't speak to them, not personally. I didn't go to their offices...

[*Interviewer*: Is it possible that they could help with your pension claim?]

EB: Yes, I think so.

[*Interviewer*: Let's hope so.] [Both laugh].

(Sra Eulogia B, Villa Azul, June 1993)

As has been shown, access to state benefits was, metaphorically speaking, something of a lottery. At times it was also a lottery in the literal sense. Chapter 3 refers to the granting of assistance pensions in the early 1950s being turned into a media extravaganza. Similar practices were apparent during the election campaign of 1988. Several elderly living in Villa Azul who had obtained assistance pensions through the *Grupo* and provincial social workers were forced to participate in a stage-managed lottery as part of an open-air political rally. Sra HF described the spectacle:

HF: Now they're giving me this pension.

[*Interviewer*: The assistance pension?]

HF: Yes, the assistance one I got in a lottery...It was a thing that the president of here [the *Grupo*] Doña María [Perez] took me to. We got these things like...coupons. Everyone was there – the girl [social worker]. And what was that thing called that I signed? The councillor was there too. I stayed put and they started the lottery. One person won, then another.

[Son interrupts: They were from the Province of Buenos Aires.]

HF: Bingo! I had the [winning] paper!...I was waiting there and María told me 'Stay put and if you're in luck they'll pick your number out.' 'Oh, please God, María.' And there was one lady, then another and then 'Sra HF!' It was me! 'Oh, look, María, it's me!' I was overcome with emotion, dear, and they were even filming it and everything. I could collect the money right away, they paid me inside a month.

[*Interviewer*: Did all the people [in Villa Azul] who got assistance pensions get them at this lottery?]

Eulogia B [secretary of *Grupo*] [interjects rather nervously]: No, no, no. I don't think there was anyone else.

HF: [disagreeing with Eulogia] No, no, no. Then they gave out plots of land. Yes, they gave us plots.

[*Interviewer*: How many people got assistance pensions there?]

Son: Twenty-four people, twenty-four, I think.

[*Interviewer*: Were there other lotteries?]

Eulogia B: No, no. There just seems to have been one. It didn't come back again. There seems to have been just the one. I don't know because I didn't go.

HF: [disagreeing with Eulogia again] No, lots. The little old lady around the corner. Lots of people got pensions...

[*Interviewer*: Were the press there?]

HF: All of them as well as the television. A plane came. The councillor came by helicopter.

Son: No, it was the governor of the Province of Buenos Aires. The old one when Alfonsín was still in power [Sr Cafiero, a Peronist].

(Sra HF, Villa Azul, June 1993)

Sra Eulogia B gave the impression of wishing to play down the importance of the lotteries. This paralleled her reticence in front of the tape recorder when describing her own political contacts. This may have been because, unlike Sra HF, she was aware of the illicit nature of such clientelistic practices and preferred discretion. Another interviewee made reference to what may have been another stage-managed pension presentation in a school.

Conversely, elderly *villeros* occasionally lost their benefits due to the corrupt practices of officials, lawyers and even relatives. Again, Sra HF recounted her experiences:

[*Interviewer*: Your father used to work for the railway?]

HF: Yes.

[*Interviewer*: And he had problems with his pension?]

HF: Yes.

[*Interviewer*: Could you give me a little more information about this?]

HF: It turned out that...father died and so they passed the pension on to my mother. My mother got me a card and kept everything [documentation] from the railway safe, she kept absolutely everything. She made a card so that I could go and collect it for her – a trustee...What happened then? ...mother died and he [her uncle] came. He said 'Look, Haidee', my uncle Salvador Corso told me 'Look, Haidee, I'm going to take you to the railway but you have to give me them [the papers] now. They're going to give you money for your mother's funeral.' Because when mother died they had to pay for the funeral...And so he took me there. We had to take the receipts for the stupid thing [funeral], because you have to have all your papers in good order there. We got the receipt for the stupid thing signed. It was the man who had attended her, the mortician.

> He [uncle] took me and we went upstairs, not to the pension offices but to the railway ones. And he said 'Here, I've brought her' he said to the main boss 'This here is the daughter of Augustín F.'...'Good', he [the official] said. 'We're going to pay you, you're due the money for your mother's funeral.' And I asked him 'Aren't I due the pension as well, sir?' 'No you're not eligible, you won't get it.' 'And why won't I get any of the pension?' 'Because you just won't, miss', he said. 'The railway already gave it to your father and mother. The *Fraternidad* [railway union] is different. If your father had been, if he had paid the *Fraternidad*, then yes you would get it.' Then he told me, he made me sign, a piece of paper like this, he made me sign, so I signed.
>
> Then it turned out that after a long time a neighbour came by. 'I'm going to take you to a lawyer of mine. You ought to be getting your father's *jubilación*. The railway should be paying it you.' Well, we went to the lawyer's and my neighbour's lawyer told me 'Yes, missus, they made you sign and now another person is receiving the pension...It should be yours, missus, you alone. Its your pension. You've got all the papers.' I've got all of them, everything. Look at them! I've still got the stuff, the date of death. Look at that! 'It should have been yours, missus. Why did you sign?' 'My uncle made me sign.'...This man who loved my mother so much. Look what he did to me. They told me that he's the one who's getting it.
>
> (Sra HF, Villa Azul, June 1993)

There are a number of possible explanations for this sequence of events. It is possible, but unlikely, that the lawyer was mistaken or lying in order to make a commission. It is more probable that Sra HF was tricked in some way, since the virtual closed shop operating in the railways during the period of her father's employment meant that opting out of membership dues to the *Fraternidad* was very difficult (Thompson, 1992:165–6). However, when her mother died, some time around 1952, Haidee was only in her early thirties and clearly not eligible for a benefit according to the criteria applied in the early 1990s. During the 1950s there were no assistance benefits at the national level targeting single mothers, although it is possible that benefits were available through trade unions or local government agencies. Thus, it is plausible that the 'railway office' was staffed by a corrupt official, who deprived Sra HF of her pension rights.

This was the only reference made by respondents to being cheated out of state benefits and so it is unlikely that this was a widespread occurrence. Nevertheless, it indicated the vulnerability of poorly educated *villeros* and provided another disincentive to actively pursue claims.

CONCLUSIONS

As has been shown, the patterns of income for elderly *villeros* and their underlying causes were complex and not always obvious. Consequently, few generalisations can be made about their economic condition. Whilst levels of insurance coverage were much lower than elsewhere in Greater Buenos Aires, *jubilados* still accounted for 28 per cent of respondents. In the great majority of cases, elderly *villeros* combined income from two or more sources. This reflected the inadequacy of benefit values and the low wages paid for such part-time employment as *changas* and laundry work. Support from family members was more commonplace than in Argentina as a whole but this did not reflect an ethic of helping or prioritising the needs of the elderly. Instead, as the various testimonies indicated, it was more usual to prioritise the needs of young children.

Whilst patterns of elderly *villero* income maintenance displayed some elements of duality between the formal/insurance and informal/assistance sectors, this generalisation did not always hold true and it disguised the existence of numerous important sub-groups of respondents. Among the most disadvantaged were women who had worked as domestic servants, those with serious health problems and those without any economically secure relatives.

The survey also indicates that there was a gap between potential entitlement to state benefits and actual access to them. This may have been larger for assistance than insurance pensions, depending on the eligibility criteria used. The 'benefit gap' was largely due to the failings of public agencies, including the inadequate dissemination of information, needless bureaucratic obstacles and delays in following up paperwork. More generally, it reflected the attitudes of responsible state bodies and government officials, who balked at taking a proactive approach, actually seeking out potential claimants, rather than waiting for them to visit offices located in the city centre.

No other studies of potential and actual access to benefits exist for other developing countries or elsewhere in Argentina. As such, it is not possible to draw comparisons between the *villas* studied here and other areas. There are, however, various reasons for concluding that the 'benefit gap' was more prominent in the *villas* than in other parts of Greater Buenos Aires. A larger proportion of elderly *villeros* had been working in the informal sector and had been either self-employed or employed in small firms which were less likely to give them assistance with paperwork and legal matters. Moreover, a number of studies have shown that levels of educational attainment among *villeros* were significantly lower than other groups (Table 4.1). As a result, the process of making an insurance pension claim was much more challenging for many *villeros*. If it is recognised that the benefit gap for assistance pensions was particularly large, the *villeros'* high degree of reliance on such support increased their vulnerability. Finally, as was shown both in this chapter and the preceding one, effective local organisations specifically targeting the needs of the elderly played a significant role in facilitating access to benefits. The absence of PAMI-funded *Centros de Jubilados* in the *villas* studied thus constituted another restriction on *villeros'* access to state support.

Both the high proportion of elderly *villeros* who had made no insurance contributions and their occasional reluctance to pursue benefit claims could, at times, be explained in terms of opportunity costs (either real or perceived). As has been shown, it may not have appeared rational for *villeros* to defer consumption or to trust a share of their income to a large, bureaucratic apparatus. Likewise, the efforts required to obtain information and overcome administrative obstacles to obtaining a benefit may have outweighed its short-term value. These opportunity costs were often greater for elderly *villeros* than for other groups because of their economically marginal status.

6 Conclusions

Since the mid-twentieth century the demographic structures of most developing countries have been transformed. Precipitous falls in mortality rates prompted extremely high levels of total population growth and the dramatic expansion of younger age cohorts. These changes generated understandable concern and have dominated debates about Third World development. More recently, however, the population dynamics of many developing countries have experienced a second radical change. Mortality rates have started to stabilise and levels of fertility have begun to drop, often sharply. In many senses these are welcome effects, since they entail a reduction in total population growth rates. However, one consequence of this change which has received little attention to date is the growing proportion of elderly in many developing countries. Whilst population ageing is a desirable process, it also poses a number of major challenges for the economic, social and political structures of these countries. This book has examined one key problem: the need to guarantee the elderly an acceptable level of economic welfare. As has been seen, elderly welfare is not just a question of effective social security provision. It is equally influenced by labour market dynamics and micro-scale social relations, as well as factors operating at the community level. Little is known about these effects and further research is urgently required to provide the basis for effective policy initiatives.

In much of the developing world, formal social security provision has been under increasing strain in recent decades. This has partly resulted from a generalised crisis of the public sector, which has prompted structural adjustment programmes and the wholesale privatisation of state services, including social welfare. At the same time, growing poverty and increased informality in labour markets have reduced the proportion of the workforce which is in a position to defer consumption until old age (through pension contributions or private savings). As such, it is likely that the welfare of tomorrow's elderly will increasingly depend upon continued employment and family support.

THE STATE AND SOCIAL SECURITY IN ARGENTINA

In the early and middle decades of the twentieth century Argentina had been a prosperous country, even by the standards of the developed world. However, a disastrous economic performance since the 1930s reduced it to 'just another middle-income developing country', facing major structural difficulties. Nevertheless, Argentina's past prosperity has left several marks. First, it caused the country to develop a demographic profile similar to that of richer nations, with a high concentration of elderly. Secondly, it saw the emergence of a large and well-developed public sector, which included a relatively embracing system of state welfare provision.

Premature demographic ageing created the need for effective welfare programmes in Argentina. The result was one of the most comprehensive social security systems to be found in the developing world. The establishment of a public sector welfare monopoly was, however, not simply a response to demographic trends, nor was it prompted by a breakdown of pre-existing welfare structures. Although mutual aid societies had run into financial difficulties during the First World War, they continued to grow rapidly until the 1940s. Church organisations had also expanded their activities. Instead, the public sector monopoly reflected the prevailing developmentalist orthodoxy which advocated high levels of state intervention in all areas of the economy. This did not involve the administrative restructuring and financial rationalisation of existing piecemeal state welfare initiatives. Rather, the expansion of the system led to the multiplication of institutional weaknesses. Within 30 years of its instigation, it had become apparent that the public sector monopoly in its current form was both financially unsustainable in the medium term (indeed, it jeopardised the success of the economy as a whole) and was failing to provide effective, universal protection to groups such as the elderly.

From the mid-1970s there were increasing indications of a shift away from the public sector welfare monopoly. Attempts to downgrade state commitment to shoring up the social security system met with stiff political resistance. Nevertheless, the change in policy orientation gradually brought about a number of significant modifications in the pattern of welfare provision. Greater opportunities were created for the participation of NGOs, community associations and private insurance companies. These were, however, unable to fully compensate for gaps in state provision. By the early 1990s more radical changes were sought, including the partial privatisation of the national social insurance fund. These trends towards greater plurality have mirrored developments across the world.

The historical evolution of welfare programmes in Argentina had bequeathed an unfortunate hybrid of statism and pluralism. Public sector agencies were of a scale and complexity associated with an embracing welfare state. However, this was not matched by the financial resources allocated to them. This problem combined with a low standard of personnel, many of whom had been recruited for political reasons, to reduce the quality and quantity of coverage afforded groups such as the elderly.

It would be dangerous to draw many comparisons between the recent pluralisation of welfare services in Argentina and conditions before the public welfare monopoly, since almost all aspects of the country's economic and social structures have been radically transformed. In the early twentieth century Argentina suffered from a general shortage of labour (hence the need for immigrants). In such a scenario, it might be expected that workers would be able to fend for themselves or make welfare conquests, either through wage increases or social legislation. More recently, the country has been suffering from a labour surplus, reflected in rising informality and unemployment. In this case, the scope for voluntary and private sector insurance initiatives is considerably reduced and the need for state welfare guarantees is greater.

It is important to assess the extent to which the failure of Argentina's state monopoly was attributable to inherent weaknesses of the public sector. Had the post-war performance of the economy been stronger and had state welfare programmes been implemented along more rational lines, it is conceivable that many of the problems which beset the social insurance system could have been avoided or resolved relatively painlessly. Some insights can be obtained with reference to the cases of Brazil and Mexico, both of which enjoyed impressive growth in the post-war era, yet whose welfare systems were also suffering severe crises by the 1980s. Moreover, the social security systems of Brazil and Mexico, as in much of Latin America, contained similar institutional weaknesses to those which afflicted the Argentine one. Many of these resulted from a failure to demarcate clearly the respective roles of state and government. This encouraged bureaucratic featherbedding and the precedence of short-term political objectives over longer-term economic rationalism. Thus, it would seem that the disorganised implementation of Argentina's state welfare monopoly was indeed to some extent the result of inherent weaknesses in the nature of the public sector in much of Latin America. It is less apparent whether these weaknesses are equally evident in other developing regions. As was seen in Chapter 1, countries such as Singapore and Malaysia have been able to establish highly effective state welfare programmes.

OLD AGE AND POVERTY IN THE *VILLAS MISERIAS* OF BUENOS AIRES

Virtually all the existing research on social security and other aspects of income maintenance in developing regions examines the impact of a single welfare institution on a broad swathe of groups. This book takes a different approach, focusing on one relatively narrow group (elderly *villeros*), but including all relevant institutions. This enables a more complete investigation which includes the historical evolution of both the group and institutions studied and a detailed analysis of their position in the early 1990s. Also it draws attention to the ways in which institutions combine to provide elderly *villeros* with a framework of resource opportunities and constraints.

There are a number of strong motives for studying *villeros*, as opposed to other sub-groups of elderly. Since they are among the poorest and most disadvantaged residents of Buenos Aires, their situation is comparable with more general living conditions in less affluent Third World cities. By studying *villeros*, it is possible to assess whether demographic ageing has been mainly confined to richer groups. Although it is to be hoped that the process has not excluded the poor, it is also the case that this scenario would entail a much greater challenge in areas such as welfare provision. Also, focusing on *villeros* enables a rigorous appraisal of social welfare programmes. On the one hand, this group should be a prime beneficiary of effective welfare safety nets and targeted programmes. On the other, *villeros* are more socially and economically vulnerable than other groups and therefore likely to suffer particularly acutely as a result of any shortcomings in welfare programmes.

The failure of the welfare system was clearly reflected by the experiences of elderly *villeros*. Among this group, contributory pensions were much less widespread than was the case for Greater Buenos Aires as a whole. This was in large part due to a greater tendency to have avoided insurance contributions in the past, although a significant minority of unprotected elderly claimed to have made some or all such payments. Low levels of insurance coverage were partly, but by no means completely, compensated for by the targeting of assistance benefits. Even so, a number of *villeros* who were clearly entitled to such assistance did not receive it. As such, it was possible to identify gaps between potential entitlement and actual access both to insurance and assistance pensions. These gaps were mainly due to the ineffectual administration of state agencies. Problems included the inadequate dissemination of information about available benefits and procedures, overly complex bureaucratic processes and a failure to take a proactive approach to identifying those most in need. At the same time, there were sharp discrepancies between the benefits promised by the system and the financial provision made for them. For insurance programmes this was reflected in pension values which fell short of legally stipulated minimums. For assistance programmes it had led to long waiting lists for benefits which should have been immediately available.

By the early 1990s, a variety of non-state institutions were seeking to improve the economic condition of elderly *villeros*. In each of the three *villas* studied, outside actors had helped establish local associations. These primarily served as conduits for resources distributed by state agencies, such as local government assistance programmes. They also served as sources of information about available benefits and their bureaucratic requirements. As such, they provided an important bridge between state agencies and the groups which were theoretically being targeted. Among such organisations knowledge of welfare programmes and contacts (formal or otherwise) with external agencies were very varied. This had led to clear discrepancies in the types of assistance benefits most frequently held in the different *villas*.

The failure of large-scale institutions to provide adequate economic support to elderly *villeros* meant that many depended upon personal strategies for a good part, if not all, of their income. Elderly *villeros* were more likely to continue in employment than those living elsewhere, although this usually entailed informal or part-time activities. Support from family members, particularly those beyond the household, was higher than that recorded by surveys of other districts. However, in the great majority of cases, elderly *villeros* received no such family support or were themselves the providers. A small but significant number of respondents had no income whatsoever and were reduced to relying on the charity of neighbours or the contents of rubbish tips. These elderly were arguably among the city's most abject and abandoned residents.

The book argues that elderly *villeros* were 'doubly marginal', in terms of their age and their residence in shanty towns. This was reflected in their education, employment (past and present), access to contributory pensions, general expectations and political attitudes. In a comprehensive, universal welfare state, such a group would receive considerable assistance to compensate for its position of relative disadvantage and vulnerability. In an economy where welfare coverage is less complete, available resources should be focused on the needs of such groups. Whilst there were some indications of assistance targeting in the three *villas* studied, several of the most acutely deprived individuals remained without any form of state support. Rather than increasing the likelihood of support, restricted mobility (through illness, disability or a fear of crime), a lack of education or even a lack of disposable income often served as barriers to obtaining benefits.

The failure of state agencies to reach the most deserving and vulnerable elderly would not have been avoided by leaving this task to the private and voluntary sectors. As has been seen, NGOs and local initiatives usually had few monetary resources of their own to fill this gap. Informal support from friends and neighbours was unsystematic and largely restricted to the most desperate cases. High unemployment reduced the capacities of both the elderly to fend for themselves and family members to provide support. Finally, the expansion of private insurance was of no relevance, since such companies only sought to include individuals with high and reliable income streams.

Rather than reducing the role of the public sector, the best prospects of improving the economic condition of the most disadvantaged elderly *villeros* were through the administrative reform of assistance agencies and the provision of funding which reflected the true number of elderly eligible for benefits. Key elements of administrative reform would have been the reduction of bureaucratic red tape and increased efforts to actively seek out needy cases, possibly by developing better links with community initiatives. Reform should also have included reversing the trend of administrative fragmentation, which increased staffing costs and led to a complex range of often overlapping benefits, with different eligibility criteria and procedures for making claims. A more unified administration and array of benefits would have greatly facilitated the dissemination of information to target groups and increased the accountability of the agencies involved.

The combined reform and upgrading of assistance for the elderly would have been a major challenge, requiring considerable planning and expertise. One way in which this might have been facilitated would have been by bringing such programmes within the activities of the INSSJP. Through the PAMI programme, the Institute had already obtained much experience of providing non-contributory services to *jubilados* and had developed a national network of community organisations. By extending its activities to include all the aged population, it would have been possible to avoid bureaucratic duplication and to reduce any dualism between insured and non-insured elderly. The privatisation of the social insurance system had not threatened the status of the Institute, which was considered a separate entity.

LESSONS FROM THE ARGENTINE EXPERIENCE

What lessons can be drawn from the Argentine case for those countries in Latin America and other developing regions which are now experiencing accelerated demographic ageing?

The first general point concerns relationships between welfare policy and economic development. Argentina provides a clear example of a country whose initially generous social policies were gradually undermined by a protracted period of economic underperformance. From this there emerged a complex vicious circle of falling wages, contracting formal employment, reduced tax and social security revenue and general institutional decline. The recent pension reform constituted an attempt to wipe the slate clean and establish a new, harmonious circle of accumulation, economic growth and, less emphatically, welfare. Thus, the Argentine case demonstrates that long-run economic buoyancy is essential for the continued effectiveness of welfare programmes. It should not, however, be assumed that economic growth alone can guarantee general welfare. The experiences of countries such as Brazil and Mexico show that, without the correct institutional structures, growth may even serve to increase the poverty and hardship faced by large sectors of society.

It is also important to consider relationships between welfare policy and politics. On one hand, ensuring that every person in a country enjoys a socially acceptable level of welfare is usually seen as a collective social responsibility and, as such, should be a key function of the state. On the other, the way the public sector has evolved in Argentina and many other developing countries has subverted its role as arbiter of general welfare and transformed it into a financial honey-pot contested by sectoral interest groups. In the context of Argentina's economic decline, this led to a zero-sum game in which more powerful groups sought to maximise their share of the spoils and in which policy reflected short-term political concerns rather than long-term economic realities.

An essential challenge is how to resolve the inherent weakness of the public sector in such countries without threatening the universal welfare guarantee. The results of this study suggest that elderly welfare is best provided by strengthening and reforming the role of the public sector, not reducing it to the bare minimum. Privatising pension programmes may be a short-cut to reducing administrative inefficiency and increasing returns on contributions, as well as stimulating capital markets. It is, however, of little relevance for groups which are unable to make insurance contributions, be they to the public or private sector. The testimonies of *villeros* indicate that neo-liberal policies which deregulate labour markets and promote the growth of the informal sector reduce the capacity of workers to make contributions. Such policies will increase the need for social assistance as these workers become elderly and may therefore simply constitute deferring the cost of provision to future generations.

Several observations can also be made about relationships between welfare policy and distributive justice. The politicised evolution of welfare in Argentina had led to a pronounced dualism in terms of the services offered and the entitlements extended to different sections of population. On paper, this dualism existed between formal sector workers, who had paid their taxes and made their pension contributions and those people who had not fulfilled such obligations, whether by choice or constraint. The actual situation was not so clear-cut, however. On one hand, governments had sometimes offered amnesties to pension contribution evaders. On the other, some of those who had made contributions, more usually the poor, self-employed and poorly educated, were unable to claim their supposed entitlements. Furthermore, since the budgetary requirements of Argentina's insurance pension programme were increasingly being met by general public funds, those individuals with full welfare entitlements were in fact being subsidised by the rest. Within this issue lies a more fundamental question. Should an individual who works as a casual rural labourer (perhaps from early adolescence), who then migrates to a city to seek industrial employment but who is forced intermittently and then more permanently into the informal sector, be denied the basic welfare rights extended to a different individual who spends 30 or so years as a white collar or factory worker? This is a question which goes to the very heart of welfare policy throughout the developing world but which has frequently been overshadowed by more technocratic concerns.

A number of more specific policy recommendations can be taken from the *villeros*' experiences. First, they highlight the need to combine welfare policy with a more comprehensive understanding of the socio-economic conditions of target groups. For example, policies should consider the elderly as part of a household unit rather than as individuals. If the welfare of other household members, particularly young children, is ignored, elderly individuals are themselves likely to suffer. The same problem will arise if employment opportunities for the main household breadwinners are restricted. A logical step would be to develop new welfare policies which seek to target households rather than individuals.

Welfare programmes should equally take account of the socio-cultural characteristics of target groups, since these may not necessarily coincide with those of the majority. In the case of *villeros*, it was necessary to consider factors such as attitudes to ageing, widespread illiteracy, a mistrust of authority and low levels of expectation. This should be linked to an understanding of the dramatic processes of social change which may have effected different sub-groups of elderly in different ways.

Welfare policy should also recognise the potential value of effective, participatory grassroots organisations for elderly, especially those experiencing severe poverty. These organisations can be used to disseminate information about available benefits and procedures. They may also draw attention to individuals in acute need and thus facilitate the targeting of assistance. It should not be assumed that these community initiatives develop spontaneously. Chapter 4 emphasised the key role which can be played by enlightened outside actors in this process. Research carried out in São Paulo, Brazil, was unable to find any similar sorts of organisation catering specifically for the city's 40000 elderly shanty town residents. This appeared to reflect the lack of interest taken by local government and local NGOs in São Paulo, rather than a reduced desire and capacity for organisation on the part of the elderly themselves.[1] With a small amount of financial backing from the state, the successful experiences of NGOs such as CEPEV could be emulated in other concentrations of urban poverty across Buenos Aires and beyond.

Finally, the Argentine experience shows that, although demographic ageing is in itself a considerable achievement, it must not be considered a costless one. Unlike other major social and economic changes, it is possible to predict ageing with a considerable degree of confidence. This gives policy-makers an opportunity to develop and adapt strategies to meet the needs of tomorrow's elderly. If this is not done, population ageing may indeed become the next social crisis to face the developing world.

Notes

CHAPTER 1

1. Whilst many studies refer to the 'problem' or 'crisis' of population ageing, it should be borne in mind that greater longevity is in fact a highly desirable process. Rather than population ageing per se, it is the economic and social ramifications of the process which should be considered as potentially problematic.
2. International Conference on Population and Development, 1995:190–1. Whilst no mention was made of the aged, a number of other groups were prioritised, including migrants, indigenous peoples, women and children.
3. For a good account of this model, see Chesnais, 1992.
4. Aghajanian, 1992:283–5 provides a more detailed account of these trends.
5. An excellent account of population ageing in China is provided in Banister, 1987.
6. The only country with a higher concentration is Uruguay, where 16.8 per cent of the population was aged 60 or over in 1990.
7. These issues are discussed in Albert and Cattell, 1994:47–50 and Araba Apt, 1996:10–11.
8. The impact of this process in Ghana is well described in Araba Apt, 1996:39–40.
9. The Spanish term for this is *seguro social*, not to be confused with *seguridad social*, which refers to social security as a whole (see Comisión Económica para America Latina, 1985:3).
10. For examples of the region's diversity, see the chapters on China, Thailand and India in Lloyd-Sherlock and Johnson, eds, 1996.
11. Information about the structure, legal basis and benefits granted by the two Indian programmes is available in Government of India, 1994:140–5.
12. Brooks and Nyirenda, 1987:258 note that the programme provided for a grand total of 55 elderly by 1981.
13. Compare the arguments put forward by Mesa-Lago, 1978:5–10 and Malloy, 1979:3–10.
14. The most extreme case of this is probably Colombia, where a recent survey found over a thousand separate public sector pension agencies (Frediani, 1989).
15. For example, unofficial estimates gauge that 40 per cent of social insurance contributions in Brazil had simply gone missing by 1991 (*El País*, 31 March 1991).
16. Vittas, 1992:2. Sadly, this point was not made with the same force by later World Bank publications, which come out strongly in favour of private sector pension administration in all economies.
17. For a strong critique of Peruvian programmes in the 1980s see Graham, 1994:98–112.
18. In 1986 the Argentine Supreme Court ordered massive increases in pension payments which threatened to bankrupt the national government. In Brazil a similar situation arose in 1988.

19. Isuani, 1985:95 provides an alternative estimate of 42 per cent for Brazilian coverage in 1979/80; Lischinsky, 1989 shows that official Argentine data were very inaccurate. Also, see Mesa-Lago, 1991a:47–49 for general criticisms of official sources.
20. For example, Lloyd-Sherlock, 1992:20 notes that whilst Chilean insurance funds allegedly included 79 per cent of the working population in 1992, only 42 per cent of the total were regularly making contributions.
21. This argument was first developed by Mesa-Lago, 1978:5–14.
22. See Hakkert and Goza, 1989:23–4 and Roberts, 1991:100 for examples of these opposed interpretations.
23. For a review of this tendency in Latin America see Stren, ed, 1995:10–12.
24. Examples of this include Mayumi Yazaki, Viera de Melo and Ramos, 1991 and Pan American Health Organisation, 1989.
25. This is clearly the case in Knopoff et al, 1991 in which the only chapter dealing with the economic welfare of the elderly is entitled '*El bienestar de los ancianos: un problema para la seguridad social*' [Elderly welfare: a problem for social security].
26. Araba Apt, 1996:34–46. Similar concerns are expressed in studies of other developing countries. For example, Vatuk, 1982:70–103.
27. Very little research has been carried out into this issue. Tout, 1989:88–90, found that remittances in India most frequently occurring between parents and their children, rather than directly to the elderly.
28. For example, Tout, 1989:63 found that 48 per cent of over-70-year-olds in parts of rural Ecuador remained in employment but that the daily workload only averaged five hours. For other examples, see Dharmalingham, 1994:12–14; Devi,1992:425–31.
29. For an excellent discussion of these problems see Cain, 1991:189–202.
30. The economically active include '...all persons in employment...as well as all the unemployed (both those with previous job experience and those seeking work for the first time)' (ILO, 1986a:5).
31. For a good analysis of the traditional roles of women in providing care to the elderly see Walker, 1992:5–18.
32. For example Tout, 1989 provides a general overview of local projects for the elderly funded by the international NGO Help Age International.
33. Leis, 1989 refers to the pivotal role played by elderly women in the human rights movement during the late 1970s. The high level of political mobilisation among Argentina's elderly in the early 1990s is reflected in the frequency of protests and demonstrations against state pensions policy.

CHAPTER 2

1. Calculated from Diaz Alejandro, 1970:6, 70; ECLAC, 1981:206–7; 1992:68–9.
2. Recchini de Lattes, 1975:115 (urban areas are defined as settlements of at least 2000 people).
3. A survey of population growth between 1840 and 1940 estimated that immigrant rates of natural increase after arrival in Argentina were only two-

thirds of the rate of native Argentines (Mortara, 1947). This indicates that immigrant fertility did not subsequently converge with national levels.

4. In 1940 the crude birth rate per 1000 was 24.0 in Argentina, compared to 33.4 in both Chile and Paraguay (Argentine Republic, 1956a:69).
5. For accounts of early healthcare development, see Isuani and Mercer, 1988:45–8 and Recalde 1991:63–84. Other social welfare developments are looked at in detail in the next chapter.
6. This point is not made in existing studies. For example, UN, 1991b:27–33, stresses the importance of various factors but makes no reference to mass immigration. Muller, 1981:9 briefly alludes to immigration but makes no mention of its impact on fertility.
7. For examples of these differences, see ECLAC, 1981:84–96.
8. As Map 2.1 shows, Greater Buenos Aires is formed by the Federal Capital district (Capital) and neighbouring municipalities in the surrounding Buenos Aires Province (the Provincial Section). In 1991 the Capital had a population of 2965403, the Provincial Section contained 7969324 people and the remaining parts of the Province not included as Greater Buenos Aires held 4625650.
9. C. Escudé, 1976:114. Regional comparisons of social security coverage are made in Chapter 3.
10. Torrado 1992:83–8 gives a detailed statistical analysis of these internal migrations. In 1947 crude reproduction rates in northern Argentina were 2.9, compared to only 1.0 in the Federal Capital and Province of Buenos Aires (Schkolnik, 1975:110–11).
11. For example Greater Buenos Aires contained 21.5 per cent of industrial establishments by 1914, compared to 25.8 per cent of the national population (Walter, 1982:95. This figure may underestimate the true importance of industry in the city since average firm sizes may have been larger than elsewhere. This indicator is used because data for personnel employed are unavailable).
12. Walter, 1982:95. More detail about the composition of industrial growth around the city is available in Provincia de Buenos Aires, 1947:67–82.
13. CEPAL, 1959:39. An important element of this was the expansion of social welfare agencies (see Chapter 3).
14. For a detailed examination of low income housing in Buenos Aires before the 1940s, see Lloyd-Sherlock, 1996b.
15. The fall in the shanty town population of the Federal Capital during the 1970s was the result of forced eradication programmes implemented by the military government of the day. These are well described in Bellardi and De Paula, 1986:23–62.
16. For example, in 1970 47 per cent of the population of Mexico City and 59 per cent in Bogotá lived in precarious, shanty town-type accommodation (Gilbert, 1993:22 and 119).
17. Between 1980 and 1993 the number of shanty town residents in São Paulo aged 60 or more rose from 4700 (1.4 per cent of the total population) to 43750 (2.3 per cent) (Prefeitura de São Paulo, 1994:79).

CHAPTER 3

1. Article 31 of the 1949 Constitution cited in Argentine Republic, 1950:21.
2. Ross, 1989:276. For an account of a similar presentation ceremony, though not specifically involving the elderly, see 'The first lady participates in the distribution of grants' *Crónica Mensual de la Secretaría de Trabajo y Previsión*, November 1946, pp.106–7.
3. *Review of the River Plate*, 9 October 1953 gives an account of the financial problems of the railway and urban transport funds. Similar accounts are given in González Galé, 1929:5 and Argentine Republic, *Caja Nacional de Jubilaciones y Pensiones*, 1914:51–63.
4. These transfers were facilitated by the establishment of a co-ordinating agency, the *Instituto Nacional de Previsión Social*, in 1944 (Lloyd-Sherlock, 1992).
5. A clear example was the pledge made by the Frondizi administration in 1958 that average pension values would be at least 82 per cent of the recipient's previous earnings (see *Review of the River Plate*, 21 August 1958, 19 September 1958 and 21 September 1959). A 1966 survey found that 26 per cent of pensioners had retired under 50 (Feldman et al, 1988:44).
6. In 1963 it was estimated that the state owed the funds a sum equivalent to half Argentina's GNP (*Review of the River Plate*, 11 November 1963).
7. In Argentine Republic, *Consejo Federal de Seguridad Social de la República Argentina*, 1967:112 it is estimated that evasion rose from 31.3 to 55 per cent of total contributions between 1950 and 1958.
8. Tenti Fanfani, 1989:83–90 provides an excellent analysis of the origins and evolution of these programmes.
9. See Golbert, 1988 for a detailed study of the Institute and its healthcare project: *el Programa de Asistencia Médica Integral* (PAMI).
10. In 1993 these discounts ranged from 30 per cent for drugs dealing with mild problems to 100 per cent for those treating serious illness.
11. Marshall, 1988 contains a good description of social policy during the *Proceso*.
12. Feldman et al, 1993:41–2 note that there were occasionally dramatic hikes in benefit values. However, Dieguez and Petrecolla, 1974 claim that over the long-run average payments fell. This was due to a failure to index pensions to inflation.
13. Data from the *Subsecretaría de Seguridad Social* presented in 'Why a social plan?' *Clarín*, Buenos Aires, 18 January 1993.
14. Mesa-Lago 1991: Table 5, p. 202. The high costs in Chile were largely the result of an intense sales and marketing drive (Lloyd-Sherlock, 1992b:18).
15. Isuani and San Martino, 1993:41–77, provide detailed descriptions of the various reform proposals put forward.
16. The PAN programme led to the creation of a complicated hierarchy of state distribution agencies ranging from municipalities to the national headquarters. The BNSE was distributed through central trade union offices (Midre, 1992:350–5).
17. Midre, 1992 gives a general critique of both programmes. Whilst Golbert, 1993:46 shows that high proportions of shanty town families participated in

the two schemes, Aguirre, 1990 claims that their impact on poor households was insignificant.

18. Waldman, 1993:90–102 effectively contrasts these two approaches.
19. Between September 1991 and September 1992 the real value of the minimum insurance pension fell by 15.8 per cent (*Clarín*, 29 September 1992).
20. 'The pensioner protest in the limelight' *Clarín*, 20 October 1992.
21. *El Cronista*, 15 October 1992 gives an account of one of the failed attempts to get the reform bill through the National Congress.
22. President Menem himself strongly advocated the private funds (*Clarín*, 3 May 1994).
23. Between 1983 and 1993, public sector employment in provincial governments rose by 40 per cent (World Bank, 1993:129).
24. For example, in 1980 the proportion of total employment in the Capital and PBA accounted for by the public sector was 19.4 and 17.3 per cent respectively, whilst domestic service accounted for 6.0 and 7.3 per cent (Argentine Republic, *Consejo Federal de Inversiones*, 1989: Volume II:45 and Volume IV:45).
25. In 1993 the Supreme Court ruled that a 93-year-old woman was too old to be made to wait to cash her bonds ('The Court ruled that a *jubilado* be paid in cash instead of bonds' *Clarín*, 30 April 1993).
26. A survey conducted by the *Universidad Argentina de La Empresa* calculated that between September 1991 and September 1992 the real value of the minimum insurance pension fell by 15.8 per cent. See 'A downturn in salaries' *Clarín*, 29 September 1992.
27. *Clarín*, 29 September, 1992. The monthly basket was defined by the *Instituto Nacional de Estadística y Censo.* Whilst the needs of an elderly individual do not correspond to those of an entire household, it should be noted that possession of such a pension usually renders a spouse ineligible for assistance benefits.
28. Sábato, 1988 and Dieguez and Petrecolla, 1977:181–92 provide detailed accounts of the development of privileged pension funds.
29. '*Deficit millionario de las cajas*' *El Cronista*, 20 September 1993. Dieguez and Petrecolla, 1977:183–4 give a brief account of the historical evolution of these funds.
30. See Blanco, 1989 for outlines of these proposals. However, these grants do not figure in data on PAMI's expenditure presented in Golbert 1988:58. PREALC, 1989:64–5 refers to PAMI's general financial difficulties in the late 1980s.
31. PAMI 1992a:8–9, proposes that grants should be provided in cases of 'urgent social emergency'. Rather than providing for the costs of family care, it simply states that household unity should be encouraged.
32. 'An announcement from PAMI' *Página 12*, 30 April 1993.
33. 'The pending allowance' *Página 12*, 28 October 1992.
34. Interview with N. Redondo of PAMI, 27 May 1993.
35. See PAMI 1992b, for PAMI guidelines for the establishment and structure of day centres.
36. 'An announcement from PAMI', *Clarín*, 30 April 1993.
37. For example, see 'A drawn-out march' *Página 12*, 12 November 1992; 'The PJ [Peronist party] resigns itself to postponing the pension reform until

February' *El Cronista*, 30 December 1992; 'Another three jubilados commit suicide' *Clarín*, 15 October 1992.

38. 'Why a social plan?' *Clarín*, 18 January 1993.
39. 'Immediate benefits for 750 000 *jubilados*' *La seguridad social en la Argentina*, January 1993. This apparent financial success was later discovered to be illusory ('PAMI: 148 million dollars missing' *Microsemanario*, 28 June 1994).
40. Article 9 of Law 13 478 and subsequent revisions (Vasquez Vialard, 1954:433).
41. 'Proof' usually required photocopies of family members' past pay slips.
42. Data concerning the proportion of these pensions granted to the elderly were unavailable. However, it is probable that they counted for the majority.
43. By 1984 these housed a grand total of 1040 elderly (Tenti Fanfani, 1989:179).
44. Interview with Cecilia Oetel, director of the DNA, 26 March 1993.
45. Data for early 1996 show that 45 per cent of pensions were awarded to people aged less than 58 years old ('The secret trade in honorary pensions' *La Nación*, 6 February 1996).
46. In 1993 the annual sums awarded were: US$ 4000 to national deputies and US$ 9000 to party leaders. In 1996 it was claimed that many of these pensions were awarded on a nepotistic basis.
47. Calculated from Table 3.2.
48. The DNA's director admitted this in an interview, 26 March 1993.
49. 'How to put out the fire' *Página 12*, 28 October 1992.
50. For example, 'The hour for social spending' *La seguridad social en la Argentina*, April 1993, lists recent initiatives for the elderly but makes no mention of the Secretaría.
51. 'Protected by law' *Página 12*, 28 October 1992 speculates that PAMI will be integrated into the *Secretaría*. 'An evening of dogs' *Página 12*, 30 October 1992 describes hurried meetings between National President Menem and the PAMI director who agree that the two agencies will remain separate.
52. See 'Chaos uncovered at Argentine ministry' *Financial Times*, London, 13 January 1994.
53. For example, in 'The secret Argentina' *Página 12*, 25 November 1992, it is claimed that half of those with basic needs dissatisfied were *jubilados* but makes no mention of other elderly.
54. For example, A. Thompson, 1991 notes that 500 PAMBA food parcels were distributed to elderly residents of the slum district of La Boca through a day centre in September 1990.
55. Interview with Sra Vázquez of the *Dirección Provincial de la Tercera Edad*, La Plata, 18 May 1993.
56. For example, the head of the DMTA had never heard of the *Subgerencia de Previsión Social*, the organisation responsible for local ANSES workers (interview with Dr R. Masobrio, Lanús, 22 April 1993).
57. This was as true for the DMTA as it was for national and provincial agencies.
58. The Spanish term *ensañarse* has no direct equivalent in English. It means both to reduce and to make more efficient.
59. Interview with Dr R. Masobrio.
60. For example, the head of the DMTA refers to beneficiaries as 'those who come here to ask for a pension...' (interview with Dr R. Masobrio).
61. For example, another municipality, Lomas de Zamora, ran a food aid programme for needy elderly instead of a pension scheme. However, by July

1992 this was only being distributed to 2700 households. There was no coordination between this initiative and PAMI's *Pro-Bienestar* programme (interview with A. de Micheli, Subsecretary of Social Assistance, Municipality of Lomas de Zamora, 5 November 1992).

62. Argentine Republic, 1917b:20. 'Working age', used in lieu of data for the economically active population, is defined here as between 15 and 64 years old.
63. Juárez, 1947:127. No figure for the economically active population is available for this period, although the 1947 National Census records a population of 10215302 aged between 14 and 59 (INDEC, 1948:104).
64. Between 1936 and 1945 union membership grew from 369969 to 528523 (Munck, 1987:115, 132).
65. Decree Law 22,946, 25 September 1945 (reported in *Revista de Trabajo y Previsión*, No.7–8, 1945:741).
66. See Escudé:1976:38–44 for a description of the *obra social* healthcare system.
67. GADIS, 1992:21, 27, shows that Caritas Argentina (a Catholic organisation) and *La Asociación Emaús de Rosario* (a left-wing organisation) were founded in 1956 and 1959, respectively and still existed in 1992.
68. It should be noted that the data do not include NGOs no longer operating in 1992 and that the register is by no means complete. Nevertheless, the trend it demonstrates is generally supported by academics (see Thompson, 1990:63–4 and Cuenya, et al, 1990:56).
69. These are well described in García Delgado and J. Silva, 1985.
70. The best-known example is Perlman, 1976.
71. Interview with anonymous projects officer, 18 January 1994.
72. Interview with anonymous projects officer 18 January 1994.
73. These include the *Fundación para la Atención Integral del Anciano y la Familia* and the *Fundación para Estudio e Investigación de la Mujer* (see below).
74. A survey of 58 NGOs carried out in the 1980s found that 92 per cent were formally registered (Cuenya et al, 1990:53).
75. The pessimistic view is put forward by Cavarozzi and Palermo, 1995:34–44. Interestingly, the following chapter of the same volume provides a markedly more optimistic interpretation (Martínez Norgueira, 1995: 45–70).
76. Pro Vida (Colombia), Pro Vida (Bolivia) and AGECO (Costa Rica): HAI *Horizontes 32*, November 1993.
77. CARITAS (Chile), Pro Vida (Peru), Pro Vida (Ecuador), ANAYA (Dominican Republic) and FAIF (Argentina); see HAI *Horizontes 32*.
78. These are, respectively, CEPEV and FOC. The other project to maintain funding, *La Fundación para la Atención Integral del Anciano y la Familia* (FAIF), was based outside GBA and is thus not of direct interest. However, descriptions of its activities can be obtained from Ball, 1992 or FAIF, 1990.
79. 'Centre for the Promotion and Study of the Elderly'.
80. Interview with S. Simone of CEPEV, Buenos Aires, 1 June 1993.
81. 'The Foundation for Community Organisation'.
82. GADIS, 1992:95. Legal recognition or *'personería juridica'* is a necessary prerequisite for formalising relations with state agencies.
83. Interview with A. de Micheli, Sub-secretary of Social Assistance, Lomas de Zamora, 5 November 1992.

84. 1980 Census data shows that in most of the enumeration districts in which FOC operated (F.23, F.24, F.26, F.27 and F.30) over-65-year-olds accounted for less than 1.5 per cent of the total population (INDEC, 1984:125).
85. A publicity leaflet issued by FOC in 1992 gives the organisation's principal aim as: 'To improve the quality of life in marginal communities, providing technical support and prioritising as the focus of its activities the mother–child binomial.'
86. According to Valler, 1970:126: 'Most pastors and bishops are orientated to the values of the social elites rather than to the workers, the agricultural labourers or the urban poor.'
87. Mignone, 1990:352–72, provides an account of relations between senior church figures and the military authorities.
88. For example, see '*Promoción, asistencia y asistencialismo.*' *Informe Caritas*, September 1992, p.17.
89. Aid targeted at northern provinces included the '*Más por menos*' programme of the 1970s and the '*Regreso con esperanza*' in the early 1990s (Passanante, 1989:156 and *Comisión Nacional de Caritas Argentina*, 1991:14).
90. The figure for households benefited by rest homes also included the activities of other community organisation projects.
91. Interview with Director of CARITAS Argentina, Buenos Aires, 24 November 1992.
92. Most Caritas publications devote considerable space to religious and moral discussions. For example, see '*Consecuencias laterales del divorcio*' [Side-effects of divorce] in *CARITAS es compartir*, September 1992.
93. Church assistance earlier in the twentieth century had sometimes reflected these criteria (Tenti Fanfani, 1989:24–34).
94. Interview with Sr Giovannini, pensions officer, Italian Embassy, Buenos Aires, 29 March 1993.
95. In 1989 US$ 150 million of such assistance was provided (Schneider, 1992:276–9).
96. By then, these were being mainly distributed by regional consulates. Two such consulates operated in GBA: one in the Federal Capital and the other in La Plata (the capital of the Province of Buenos Aires).
97. Interview with Sra Tussini, Asistenzi Soziali, Italian Consulate, La Plata, 18 May 1993.
98. '*España equipará pensiones mínimas para los residentes*' *Ambito Financiero*, 15 October 1993.
99. See *Ambito Financiero*, Buenos Aires, 24 September 1993 for the full text of the reform bill and Isuani and San Martino, 1993 for a detailed account of the reform process itself.
100. For example, see '*AFJP: preparadas, listas, ya.*' *El Cronista*, 13 September 1993.
101. Jelín, 1991:173–6, provides a good categorisation of different household and family structures.
102. INDEC defined the different household structures as follows: (1) *Nuclear*: father and/or mother with/without single children; (2) *Extended*: nuclear containing other relatives; (3) *Composite*: nuclear or extended also containing non-relatives (INDEC, 1973:7).

103. Jelín, 1991 and Lomnitz and Peréz-Lizaur, 1991 provide good accounts of this process in Latin America. For a more general discussion, see Albert and Cattell, 1994:89–100.
104. Ramos, 1992:224--32 found that this was considered the ideal option by most of the elderly individuals he studied, who felt that it combined independence with security.
105. '*Casi 15 millones de pobres*' *Clarín*, 22 September 1992.
106. Oddone, 1991:13–14, includes a personal testimony of such a case.
107. See the testimonies of 'Bernarda' and 'Celina' cited in Oddone, 1991:12.
108. Scipione et al, 1992:36 qualify their findings by stressing that those in receipt of family support were vulnerable to variations in the amounts received over time.
109. This agrees with the findings of Kaplan and Redondo, 1992:115.
110. Compare the testimonies of Celina and Antonio in Oddone, 1991:12 and 14.
111. Between 1970 and 1980 the proportion of the total population attending tertiary education rose from 14.9 to 21.6 per cent (ECLAC, 1993:57).
112. See Table 2.9 and Marshall, 1991:18–46.
113. Isuani and San Martin, 1993:25, claim that no underemployed workers participated in social insurance programmes. See Carpio et al, 1991:196–218 for data on income security.
114. This is supported by the results of another survey of elderly employment based on 1985 household survey data (Oddone, 1994:10–11).
115. This is reflected in the results of a 1988 survey of self-employed workers in GBA which found that the great majority (84.9 per cent) of over-65-year-olds working in this sector had been doing so for more than seven years. This indicates that self-employment was not primarily a refuge for the recently retired (calculated from INDEC, 1989:47).
116. In 1983 contributory pension schemes accounted for 85.7 per cent of total social security expenditure in Argentina (ILO, 1992:112).

CHAPTER 4

1. Some general information about *villas miserias* is provided in Chapter 2. Whilst it would be wrong to assume that these neighbourhoods have the monopoly of poverty in Greater Buenos Aires, it is generally recognised that the great majority of their populations are lacking in basic needs. Consequently, *villas* provide more convenient locations for case studies than other neighbourhoods where poverty is more diffuse.
2. These included: (1) Villa Albertina in Lomas de Zamora. Contacts were made with a local NGO working there, but the total elderly population was small. (2) Isla Maciel in Avellaneda. This contained a high concentration of both elderly residents and poverty, but was too dangerous to permit effective research. (3) Las Cavas in San Isidro. This was very difficult to reach by public transport from central Buenos Aires.
3. Argentine Republic, *Ministerio de Trabajo y Seguridad Social*, 1987:11. The report does not provide literacy rates for elderly *villeros*, but notes that men aged 50 and over accounted for 9.7 per cent of all male illiterates and

that for women this was 16.7 per cent. Since over-50-year-olds only accounted for 9.2 per cent of over-fives in the total population, it is evident that a disproportionate number of them were illiterate.

4. This sector of Buenos Aires attracted a particularly large concentration of industry between the 1930s and 1950s, including a military steel works as well as several metallurgical and meat-packing plants. These factories, along with the nearby docks, accounted for the vast majority of male employment until the deindustrialisation of the 1970s.
5. Much of the literature on poor urban neighbourhoods such as shanty towns seeks to distinguish between 'slums of hope' or self-help housing and 'slums of despair'. It is claimed that the former are upgraded over time and provide a temporary staging post to improved accommodation. Conversely, the latter are characterised as comprising of downwardly mobile 'dregs and drop-outs' (Ward, 1976; Lloyd, 1979:39 are examples of this approach).
6. These indicators are the same as those used in Table 3.19.
7. This led to the formation of the first '*Unión Vecinal de Villa Jardín*', usually referred to as the '*Junta Vecinal*'.
8. Villa Itatí was used as a case-study by Golbert et al, 1992:33–6 who provide a general description.
9. According to the Province of Buenos Aires, 1985 the settlement was first known as 'Villa Fa-mac', before taking the name 'Azul' from a local dance hall. See Chapter 2, for background information on the general expansion of industries in the provincial part of the city.
10. López, 1992:36 observes that fertility rates were just under three. National levels were estimated to be 2.96 in 1990.
11. Despite there being no mention of Villa Azul in the published version of the census, a separate survey (Province of Buenos Aires, 1985) claims the census found it had a population of 1039. As will be seen, this figure sharply contradicts the findings of other surveys and should be discounted. It is possible that this figure only referred to the part of the *villa* lying in Avellaneda, whilst the rest was included with neighbouring Villa Itatí in Quilmes. However, it was impossible to confirm this with those responsible for the census.
12. The inaccuracy of the 1981 figure is explained in note 11 above. Various studies, including Midre, 1992, have drawn attention to the tendency of PAN workers to overestimate beneficiary populations in order to acquire additional food parcels.
13. A further survey conducted by the *Sociedad de Fomento* in 1992 recorded a total of 42 over-65s living in the Quilmes section alone. Given that roughly three-quarters of the *villa*'s land is on this side of the municipal divide, this figure might be interpreted as signifying a reduction in the number of elderly in Villa Azul since the UNICEF survey. However, as mentioned earlier, the earlier settlement of the Avellaneda side may have led to greater concentrations of elderly in this section. This view was supported by the researcher's own direct observations of the *villa*. The *Sociedad*'s survey of the Quilmes sector indicates that there is a much larger number of people aged between 50 and 59 (102) than those aged over 60. This suggests that, as in Villa Jardín, the ageing of Villa Azul's population will continue apace through the next decade.
14. This is the term used by the *villeros* themselves. Friedrich, 1978 defines *caciques* as 'a strong and autocratic leader in local and/or regional politics whose char-

acteristically informal, personalistic, and often arbitrary role is buttressed by a core of relatives, "fighters", and dependents, and is marked by the diagnostic threat and practice of violence'. Cornelius, 1973:119–34, gives an excellent account of such practices.

15. Gillespie, 1982:89–159 provides a detailed examination of this and similar guerrilla groups.
16. According to the ex-president of the *Grupo de Tercera Edad*, it was impossible for local people to obtain any support from local government without dealing through these *caciques* (interview with Sra MP, May 1993).
17. Reference was made to these during informal conversations with several *villeros*. The same interviewees became much more reticent about this issue when a tape recorder was switched on, indicating that they had still not conquered the fears engendered in earlier periods.
18. This was known as the '*Plan Arraigo*'. Information about the Plan is available in Argentine Republic, *Presidencia de la Nación*, 1993.
19. For example, one family contained the treasurer of the *Sociedad*, the president of the Quilmes co-operative and a senior member of the *Unidad Básica*.
20. This contradicts proposals made in the original plans (see Argentine Republic, *Ministerio de Bienestar Social*, 1968:25).
21. Law 17.561, cited in Argentine Republic, *Ministerio de Bienestar Social*, 1968:35. Interestingly, these loans were to be financed by the *Instituto Nacional de Seguridad Social* and, consequently, may have exacerbated the financial positions of national pension funds.
22. This included a reduction both in general economic opportunities to 'make good and get out' and in the relocation of *villeros* to better sites by the CMV. The latter had not occurred since 1984.
23. For example, Sra MB claimed that she was the only ex-committee member of the *Consejo Deliberante* remaining in the *villa*.
24. Many of the members registered by a local church group gave false addresses, perhaps reflecting a fear of both the outside authorities and other *villeros*.
25. *Municipalidad de la Ciudad de Buenos Aires*, which is responsible for the Federal Capital section of the city.
26. *El Programa Alimentario de la Municipalidad de la Ciudad de Buenos Aires* (PAMBA), a similar programme to the PAN mentioned in Chapter 3.
27. Unfortunately, the NCV's minutes book was unavailable and so it was unable to obtain more precise information about its activities and the numbers who benefited from them.
28. This term was used by Sra CB.
29. 'The Youngsters of 1990'.
30. '"Union and Hope" Group for the Elderly'.
31. In the minutes book no mention is made of these social workers after December 1988.
32. For a good account of the respective histories and policies of these two parties see *Centro Interdisciplinario de Estudios Sobre el Desarrollo Latinoaméricano*, 1990.
33. The President of the *Grupo* had been working alone for several years to obtain food parcels and blankets from both councils. The *Departamento de Entidades de Bien Público* of Quilmes council formally registered the *Grupo* in February 1987, whilst the Province granted it legal status in March 1988.

34. Of the original 28 members, 15 were women.
35. For example, the first goal was simply to: 'Give an organisational structure for the aspirations of progress in the neighbourhood and for improvements in material levels.'
36. For example, *El Grupo de la Tercera Edad* refers to attendances of 52 members on 22 July 1988 and only six on 2 March 1990.
37. Cavarozzi and Grossi, 1992:178–86 provide a good analysis of political developments during this period.
38. *El Grupo de la Tercera Edad*, 14 September 1990. No reason was given for the Church's actions.
39. *El Grupo de la Tercera Edad*, 19 February 1990, mentions the visit of two social workers from Avellaneda council to the president's wife, offering help. It would appear that the *Grupo* failed to take advantage of this offer, as no further mention is made of it. This was probably because the *Grupo* had already gone into decline.
40. '"The Virgin of Luján" Centre for the Elderly'.
41. The latter was Sra CB, interviewed in May 1993. Her work with the CVL was not part of her PAMI responsibilities and she did not represent the organisation in this capacity.
42. Elderly inhabitants were initially identified by going through index cards from the local Caritas branch. Unfortunately, the survey was left incomplete as the CVL went into decline.
43. These allegations were made by Sra CB and a number of volunteers but they refused to be recorded.
44. For example, the meetings held on 17 March 1993 and 31 March 1993 only attracted 15 and 12 elderly respectively.
45. For example, they had no knowledge of the ANSES assistance pension.
46. See Chapter 2 for a description of the organisational structure of Caritas in Argentina and its general objectives.
47. For example, at the end of 1992 Caritas was helping five families of evangelical Christians.
48. For example, one interviewee complained that she had not received any visits from a Caritas volunteer, despite her bad economic position. Another respondent mentioned going to the church in person to get Caritas aid, suggesting that the network of volunteers was not always effective.
49. These token payments were not well received by many beneficiaries. One interviewee complained that if she had any cash she would buy the food for herself. Another claimed that she was exempt from making payments.
50. Unfortunately, local Caritas archives going back to its foundation were destroyed in 1991.
51. CEPEV, 1990:11 describes Caritas activities in 1990 but makes no reference to any specifically targeting the elderly.
52. The number of assistance pensions granted never exceeded 10 and only three people were placed in homes.
53. Informal interview, Villa Jardín February 1993.
54. Minujim, 1992:33–8 provides a clear account of these trends.
55. The director complained that used clothing was rarely passed on to *villeros* since they would 'send it to relatives back in Paraguay'. He went on to claim: 'They ask out of habit...They haven't learnt anything except how to beg...They

have a lot of time. What do they do with it all?' (Informal interview, Villa Azul, April 1993).

56. These were: *La Iglesia Evangélica Metodista, La Iglesia Evangélica Valdense, La Iglesia Discípulos de Cristo and El Instituto Superior Evangélico de Estudios Teológicos*. For a good overview of the history of the Protestant Church in Argentina see Martin, 1990:73–6.
57. In an informal conversation, one of the CUNP's directors hinted that this was partly because some members had had Peronist ties.
58. Between 1960 and 1985 the proportion of Argentines who were evangelical Protestants rose from 1.63 to 4.69 per cent. This phenomenon is examined in Stoll, 1990.
59. The Argentine Federation of Evangelical Churches.
60. For a historical account of community organisation, see García Delgado and Silva, 1985:68–74.
61. This was a 60-year-old single working mother of three, who succeeded in obtaining a municipal assistance pension.
62. Whilst they were aware of the municipal assistance pensions, they had never heard of the DNA benefit.
63. Lanús Council only recognised its right to operate in six blocks. The *Junta* was hoping to get the authorisation to extend this.
64. The Housing and Community Foundation.
65. This programme was funded through a 10 per cent profit tax imposed by the national government. Its objective was to upgrade the 'social infra-structure' of greater Buenos Aires, including health clinics and the improvement of basic utilities (see *Movimiento: revista de la agrupación '11 de Marzo'*, April 1993).
66. These relationships are well portrayed in Izaguirre, 1984.
67. It should be noted that, as the prime mover behind the establishment of the *Centro*, CEPEV's views would have a major effect on its relations with other organisations.
68. In the case of the *Centro*, this occurred because not enough *jubilados* could be persuaded to join up for it to obtain formal support from PAMI.
69. This is evidenced by a lack of reference to women in the literature on contemporary Argentine unionism. For example, Palomino, 1991:36–60 makes direct reference to 16 prominent union leaders in the 1980s, none of whom were women.
70. Brumer, 1993:412–18 notes that a failure to provide welfare benefits to women in Brazil prompted them to form pressure groups.
71. The weakness of local initiatives as pressure groups fits with Gilbert and Ward's view that community organisations are rarely allowed to challenge the existing structure of power and resources (Gilbert and Ward, 1985:175–7, 237–9).
72. This perceived distinction was borne out by official data for insurance coverage in the Federal Capital and Province (Table 3.5).
73. During the re-election of the Villa Azul *Grupo*'s committee in May 1993, a proposal was made to model the organisation along PAMI lines. This was met with general derision when it pointed out that around 80 per cent of its elderly lacked contributory pensions.
74. This rivalry and fragmentation is also observed by Tenti, 1993:137.

75. For an example of this, see the article 'Close to poverty, far from power' in *Clarín*, 9 March 1993, written by Monseñor J. Casaretto, a senior Church figure at the national level.

CHAPTER 5

1. The sequence of questions was designed with the respondents in mind. Thus, less sensitive topics such as household structure and labour history come before more sensitive issues such as monetary income. This chapter follows a different sequence from the questionnaire, making a more logical progression through the issues. For example, data on household structure are analysed in the section about economic relations with family members.
2. The interviewer received eight refusals from prospective households. The reasons, when apparent, were varied, including the intervention of an intoxicated relative and a claim to be on the verge of moving away from the *villa*.
3. In 1990 Argentina contained 16285000 men aged 60 or more, compared to 16 595 000 women (UN, 1990:21).
4. Chapter 2 shows that historically many residents from neighbouring countries had not obtained formal registration.
5. Twenty-three of a total of 62 pre-1960 arrivals (37 per cent) worked in the formal sector, compared to 5 out of 27 (19 per cent) for the other group. It was decided to exclude Villa Azul from the analysis, since so few of its elderly came in the earlier period and so this could have introduced a locational effect.
6. The respective numbers are 19 (31 per cent) and 16 (60 per cent).
7. Two respondents failed to give satisfactory answers and are not included.
8. In the *villas* this type of employment is often known as *changas*. It includes street hawking and a wide range of odd jobs, usually performed on a casual, part-time basis.
9. The survey found that eight definitely did, two definitely did not and six did not provide a clear answer.
10. This is a form of annual bonus, known as an '*aguinaldo*' which is ubiquitous in Argentina's formal sector.
11. This argument is well developed in Chant, 1991:202–5.
12. In 1990 only 39.1 per cent of the national population aged over the minimum retirement age were without an insurance benefit (see Table 3.2).
13. National assistance coverage of the elderly was estimated to be roughly 5 per cent in 1992 (Chapter 3).
14. See Chapter 3. The size and structure of elderly *villeros'* households is examined below.
15. Interview with Sr JJ, Villa Azul, June 1993. The confusion about monetary values resulted from a series of currency changes. The most recent of these had been in 1991, when the new peso (worth 10000 of the old currency unit) was established.
16. Interview with Sra AM, Villa Jardín, March 1993. This was probably the month-long dock strike of 1966, which was part of a general campaign of labour

unrest known as the '*Plan de Lucha*' [Plan of struggle] (see Munck, 1987:161–2).

17. For example, between March 1991 and November 1995 the cost of rental accommodation in Argentina as a whole rose by 185 per cent, whereas average inflation was less than 60 per cent.
18. Interview with Sra Eugenia B, Villa Azul, June 1993. This is corroborated by Jelín, 1991:173–9 who notes that the use of *libretas* is most frequent among households with low but stable monthly incomes.
19. For example, '*En las cajas hay 100 000 trámites jubilatorios esperando definición*' [In the pension funds there are 100000 claims waiting to be processed] *Clarín*, 23 March 1994.
20. Interview with Sra AG, Villa Jardín, March 1993. Her claim that she had to pay outstanding pension contributions is confusing, since her husband had obtained a *jubilación* some years previously. It is possible that she confused this with the 'fee' for obtaining the sworn statement. Such a 'fee' may have been a formal bureaucratic requirement or may have simply been a requisite bribe.

CHAPTER 6

1. The São Paulo project was carried out by the author in 1995 and was funded by the Leverhulme Foundation.

Bibliography

SECONDARY SOURCES

Aghajanian, A. 'Elderly population in Iran: an overview' in P. Krishnan and K. Mahadevan, eds, *The elderly population in the developed and developing world*, Delhi (1992).

Aguirre, P. *Impacto de la hiperinflación en la alimentación de los sectores populares*, FUCADE documento no. 2, Buenos Aires (1990).

Albert, S. and M. Cattell *Old age in global perspective. Cross-cultural and cross-national views*, New York (1994).

Alschuler, L. 'Argentina: from egalitarian stagnation to authoritarian growth' in L. Alschuler, ed., *Multinationals and maldevelopment*, London (1987).

Anis, S. 'Can small-scale development be a large-scale policy? The case of Latin America.' *World Development*, volume 15 (1987).

Araba Apt, N. *Coping with old age in a changing Africa. Social change and the elderly Ghanaian*, Aldershot (1996).

Araba Apt, N. and M. Grieco 'Urbanization, caring for elderly people and the changing African family: the challenge to social policy' *International Social Security Review*, 47, 3–4 (1994).

Araujo Oliveira, J. and S. Fleury Teixeira *(Im)previdência social. 60 anos da previdência no Brasil*, Petrópolis (1986).

Arellano, J. *Políticas sociales y desarrollo en Chile: 1924–1984*, Santiago (1985).

Assies, W. 'Of structured moves and moving structures' in W. Assies et al, eds, *Structures of power, movements of resistance. An introduction to the theories of urban movements in Latin America*, Amsterdam (1990).

Assies, W., G. Burgwal and T. Salman *Structures of power, movements of resistance. An introduction to the theories of urban social movements in Latin America*, Amsterdam (1990).

Badoza, S. 'Typographical workers and their mutualist experience: the case of the Sociedad Tipográfica Bonaerense, 1857–80' in J. Adelman, ed., *Essays in Argentine labour history, 1870–1930*, London (1992).

Baeza, S. and A. Simonetti 'Cinco años de operación del nuevo sistema previsional' in S.Baeza, ed., *Analisis de la previsión en Chile*, Santiago (1986).

Baily, S. 'Las sociedades de ayuda mutua y el desarrollo de una comunidad italiana en Buenos Aires, 1858–1918.' *Desarrollo Económico* (1982).

Ball, C. 'The experience of FAIF in Argentina' *Community Development Journal*, Vol. 27, No. 2 (1992).

Banister, J. *Changing China's population*, Stanford (1987).

Bellardi, M. and A. De Paula *Villas miseria: origen, eradicación y respuestas populares*, Buenos Aires (1986).

Blanco, R. 'Social welfare programmes for the elderly in Argentina' in Pan American Health Organisation (PAHO) *Mid-life and older women in Latin America and the Caribbean*, Washington (1989).

Bouzas, R. 'Más allá de la estabilización y la reforma? Un ensayo sobre la economía argentina a los comienzos de los '90' *Desarrollo Económico* (April 1993).

Brooks, E. and V. Nyirenda 'Zambia' in J. Dixon, ed., *Social welfare in Africa*, London (1987).

Brumer, A. 'Mobilization and the quest for recognition: the struggle of rural women in southern Brazil for access to welfare benefits' in C. Abel and C. Lewis, eds, *Welfare, poverty and development in Latin America*, London (1993).

Bulatao, R., E. Bos, P. Stephens and M. Vu *World population projections. 1989–90 edition*, Baltimore (1990).

Bunge, A. *El seguro nacional*, Buenos Aires (1917).

Cain, M. 'The activities of the elderly in rural Bangladesh', *Population Studies* 45 (1991).

Carpio, J. et al, 'Precariedad laboral en el conurbano bonaerense. Resultados de un estudio sobre pobreza' in P. Galin and M. Novick, eds, *La precarización del empleo en la Argentina*, Buenos Aires (1991).

Castañeda, T. *Combating poverty: innovative social reforms in Chile during the 1980s*, San Francisco (1992).

Castells, M. *The city and the grassroots*, Berkeley (1983).

Cavarozzi, M. and M. Grossi 'Argentine parties under Alfonsín: from democratic reinvention to political decline and hyperinflation' in E. Epstein, ed., *The new Argentine democracy. The search for a successful formula*, London (1992).

Cavarozzi, M. and V. Palermo 'State, civil society and popular neighbourhood organisations in Buenos Aires: key players in Argentina's transition to democracy' in C. Reilly, ed., *New paths to democratic development. The rise of NGO-municipal collaboration*, London (1995).

Chant, S. *Women and survival in Mexican cities*, Manchester (1991).

Chesnais, J. *The demographic transition. Stages, patterns and economic implications*, Oxford (1992).

Cochrane, S. 'Effects of education and urbanisation on fertility' in R. Bulato and R. Dee, eds, *Determinants of fertility in developing countries. Volume 2. Fertility regulation and institutional influences*, London (1983).

Contreras de Lehr, E. 'Aging and family support in Mexico' in H. Kendig et al, eds, *Family support for the elderly*, Oxford (1992).

Cornelius, W. Jr 'Contemporary Mexico: a structural analysis of urban caciquismo' in R. Kern, ed., *The caciques. Oligarchical politics and the system of caciquismo in the Luso-hispanic world*, Albuquerque (1973).

Cortes, R. 'El empleo urbano argentino de los '80. Tendencias recientes y perspectivas' in E. Bustelo and E. Isuani, eds, *Mucho, poquito o nada. Crisis y alternativas de política social en los '90*, Buenos Aires (1990).

Cotts Watkins, S. 'Conclusions' in A. Coales and S. Cotts Watkins, *The decline of fertility in Europe*, Princeton (1986).

Cowgill, D. 'Aging and modernization: a revision of the theory' in J. Gubrium, ed., *Late life: communities and environmental policy*, Springfield (1974).

Cuenya, B., A. Rofman, M. Di Loreto and C. Fidel 'Proyectos alternativos de habitat popular y ONGs en la Argentina', *Medio Ambiente y Urbanización* (1990).

Davalos, P., M. Jabbaz and E. Molina *Movimiento villero y estado (1966–1976)*, Buenos Aires (1987).

Devi, R. 'Work participation of the aged in India' in P. Krishnan and K. Mahadevan, eds, *The elderly population in the developed and developing world*, Delhi (1992).

Dharmalingham, A. 'Old age support: expectations and experiences in a south Indian village', *Population Studies* 48 (1994).

Diaz Alejandro, C. *Essays on the economic history of the Argentine Republic*, London (1970).

Dieguez, H. and H. Petrecolla 'La distribución funcional del ingreso y el sistema previsional en la Argentina', *Desarrollo Económico*, 14:55 (1974).

Dieguez, H. and H. Petrecolla 'Estudio estadístico del sistema previsional argentina en el periodo, 1950–1972', *Económica*, 23:3 (1977).

Escudé, C. *Aspectos ocultos de la salud en la Argentina*, Buenos Aires (1976).

Escudé, G. and S. Guerberoff 'Ajuste macroeconómico, deuda externa y ahorro en la Argentina' in C. Massad and N. Eyzaguirre, eds, *Ahorro y formación de capital: experiencias latinoamericanas*, Buenos Aires (1990).

Fennel, S. and L. Zhu 'Ageing and pensions in China' in P. Lloyd-Sherlock and P. Johnson, eds, *Ageing and social policy. Global comparisons*, London (1996).

Fernández, A. 'NGOs in South Asia: peoples' participation and partnership' *World Development*, volume 15 (1987).

Fernández, A. 'Mutualismo étnico, liderazgo y participación política. Algunas hipótesis de trabajo' in D. Armús, ed., *Mundo urbano y cultura popular. Estudios de historia social argentina*, Buenos Aires (1990).

Fogarty, J. 'Social experiments in regions of settlement' in D. Platt, ed., *Social welfare 1850 to 1950: Australia, Argentina and Canada compared*, London (1989).

Foweraker, J. *Theorizing social movements*, London (1995).

Frediani, R. *La seguridad social en Latinoamerica: un estudio comparativo del seguro social en Argentina y Colombia*, Buenos Aires (1989).

Friedrich, P. 'The legitimacy of the cacique' in M. Swartz, ed., *Local level politics: social and cultural perspectives*, London (1978).

García Delgado, D. and J. Silva 'El movimiento vecinal y la democracia: participación y control en el Gran Buenos Aires' in E. Jelín, ed., *Los nuevos movimientos sociales/2. Derechos humanos, obreros, barrios*, Buenos Aires (1985).

Germani, G. *La estructura social de la Argentina*, Buenos Aires (1955).

Germani, G. 'Mass immigration and modernisation in Argentina' in I. Horowitz, ed., *Masses in Latin America*, New York (1970).

Gilbert, A. *In search of a home. Rental and shared housing in Latin America*, London (1993).

Gilbert, A. and P. Ward *Housing, the state and the poor. Policy practice in three Latin American cities*, Cambridge (1985).

Gillespie, R. *Soldiers of Perón: Argentina's montoneros*, Oxford (1982).

Golbert, L. 'El envejecimiento de la población y la seguridad social' *Boletín Informativo Techint* (1988).

Golbert, L. 'La asistencia alimentaria: un nuevo problema para los argentinos' in S. Lumi et al, eds, *La mano izquierda del estado: la asistencia social según los beneficiarios*, Buenos Aires (1993).

González Galé, J. *Jubilaciones y seguro social*, Buenos Aires (1929).

Graham, C. *Safety nets, politics and the poor. Transitions to market economies*, Washington (1994).

Grassi, C. 'Dónde viven los trabajadores? Condiciones de trabajo, reproducción y la cuestión de los prejuicios' in S. Hintze et al, *Trabajos y condiciones de vida en sectores populares urbanos*, Buenos Aires (1991).

Hakkert, R. and F. Goza 'Demographic consequences of austerity in Latin America' in W. Canak, ed., *Lost promises: debt, austerity and development in Latin America*, Colorado (1989).

Hall, A. 'Non-governmental organisations and development in Brazil under dictatorship and democracy' in C. Abel and C. Lewis, eds, *Welfare, poverty and development in Latin America*, London (1993).

Huff, W. *The economic growth of Singapore: Trade and development in the twentieth century*, Cambridge (1994).

Isuani, E. 'Social security and public assistance' in C. Mesa-Lago, ed., *The crisis of social security and healthcare: Latin American experiences and lessons*, Pittsburgh (1985).

Isuani, E. 'Los orígenes' in J. Feldman, L. Golbert and E. Isuani, eds, *Maduración y crisis del sistema previsional argentino*, Buenos Aires (1988).

Isuani, E. and H. Mercer *La fragmentación institucional de sector salud. Pluralismo o irracionalidad?,* Buenos Aires (1988).

Isuani, E. and J. San Martino *La reforma previsional argentina. Opciones y riesgos,* Buenos Aires (1993).

Ivereigh, A. *Catholicism and politics in Argentina 1810–1960*, Basingstoke (1995).

Izaguirre, I. *Los asalariados del aparato del estado: 1945–76*, Buenos Aires (1984).

Jelín, E. 'Family and household: outside world and private life' in E. Jelín, ed., *Family, household strategies and gender relations in Latin America*, London (1991).

Jelín, E. 'The social relations of consumption: the urban popular household' in E. Jelín, ed., *Family, household strategies and gender relations in Latin America*, London (1991).

Johnson, P. and J. Falkingham *Ageing and economic welfare*, London (1992).

Juárez, J. *Los trabajadores en función social*, Buenos Aires (1947).

Kaplan, R. and N. Redondo 'Family care of the elderly in Argentina' in J. Kosberg, ed., *Family care for the elderly: social and cultural changes*, London (1992).

Keith, J. et al, *The aging experience. Diversity and commonality across cultures*, London (1994).

Kertzer, D. and P. Laslett, eds, *Aging in the past. Demography, society and old age*, Berkeley (1995).

Kimberly, J. 'The life cycle analogy and the study of organizations: introduction' in J. Kimberly et al, eds, *The organizational life cycle. Issues in the formation, transformation, and decline of organizations*, London (1980).

Knopoff, R. et al, *Dimensiones de la vejez en la sociedad argentina*, Buenos Aires (1991).

Landim, L. 'Non-governmental organisations in Latin America', *World Development*, volume 15 (1987).

Lattes, A. 'El crecimiento de la población y sus componentes demográficos entre 1870 y 1970' in Z. Recchini de Lattes and A. Lattes, eds, *La población de Argentina*, Buenos Aires (1975).

Leis, H. *El movimiento por los derechos humanos y la política argentina*, Buenos Aires (1989).

Lewis, C. 'Social insurance: ideology and policy in the Argentine, c.1920–66' in C. Abel and C. Lewis, eds, *Welfare, poverty and development in Latin America*, London (1993).

Lewis, O. *Five families: Mexican case-studies in the culture of poverty*, New York (1959).

Lewis, O. *Life in a Mexican village: Tepoztlan revisited*, Urbana (1963).

Lewis, O. *A death in the Sánchez family*, London (1969).

Lewis, P. *The crisis of Argentine capitalism*, London (1990).

Liebenstein, H. *Economic backwardness and economic growth*, New York (1957).

Lindert, P. 'Changing costs and benefits of having children' in R. Bulatao and R. Lee, eds, *Determinants of fertility in developing countries*, New York (1983).

Livi Bacci, M. *A history of Italian fertility during the last two centuries*, Princeton (1977).

Lloyd, P. *Slums of hope?*, London (1979).

Lloyd-Sherlock, P. *The Instituto Nacional de Previsión Social and social insurance reform in Argentina, 1944 to 1953*, London (1992a).

Lloyd-Sherlock, P. *Social insurance reform in an ageing world: the case of Latin America*, London (1992b).

Lloyd-Sherlock, P. 'Policy, distribution and poverty in Argentina since redemocratisation', (mimeo) Glasgow (1996a).

Lloyd-Sherlock, P. 'The growth of and socio-economic conditions in shanty towns within Greater Buenos Aires', Occasional Paper, Institute of Latin American Studies, Glasgow (1996b).

Lloyd-Sherlock, P. and P. Johnson, eds, *Ageing and social policy. Global comparisons*, London (1996).

Lomnitz, L. *Networks and marginality. Life in a Mexican shanty town*, New York (1977).

Lomnitz, L. and M. Peréz-Lizaur 'Dynastic growth and survival strategies: the solidarity of the Mexican grand families' in E. Jelín, ed., *Family, household strategies and gender relations in Latin America*, London (1991).

López, N. *Censo de Villa Azul: metodologia y primeros resultados*, Buenos Aires (1992).

Lo Vuolo, R. 'Structural reforms and labour markets in Argentina', *Scandinavian Journal of Social Welfare* 4 (1995).

MacEwan, A. 'Differentiation among the urban poor: an Argentine study' in E. De Kadt and G. Williams, eds, *Sociology and development*, London (1974).

Mallon, R. and J. Sourrouille *Economic policy making in a conflict society: the Argentine case*, Cambridge, Mass. (1975).

Malloy, J. *The politics of social security in Brazil*, Pittsburgh (1979).

Marshall, A. *Políticas sociales: el modelo neoliberal*, Buenos Aires (1988).

Marshall, A. 'Contrataciones flexibles o trabajo precario? El empleo temporario y a tiempo parcial' in G. Galín and M. Novick, eds, *La precarización del empleo en la Argentina*, Buenos Aires (1991).

Martin, D. *Tongues of fire. The explosion of Protestantism in Latin America*, Oxford (1990).

Martínez Norgueira, R. 'Lifecycle and learning in grassroots development organisations', *World Development*, volume 15 (1987).

Martínez Norgueira, R. 'Negotiated interactions: NGOs and local government in Rosario, Argentina' in C.Reilly, ed. *New paths to democratic development. The rise of NGO-municipal cooperation*, London (1995).

Mayumi Yazaki, L., A. Viera de Melo and L. Ramos 'Perspectivas actuais do papel da familia frente ao envelhecimento populacional: um estudo de caso' in SEADE, *Informe demográfico, no.24. A população idoso e o apoio familiar*, São Paulo (1991).

Mensa, J. 'Algunas consideraciones sobre legislación mutual' *Crónica Mensual de la Secretaría de Trabajo y Previsión*, Buenos Aires (January 1946).

Mesa-Lago, C. *Social security in Latin America: pressure groups, stratification and inequality*, Pittsburgh (1978).

Mesa-Lago, C. 'Social security and extreme poverty in Latin America', *Journal of Development Economics* (1983).

Mesa-Lago, C. *Social security and prospects for equity in Latin America*, World Bank Discussion Paper, Washington (1991a).

Mesa-Lago, C. 'Social security: ripe for reform' in Inter-American Development Bank, *Economic and social progress in Latin America. 1991 annual report*, Washington (1991b).

Midgely, J. *Social security, inequality and the Third World*, London (1984).

Midre, G. 'Bread or solidarity: Argentine social policies, 1983–1990', *Journal of Latin American Studies*, 24:2 (1992).

Mignone, E. 'The Catholic church, human rights and the "dirty war" in Argentina' in D. Keogh, ed., *Church and politics in Latin America*, London (1990).

Minois, G. *History of old age. From antiquity to renaissance*, Oxford (1987).

Minujin, A. 'En la rodada' in A. Minujin, ed., *Cuesta abajo. Los nuevos pobres: efectos de la crisis en la sociedad argentina*, Buenos Aires (1992).

Minujin, A. and P. Vinocur 'Quiénes son los pobres del Gran Buenos Aires?', *Comercio Exterior* (1992).

Mitchell, B. *Abstract of British historical statistics*, Cambridge (1962).

Mortara, G. 'Pesquisas sobre populações americanas' *Estudos Brasilieros de Demografia*, No. 3 (1947).

Moser, C. *Confronting crisis: household responses to poverty and vulnerability. A comparative study of four urban communities*, Washington (1995).

Muller, M. *La población anciana de la Argentina: tendencia secular y características recientes*, Buenos Aires (1981).

Munck, R. *Argentina. From anarchism to Peronism. Workers, unions and politics, 1855–1985*, London (1987).

Navarro, M. 'Evita and Peronism' in F. Turner and J. Miguens, eds, *Juan Perón and the reshaping of Argentina*, Pittsburgh (1983).

Oddone, M. *Los trabajadores de mayor edad: empleo y desprendimiento laboral*, Buenos Aires (1994).

Palomino, H. 'El movimiento de democratización sindical' in E. Jelín, ed., *Los nuevos movimientos sociales/2*, Buenos Aires (1985).

Passanante, M. *Pobreza y acción social en la historia argentina: de la beneficencia a la seguridad social*, Buenos Aires (1987).

Pastrana, E. 'Historia de una villa miseria de la ciudad de Buenos Aires', *Revista Interamericana de Planificación*, (1980).

Peluffo, D. 'El desarrollo del seguro de retiro en la Argentina', *Mercado Asegurador*, Buenos Aires (September 1991).

Perlman, J. *The myth of marginality*, Berkeley (1976).

Ramos, L. 'Family support for elderly people in São Paulo, Brazil' in H. Kendig, H. Hashimoto and L. Coppard, eds, *Family support for the elderly*, Oxford (1992).

Ramos, S. *Las relaciones de parentesco y de ayuda mutua*, Buenos Aires (1981).

Recalde, H. *Beneficencia, asistencialismo estatal y previsión social/1*, Buenos Aires (1991).

Recchini de Lattes, Z. 'Urbanización' in Z. Recchini de Lattes and A. Lattes, eds, *La población de Argentina*, Buenos Aires (1975).

Redondo, N. *Ancianidad y pobreza: una investigación en sectores populares urbanos*, Buenos Aires (1990).

Roberts, B. 'The changing nature of informal employment: the case of Mexico' in G. Standing and V. Tokman, eds, *Towards social adjustment: labour market issues in structural adjustment*, Geneva (1991).

Rock, D. 'Argentina, 1930–46' in L. Bethell, ed., *The Cambridge History of Latin America. Volume VIII*, Cambridge (1991).

Rock, D. 'From the First World War to 1930' in L. Bethel, ed., *Argentina since independence*, Cambridge (1993).

Rojo, A. *Las villas de emergencia*, Buenos Aires (1976).

Roxborough, I. 'Urban wages and welfare' in C. Lewis and C. Abel, eds, *Welfare, poverty and development in Latin America*, London (1993).

Sábato, J. 'Jubilados con coronita', *Humor*, Buenos Aires (October 1988).

Sanchez Albornoz, N. *The population of Latin America*, Berkeley (1974).

Schkolnik, S. 'Los cambios en la composición de la población' in Z. Recchini de Lattes and A. Lattes, eds, *La población de Argentina*, Buenos Aires (1975).

Silverman, P. and R. Maxwell 'Cross-cultural variations in the status of old people' in P. Steans, ed., *Old age in preindustrial society*, London (1982).

Stren, R. ed., *Urban research in the developing world. Volume three: Latin America*, Toronto (1995).

Stoll, D. *Is Latin America turning protestant? The politics of evangelical growth*, Oxford (1990).

Tenti, E. 'Representación, delegación y acción colectiva en comunidades urbanas pobres' in L. Golbert et al, eds, *La mano izquierda del estado. La asistencia según los beneficiarios*, Buenos Aires (1992).

Tenti Fanfani, E. *Estado y pobreza: estrategias de intervención*, Buenos Aires (1989).

Thompson, A. *The voluntary sector in transition. The case of Argentina*. Serie Estudios GADIS, no.4, Buenos Aires (1989).

Thompson, A. 'El tercer sector y el desarrollo social' in E. Bustelo and E. Isuani, eds, *Mucho, poquito o nada. Crisis y alternativas de política social en los '90*, Buenos Aires (1990).

Thompson, R. 'Trade union organisation: some forgotten aspects' in J. Adelman, ed., *Essays on Argentine labour history, 1870–1930*, London (1992).

Tokman, V. 'The informal sector in Latin America: from underground to legality' in G. Standing and V. Tokman, eds, *Towards social adjustment: labour market issues in structural adjustment*, Geneva (1991).

Torrado, S. *Estructura social de la Argentina, 1945–1983*, Buenos Aires (1992).

Tout, K. *Ageing in developing countries*, Oxford (1989).

Vallier, I. *Catholicism, social control and modernisation in Latin America*, Santa Cruz, California (1970).

Vargas de Flood, M. *El gasto público consolidado*, Buenos Aires (1992).

Vasquez Vialard, A. *Derecho del trabajo y de la seguridad social, tomo 2*, Buenos Aires (1954).

Vatuk, S. 'Old age in India' in P. Stearns, ed., *Old age in preindustrial society*, London (1982).

Vittas, D. *Swiss Chilanpore. The way forward for pension reform?*, Washington (1992).

Waldman, P. 'The Peronisms of Perón and Menem: Justicialism to Liberalism?' in C. Lewis and N. Torrents, eds, *Argentina in the crisis years (1983–1990)*, London (1993).

Walker, A. 'The care for elderly people in industrial society: a conflict between the family and the state' in P. Krishnan and K. Mahadevan, eds, *The elderly population in the developed and developing world*, Delhi (1992).

Walter, R. 'The socio-economic growth of Buenos Aires in the twentieth century' in S. Ross and T. McGann, *Buenos Aires: 400 years*, Austin (1982).

Ward, P. 'The squatter settlement as slum or housing solution: the evidence from Mexico City', *Land Economics* (1976).

Yujnovsky, O. *Claves políticas del problema habitacional argentino, 1955/1981*, Buenos Aires (1984).

OFFICIAL REPORTS AND SURVEYS

Argentine Republic

Argentine Republic *Censo Nacional 1914. Tomo III: población*, Buenos Aires (1916).

Argentine Republic *Censo Nacional 1914. Tomo X: valores mobiliarios y estadísticas diversas*, Buenos Aires (1917).

Argentine Republic *Primera Conferencia Nacional de Asistencia Social*, Buenos Aires (1934).

Caja Nacional de Jubilaciones y Pensiones *La situación de los funcionarios de la administración nacional en la actividad y la pasividad*, Buenos Aires (1914).

Comisión Nacional de la Vivienda (CNV) *Plan de emergencia*, Buenos Aires (1956).

Consejo Federal de Inversiones *Algunos aspectos cuantitativos de la población orginaria de paises limítrofes*, Buenos Aires (1973).

Consejo Federal de Inversiones *Estructura social de la Argentina. Volumen 2: Capital Federal*; *Volumen 4: Buenos Aires*, Buenos Aires (1989).

Consejo Federal de Seguridad Social de la República Argentina *Informe acerca de la factibilidad financiera del plan argentino de seguridad social*, Buenos Aires (1967).

Instituto Nacional de Estadística y Censo (INDEC) *Cuadros inéditos. IV censo general 1947. Características de familia y convivencia, estado civil y fecundidad*, Buenos Aires (1948).

INDEC *Censo nacional de población, 1960. Tomo 1: total del país*, Buenos Aires (1961).

INDEC *Censo nacional de población, familias y viviendas – 1970. Resultados obtenidos por muestra (total del país)*, Buenos Aires (1973).

INDEC *Censo nacional de población y vivienda*, Buenos Aires (1981a).

INDEC *Anuario estadístico de la Republica Argentina. 1979.1980*, Buenos Aires (1981b).

INDEC *La pobreza en la Argentina*, Buenos Aires (1984).

INDEC *La pobreza en el conurbano bonaerense*, Buenos Aires (1989a).

INDEC *Trabajadores por cuenta propia. Encuesta del Gran Buenos Aires 1988*, Buenos Aires (1989b).

INDEC *Censo nacional de población y vivienda, 1991 (total del país)*, Buenos Aires (1993a).

INDEC *Censo nacional de población y vivienda 1991. Resultados definitivos, características de Lanús*, Buenos Aires (1993b).

Instituto Nacional de Previsión Social *Previsión social*, Buenos Aires (April 1991).

Ministerio de Bienestar Social, *Plan de erradicación de las villas de emergencia de la Capital Federal y del Gran Buenos Aires*, Buenos Aires (1968).

Ministerio de Economia y Obras y Servicios Públicos *Economic report. Second quarter 1995*, Buenos Aires (1995).

Ministerio de Finanzas de la Nación, Caja Nacional de Ahorro Postal *Ahorro obrero: manual para el dirigente*, Buenos Aires (1950).

Ministerio de Hacienda, Dirección Nacional de Estadística y Censos *Informe demográfico, 1944–55*, Buenos Aires (1956).

Ministerio de Trabajo y Seguridad Social *Sistema nacional de previsión social: su evaluación y situación a fines de la década del '80*, Buenos Aires (1990).

Programa de Atendamiento Médico Integral (PAMI) *El centro de jubilados*, Buenos Aires (1992).

PAMI *Programa social integral*, Buenos Aires (1992).

Presidencia de la Nación, Comisión de Tierras Fiscales Nacionales *Programa Arraigo. Un país para siempre*, Buenos Aires (1993).

Secretaría de Economía, Superintendencia de Seguros de la Nación *Información estadística. Seguro de retiro*, Buenos Aires (12 November 1991 to 26 February 1993).

Secretaría de Seguridad Social *Acciones significativas desarrolladas en el año 1992*, Buenos Aires (1993).

Subsecretaría de Seguridad Social presented in 'Why a social plan?' *Clarín*, Buenos Aires (18 January 1993).

Other official sources

Centro Latinoamericano de Demográfia (CELADE) *Argentina: situación y necesidades de la tercera edad. Algunas ciudades seleccionadas*, Santiago de Chile (1989).

Comisión Económica para America Latina (CEPAL) *Analisis y proyecciones del desarrollo económico, V. El desarrollo económico de la Argentina*, Mexico (1959).

CEPAL *El desarrollo de la seguridad social en America Latina*, Santiago (1985).

Economic Commission for Latin America and the Caribbean (ECLAC) *Statistical bulletin for Latin America, volume 8*, Santiago (1969).

ECLAC *Statistical yearbook for Latin America and the Caribbean, 1980*, Santiago (1981).

ECLAC *Economic survey of Latin America and the Caribbean, 1988*, Santiago (1989).

ECLAC *Statistical yearbook for Latin America and the Caribbean, 1991*, Santiago (1992).

ECLAC *Statistical yearbook for Latin America and the Caribbean 1992*, Santiago (1993a).

ECLAC *Economic survey of Latin America and the Caribbean, 1991*, Santiago (1993b).

Government of India, Labour Bureau, Ministry of Labour *Pocket book of labour statistics 1990*, Delhi (1990).

Government of India, Labour Bureau, Ministry of Labour *Indian Labour Year Book 1995*, Delhi (1994).

International Labour Office (ILO) *Introduction to social security*, Geneva (1984).

ILO *Economically active population estimates: 1950–1980. Projections: 1985–2025. Volume IV, methodological supplement*, Geneva (1986a).

ILO *Economically active population estimates: 1950–1980. Projections: 1985–2025. Volume V, world summary*, Geneva (1986b).

ILO *Economically active population estimates: 1950–1980. Projections: 1985–2025, Volume III, Latin America*, Geneva (1986c).

ILO *The cost of social security. Thirteenth international enquiry, 1984–1986. Basic tables*, Geneva (1990).

International Conference on Population and Development 'Documents. Programme of action of the 1994 International Conference on Population and Development' *Population and Development Review*, 21:2 (1995).

International Social Security Association 'Developments and trends in social security 1990–1992' *International Social Security Review*, 45, 4 (1992).

Municipality of Lomas de Zamora, Subsecretaría de Acción Social 'Comunicación de la Subsecretaría de Acción Social. Información para los C.O.C.' (mimeo) Lomas de Zamora (1992).

Organisation for Economic Cooperation and Development (OECD) *Ageing populations. The social policy implications*, Paris (1988).

Pan American Health Organisation *Mid-life and older women in Latin America and the Caribbean*, Washington (1989).

Programa Regional de Empleo de America Latina y el Caribe (PREALC) *Mercado de Trabajo en cifras, 1950–1980*, Santiago (1982).

PREALC *El desafío de la seguridad social: el caso Argentino*, Santiago (1989).

PREALC *Newsletter number 32*, Santiago (1993).

Prefeitura de São Paulo *Favelas e cortiços da cidade de São Paulo*, São Paulo (1994).

Provincia de Buenos Aires, Ministerio de Hacienda, Economia y Previsión *Buenos Aires en cifras*, La Plata (1947).

Provincia de Buenos Aires *Censo socioeconomico en villas de emergencia*, La Plata (1981).

Provincia de Buenos Aires 'Misión de aproximación rápida. Asentamiento Villa Azul' (mimeo) La Plata (1985).

United Kingdom, Central Statistical Office *Social trends 24*, London (1994).

United Nations (UN) *World population prospects 1990*, New York (1991a).

UN *Economic and social aspects of population ageing in Argentina*, New York (1991b).

UN *Economic survey of Latin America and the Caribbean. 1990, volume 2*, Santiago (1992).

UN *World population prospects the 1992 revision*, New York (1993).

UN *The sex and age distribution of the world populations. The 1994 revision*, New York (1994).

UNESCO *Statistical yearbook 1991*, Paris (1991).

World Bank *World Development Report 1991. The challenge of development*, Oxford (1991).

World Bank *Argentina: from insolvency to growth*, Washington (1993).

World Bank *Averting the old age crisis. Policies to protect the old and promote growth*, Oxford (1994).

REPORTS BY NON-GOVERNMENTAL ORGANISATIONS

Academia Nacional de Ciencias Económicas *Estadísticas historicas argentinas. Compendio 1873–1973*, Buenos Aires (1988).

CEPEV *Evaluación de la situación de los ancianos en Villa Jardín y diseño de una estrategia de abordaje. Trimestre junio–agostso 1990*, (mimeo) Buenos Aires (1990).

Centro Interdisciplinario de Estudios Sobre el Desarrollo Latinoamericano *Los partidos políticos en América Latina. Desarrollo, estructura y fundamentos programáticos. El caso argentino*, Buenos Aires (1990).

Comisión Nacional de Caritas Argentina 'Memoria y balance, periodo 1987–1990' (mimeo) Buenos Aires (1991).

La Fundación para la Atención Integral del Anciano y la Familia (FAIF), *Talleres para la tercera edad: testimonios de sus protagonistas*, Córdoba (1990).

La Fundación de Investigaciones Económicas Latinoamericanas (FIEL) *El gasto público en la Argentina 1960–1985*, Buenos Aires (1987).

FIEL *Argentina: la reforma económica 1989-1991. Balance y perspectivas*, Buenos Aires (1991).

La Fundación de Organización Communitaria (FOC) 'Las educadoras sanitarias comunales de Lomas de Zamora: síntesis y experiencia de los programas' (mimeo), Lomas de Zamora (1981).

FOC 'Proyecto de integración de la tercera edad como educadores sanitarios comunales' (mimeo), Lomas de Zamora (1990).

FOC 'Informe de avance del proyecto de tercera edad, julio-noviembre 1991' (mimeo), Lomas de Zamora (1991).

Grupo de análisis y desarrollo institucional y social (GADIS) *Directorio de organizaciones no gubernmentales de promoción y desarrollo de Argentina, June 1992*, Buenos Aires (1992).

Help Age International *Horizontes 32*, London (November 1993).

NEWSPAPERS AND MAGAZINES

Ambito Financiero, Buenos Aires (15 October 1993).

CARITAS es compartir, Buenos Aires (September 1992).

Clarín, Buenos Aires (various editions 1992–5).

Crónica Mensual de la Secretaría de Trabajo y Previsión, Buenos Aires (November 1946).

El Cronista, Buenos Aires (various editions 1992–3).

El País, Montevideo (1991).

Informe Caritas, Buenos Aires (September 1992).

La Nación, Buenos Aires (6 February 1996).

La seguridad social en la Argentina, Buenos Aires (January and April 1993).

Latin American Weekly Reports, London (20 November 1986).

Microsemanario, Buenos Aires (28 June 1994 and 20 May 1996).

Movimiento: revista de la agrupación '11 de Marzo', Buenos Aires (April 1993).
Página 12, Buenos Aires (various editions 1992–4).
Previsión Social, No. 3 Buenos Aires (April 1991).
Review of the River Plate, Buenos Aires (various editions 1952–63).
Revista de Trabajo y Previsión, Nos. 7–8, Buenos Aires (1945).

ADDITIONAL UNPUBLISHED MATERIAL

El Grupo de la Tercera Edad 'Unión y Esperanza' *Minutes book*, Villa Azul, Buenos Aires (1988–93).

Lezcano, C. 'La historia de la consolidación de Villa Jardín', Buenos Aires (1982).

Lischinsky, S. in 'La afiliación al sistema previsional (1944–1955). Logros y dificuldades en su expansión', Rosario (1989).

Matijasic. M. 'Fundos de pensão brasilieros: parafinanciamento', unpublished masters dissertation, Instituto de Economia, Universidade Estadual de Campinas (1993).

Oddone, M. 'Ancianidad, contextos regionales y redes de intercambio', Buenos Aires (1991).

Padrón, M. 'Los centros de promoción y la cooperatión internacional al desarrollo en America Latina', Buenos Aires (1986).

Pantelides, E. 'Servicios sociales para la tercera edad en el Gran Buenos Aires', Buenos Aires (1988).

Ross, P. 'Policy formation and implementation of social welfare in Peronist Argentina', PhD thesis, University of New South Wales (1989).

Schneider, A. 'Italian immigrants in contemporary Buenos Aires: their responses to changing political, economic and social circumstances', PhD Thesis, University of London (1992).

Scipione, J. et al, *Situación de los beneficiarios del sistema nacional de previsión social, Informe de GALLUP*, Buenos Aires (1992).

Setapa, S. 'Old age support and security in Malaysia' PhD thesis, University of California at Berkeley (1993).

Thompson, A. 'Segundo informe de monitoreo: el Centro de Estudios y Promoción de la Vejez', Buenos Aires (1991).

Index